The British Army, 1714-1783

The British Army, 1714–1783

An Institutional History

Stephen Conway

The Pen & Sword
History of the British Army

Series editor
Professor Ian Beckett

Pen & Sword
MILITARY

An imprint of
Pen & Sword Books Ltd
Yorkshire - Philadelphia

First published in Great Britain in 2021 by
PEN & SWORD MILITARY
An imprint of
Pen & Sword Books Ltd
Yorkshire – Philadelphia

ISBN 978-1-52671-140-3

Typeset in India by Lapiz Digital Services

Printed and bound by CPI Group (UK) Ltd, Croydon, CR0 4YY

Pen & Sword Books Ltd incorporates the imprints of Pen & Sword
Archaeology, Atlas, Aviation, Battleground, Discovery, Family History, History, Maritime,
Military, Naval, Politics, Social History, Transport, True Crime, Claymore Press,
Frontline Books, Praetorian Press, Seaforth Publishing and White Owl
For a complete list of Pen & Sword titles please contact

PEN & SWORD BOOKS LTD
47 Church Street, Barnsley, South Yorkshire, S70 2AS, England
E-mail: enquiries@pen-and-sword.co.uk
Website: www.pen-and-sword.co.uk

Or

PEN AND SWORD BOOKS
1950 Lawrence Rd, Havertown, PA 19083, USA
E-mail: Uspen-and-sword@casematepublishers.com
Website: www.penandswordbooks.com

Contents

List of Illustrations

Foreword

There has been no multi-volume history of the British Army since the completion of Sir John Fortescue's monumental history in 1930 and Fortescue effectively ended his story of the army in 1870. A new series was begun in the 1990s by another publisher but it was never completed. Only three of a projected nine volumes were published: two of these were subsidiary volumes on the auxiliary forces and the British army in India and only one of the seven chronological volumes. As it happens, these two supporting volumes have been republished with new introductions by Pen & Sword as *Britain's Part-time Soldiers* (2011) and *The Military in British India* (2013).

The aim of the revived series remains that of the original concept: to draw on the most recent scholarship to present the army's story in the context of wider military, political, socio-economic and cultural developments. While each volume will stand alone, they will all deal with such institutional aspects as organisation, training, the recruitment of officers and men, conditions of service, and the relationship of army with society and state.

Over the last 30 years research has advanced still further with a multiplicity of interdisciplinary approaches being applied to the impact of war on states, societies, institutions and individuals. The series will be an invaluable guide to the new scholarship for undergraduates and postgraduates and will appeal equally to specialists and the wider readership interested in military affairs.

This first volume of the new series covers a period from 1714 to 1783 that is still comparatively under-researched compared to the Stuart era preceding it and the French Revolutionary and Napoleonic Wars that followed. It is contributed by an acknowledged expert in Professor Stephen Conway and stands as an exemplar of the expectations of the series as a whole in transforming our understanding of the evolution of Britain's army.

Professor Ian F.W. Beckett,
General Editor

Preface

Every author incurs a multitude of debts in writing a book. In my case, those debts go back a long way, as this work is the fruit of many years labour in archives, in this country and overseas, stretching back to my time as a research student. My first debt, appropriately enough, is therefore to the people who have facilitated my use of this archival material. Here I want to thank the owners, who kindly granted me access to their collections, particularly Her Majesty the Queen (the Cumberland Papers, at Windsor Castle), Mr A.C. Bell-Macdonald (Bell-Macdonald Papers), Lieutenant Colonel R.M.P. Campbell-Preston (Campbell Preston of Ardchattan Papers), Sir John Clerk of Penicuik (the Clerk of Penicuik Muniments), Mr F.E. Hart (Hart Letters), the Rt. Hon. Lady Lucas (Lucas of Wrest Park Collection), the Duke of Northumberland (Percy Papers) and Oliver Russell (the Macpherson Grant Papers, now deposited in the National Records of Scotland at Edinburgh). My thanks are also due to the librarians and archivists whose knowledge of the documents in their care made my task much easier. I am no less grateful to colleagues and former students in my own department and in other universities, who have provided information, clarification and encouragement. Tony Hayter, who has worked extensively on the army, deserves a special mention; he very kindly gave me some of the material he had accumulated over many years of research. The debt I owe to all those who have written on the eighteenth-century British Army will be obvious from my text and my notes. If I have failed to give sufficient acknowledgement to all the authors who have gone before me, I can only plead the need to limit my references as my excuse.

Parts of this book have appeared in earlier versions in essays and articles published before. In all cases, I have revised them, but I should acknowledge my thanks to the editors and publishers for permission to reproduce them, albeit in modified form, in this book. In particular, parts of Chapter 1 draw on my essay on the impact on civilians of the British Army at home in

Civilians and War in Europe, 1618-1815, ed. Erica Charters, Eve Rosenhaft and Hannah Smith (Liverpool, 2012); parts of Chapter 3 are based on sections of my essay on the British Army as a European institution in *Britain's Soldiers: Rethinking War and Society, 1715-1815*, ed. Kevin Linch and Matthew McCormack (Liverpool, 2014); and parts of Chapter 5 appeared first in my article 'Moral Economy, Contract and Negotiated Authority in Eighteenth-Century American, British and German Militaries, *c.*1740-1783', *Journal of Modern History*, 88 (2016), 34–59.

This book has taken longer to write than I had hoped. My tardiness has been at least partly due to events beyond my control – a heavy teaching load, significant administrative responsibilities, a period of illness and, not least, the public health crisis that has posed many challenges since the early spring of this year. Stephen Chumbley deserves my thanks for his eagle-eyed copy-editing. I am also indebted to Agata Rutkowska of the Royal Collections Trust and Pip Dodd of the National Army Museum for facilitating access to images used in the plates. I am enormously grateful for the patience and good humour of Rupert Harding, the commissioning editor for the publishers, who stuck with me and was willing to wait. I hope his faith is justified.

Finally, I want to thank my family. If Rupert Harding showed a saint-like patience in the face of my pleas for more time, my wife and my son and his girlfriend, all of who have been closeted with me during the 'lockdown', deserve a medal. They have put up with my preoccupation with the past and particularly with the eighteenth-century British Army, for far longer than any reasonable human being could expect. I thank them for that and for much more besides.

Stephen Conway
May 2020

Abbreviations

I have tried to avoid overuse of abbreviations in the notes identifying the sources of quotations or specific information, but the following have been employed to avoid undue repetition and to save space:

Add. MS: Additional Manuscript
BL: British Library, London
TNA: The National Archives of the United Kingdom, Kew.

Note on Quotations

When I quote from archival sources, I have followed the practice of reproducing the texts as they appear, without adding or subtracting punctuation or correcting grammatical slips or spelling errors (eighteenth-century authors seem to have been rather cavalier in this regard) and what to us is eccentric capitalization (an area in which eighteenth-century writers were exceedingly generous). When I have quoted from published sources, I have reproduced the passages in the form in which they appear in those published sources, which may mean that an editor has intervened to correct spelling mistakes and regularize punctuation and capitalization.

Timeline

1714: George, Elector of Hanover, succeeds to the British thrones.

1715: Jacobites (supporters of the deposed Stuart monarchy) begin a rebellion in Scotland.

1716: Defeat of the Jacobite uprising.

1719: Another Jacobite uprising in Scotland, on this occasion supported by Spain; British forces capture Vigo and Portevedra in northern Spain.

1720: Royal warrant seeks to regulate price of army commissions; Sir Robert Walpole becomes effective first or prime minister.

1727: George II succeeds his father.

1739: Start of new war with Spain.

1740: British expedition sent to the West Indies; Prussian invasion of Austrian Silesia begins the War of the Austrian Succession.

1742: British troops sent to Flanders to support the Austrians and Dutch in conflict with France; Walpole resigns; clothing regulations refer for the first time to regiments solely by number.

1743: British, Austrian, Hanoverian and Hessian army defeats the French at Dettingen in Germany; George II is present – the last British monarch to lead his forces on the battlefield.

1745: Allied army in Flanders, led by the Duke of Cumberland, defeated at the Battle of Fontenoy; start of another Jacobite rebellion in Scotland.

1746: Defeat of Jacobites at Culloden by army led by the Duke of Cumberland

1747: Clothing regulations prohibit use of colonels' private insignia on uniforms and flags; British garrison at recently-captured Louisbourg mutinies over pay deductions.

1748: War against France and Spain ends; Peace of Aix-la-Chapelle.

1751: Royal warrant declares that henceforth regiments must be known only by number.

1754: British regiment and a Royal Artillery contingent sent to India; two further regiments ordered to embark for North America.

1755:   British regiments in North America defeated at the Battle of the Monongahela.

1756:   Outbreak of the Seven Years War in Europe.

1758:   British troops sent to western Germany; British forces capture Louisbourg, the French fortress on Cape Breton Island, taken in the previous war, but returned to France at the Peace of Aix-la-Chapelle.

1759:   Allied victory at Minden in Germany; fall of Quebec in Canada.

1760:   Surrender of Montreal and all of New France; George III becomes king.

1763:   Peace of Paris ends Seven Years War; mutinies in British army in North America over new pay deductions.

1766:   New royal warrant regulating price of commissions.

1775:   Outbreak of fighting in North America between British regulars and New England militiamen; start of the War of American Independence.

1776:   Thirteen of the rebel colonies declare independence; American forces defeated by General William Howe's army at the Battle of Long Island.

1777:   Defeat and surrender of a British field army under General John Burgoyne at Saratoga, New York.

1778:   France enters the War of Independence as an ally of the United States; major redeployment of the British Army to West Indies and home defence.

1779:   Spain enters the war as an ally of France.

1780:   The Dutch become belligerents after a British declaration of war.

1781:   Surrender of a second British field army at Yorktown, Virginia, leads to effective end of the war in North America, but it continues in other theatres – the West Indies, West Africa, the Mediterranean and South Asia.

1783:   Peace of Paris ends the War of American Independence; Britain acknowledges the United States.

Introduction

This book is intended as an institutional history of the British Army from the accession of the first Hanoverian monarch, George I, in 1714 until the end of the War of American Independence and British acknowledgement of the United States in 1783. Before I explain what I mean by 'an institutional history', the British Army itself needs to be defined, as what it constituted is by no means self-evident. In this study, I focus on the professional or regular army. The marines are included when they served on land as part of that army, but not when they were on board ship, when they can be seen as part of the navy. The artillery, though administered separately from the infantry and cavalry by the Board of Ordnance, is regarded here as an integral element of the army (artillery officers, as well as marine officers, appear in contemporary compendia of the army's commissioned ranks, known as the *Army Lists*). The book tangentially mentions the militia, which increasingly served alongside the army at home after its wartime reform and mobilization in 1756–7; but the militia are not included in my definition of the army.[1] Nor does the book consider the assorted units of volunteers, formed by local initiatives to defend their communities at time of external threat.[2] Most importantly, it excludes the auxiliary units that fought alongside British regulars abroad – on the Continent and in the empire – and even served with them at home when domestic insurrection or foreign invasion threatened in 1715–16, 1722–3, 1745–6 and 1756. These Dutch and especially German soldiers organized in their own units, though under overall British command and in British pay, never in contemporary estimation formed part of the army itself.[3]

Histories of the British Army, for all or parts of the period covered by this book, are plentiful. On the operational side, Sir John Fortescue's multi-volume shelf-filler, published between 1899 and 1930, though it now seems very old-fashioned in approach and attitudes, still provides a basic guide to battles and campaigns.[4] Charles Clode's even older account of the army's

administration (and the legal and political framework within which it operated) first appeared in 1869, but similarly remains a useful, if dated, starting
point.[5] In 1926, Edward Curtis produced a short yet informative book on the
organization of the army at the time of the War of American Independence
(1775–83).[6] More recently, H.C.B. Rogers, a career soldier, wrote an accessi-
ble general overview of the Georgian army, which relied heavily on existing
scholarship rather than original research.[7] By contrast, Tony Hayter's monograph on the army's deployment against local disturbances, from the middle
decades of the eighteenth century to London's Gordon Riots of 1780, rests
on extensive work in the archives.[8] The same can be said for John Houlding's
impressive study of the training of the army, which presented its readership
with a much fuller picture of the British military than its title suggested.[9]
Glenn Steppler's (sadly unpublished) Oxford doctoral dissertation on the
army in the reign of George III is similarly wide-ranging and grounded again
in a heroic trawl through a great range of archives.[10] Alan Guy's valuable
study of the administration and finance of the mid-eighteenth-century army
is no less impressive and insightful and no less well informed by archival
labours.[11] Peter Way, from a Marxian perspective, has mined the archives to
produce interesting work on the army's common soldiers, conceiving them
as having much in common with other working men.[12] Hannah Smith, for
her part, is conducting research for a social history of the army, the first
fruits of which are interesting accounts of the army's interactions with local
communities and particularly the socializing of officers with local elites.[13]
Recent collections of essays on the army are a further testament to the way
historians are engaging with a wide variety of facets of its eighteenth-century
story.[14] The work that most closely anticipates this book is Tony Hayter's
planned but unfortunately never-finished study of the army's organization.[15]

No scholar, however, to the best of my knowledge, has tried to produce an
institutional history of the kind offered here. To me, an institutional history
is not the same as an administrative history. Administrative histories aim primarily to describe and analyse organization and structure or what we might
call the mechanics of the subject of study. An institutional history will almost
certainly concern itself with such matters – it can hardly avoid them – but
it also strives to capture the essence of how an organization functioned; its
customs, ethos and unwritten rules. My book, then, is essentially a study of
the army as a living organism, with its own ways of doing things, which are

often difficult for the outsider to comprehend without someone to decode the world of both officers, common soldiers and the vitally important intermediaries between them – the little understood non-commissioned officers or corporals and sergeants. The aim, in short, is not simply to enable the reader to become familiar with the structure of the army, but to reveal its inner life.

To this end, I have used the insights of other historians, some mentioned already, but many more of whom receive credit only in my notes. Not all of these historians are military specialists; indeed, some of the most influential on my thinking have produced work seemingly very remote from the subject of this book. I owe much, for instance, in my attempt to uncover the army's ethos and customs, to work on contractual and quasi-contractual relationships in non-military settings, which provided me with a route into the mind-set of the common soldier. Here E.P. Thompson's pioneering study of the attitudes of eighteenth-century food rioters about the just functioning of provision markets, encapsulated in his concept of 'the moral economy', proved particularly stimulating.[16] I am equally indebted to studies of the negotiated nature of British imperial authority in the eighteenth century, especially the work of the American historian Jack P. Greene, which suggested to me that the army's officers could not have imposed their will simply by the use of brutal violence or its threat.[17] Their authority, like all authority, ultimately depended upon consent and that consent was built not just by fear but also by respect for officers who treated the soldier as a thinking being, able to respond to encouragements and appeals. The most successful officers, it seems, were not the martinets who relied on punishment alone (who could provoke mutinies rather than instil obedience), but those who respected the rank and file's customs and belief in the contractual nature of military service.

But if this book draws on concepts originally deployed in different fields of historical study, it is most obviously informed by many years of my own emersion in the world of the eighteenth-century British Army, as glimpsed in a wide range of archives in this country, Ireland and the United States. The official records of the army, in the voluminous War Office collection, housed at The National Archives of the United Kingdom at Kew, give an invaluable insight into how things were supposed to work and some interesting views of what happened when they went wrong. Particularly important for this study were the in- and out-letters of the Secretary at War, the minister responsible for the army, and the records of the Judge-Advocate General, including proceedings of general courts martial. Other official papers, not primarily focused on the army, such as the Lord Lieutenant of Ireland's reports to London, also in The National Archives, tell us about the importance of patronage in the military. Similarly, the Colonial Office Papers give us a top-level view of the army in various imperial settings, as reported to the secretary of state in London by commanders-in-chief in distant outposts and theatres of war. But the best sources for capturing a flavour of the army's inner life come in the many collections of private papers consulted for this study. Some of these are based on the correspondence and other documents preserved by serving officers, senior and junior, such as Jeffrey Amherst and Sir Henry Clinton in the senior officer category and a whole host of less well-known lieutenant colonels, majors, captains, lieutenants and ensigns (the lowest officer rank in the infantry). We even have a few records left by common soldiers, particularly diaries and memoirs. The papers of key administrators are often no less valuable. The sprawling collection amassed by Robert Wilmot, secretary to successive Lord Lieutenants of Ireland from 1737 to 1772, contains copies and originals of many communications from officers of the regiments stationed in Ireland. Just as informative are the private papers of Henry Fox, Secretary at War, 1746–55; of his successor, Lord Barrington, Secretary at War, 1755–61 and 1765–78; and of Barrington's successor, Charles Jenkinson, who held office from 1778 until 1782. Letters, memorials, diaries and regimental order-books in various private collections often reveal much about motives, relationships and the exercise of command that remains invisible in the official record.

A few words about the book's structure may be helpful. The opening chapter seeks to establish the context for what follows. It considers the army and the state (civil-military relations in theory and practice) and the army and society (the relationship between the army and wider society). The second chapter provides some military background to make the subsequent analysis more comprehensible; it focuses on the size, structure and deployments of the army, in peace and in war. Chapter 3 looks at the way in which officers and common soldiers entered the army and explores their motives and ambitions, which seem to have ranged from family tradition to local loyalties and national identification, but also included escape from difficult personal situations and the desire for financial betterment. Chapter

4 considers the institution that the entrants had joined. We examine the case for seeing it as a self-contained community, with its own norms and rules, language and etiquette. The profession of arms, as with all other professions, was in some senses like a caste separate from the rest of society, even if, as we saw in the first chapter, its members remained, in important ways, part of that wider society. This fourth chapter also shows that British soldiers had much in common with soldiers in other European armies; they were part of a European military fraternity, capable of linking enemies as well as allies and auxiliaries.

The fifth chapter turns to the 'military moral economy' and comes to the heart of my investigation of the inner life of the army. It examines first the common soldiers' sense of their rights and entitlements and then turns to the techniques used by officers to manage their units – from capital and corporal punishments to incentives, encouragements, appeals to patriotism and soldierly pride and accommodation of the ordinary soldier's sense of the contractual nature of his service. Chapter 6 looks at the matters that surviving sources tell us preoccupied the army's officers and rank and file – promotion, pay and perquisites, food and drink, hardships and overcoming the tedium that was inseparable from military life.

Chapter 7, on women and the army, focuses on the females associated with what was an essentially male institution. Its subjects are the few women who defied the conventions of the age and actually served (clandestinely) as soldiers, the more numerous body of women married to officers and soldiers and the upper-class women who helped advance the military careers of friends and relatives. The eighth chapter looks, appropriately for the final one, at the ways in which officers and common soldiers left the service. The chapter also says a little about what happened next. It gives some attention to the subsequent lives of deserters; and to those whose services were no longer required – particularly the discharged soldiers, but also to the officers who were removed from active service in their regiments or corps and placed on the half-pay list, a kind of dole for gentlemen.

I should acknowledge that my coverage is far from comprehensive in chronological terms. The early part of the period is not given much attention compared with the 1740s onwards, the decades marked by repeated – and demanding – warfare. Attentive readers will notice a disproportionate number of examples drawn from the era of the American Revolution; this is the period with which I am most familiar and have researched the most extensively over the majority of my career. But I include illustrations from the time of the Seven Years War and the War of the Austrian Succession and from the years of peace preceding and following these major conflicts, in the 1730s, late 1740s, early 1750s, the 1760s and early 1770s.

Nor is my coverage comprehensive in thematic terms. Inevitably, I have had to be selective. Much that might have been included is omitted or dealt with only briefly. Even in a much larger book, full coverage would not be possible. I say very little about what many readers may regard as the main business of military history – the story of battles and campaigns. I treat military operations as part of the background, rather than my main focus, in part because many fine studies of particular wars, campaigns and battles are already available and I see little point in repeating the same narrative when I can add nothing of value. But the army's conduct of military operations is not my central concern for another and more important reason. My approach is that of an exponent of the so-called new military history (though in truth it is now not so 'new', but has been around long enough to be regarded as middle-aged or even elderly). My interest is in how we might understand the army as an institution both connected to and, in important ways, separate from wider society. The ambitions I have for this book are therefore modest. I do not present it as a total history of the British Army between 1714 and 1783. It aims to highlight aspects of the army that usually receive much less attention than battles and campaigns. I hope that through what I have chosen to emphasise the book paints a picture – perhaps an unfamiliar and therefore intriguing picture – of the inner life of the British Army in a crucial period of its development.

Chapter 1

The Political and Social Background

Before we look at the army itself, we need to know something of the broader setting within which it operated. In particular, we should be aware of the political and social context of the home islands. This chapter will accordingly sketch out the relationship of the army to the state and the army to society. In considering the relationship with the state, we will focus particularly on the political fears about the army and the political controls imposed upon it. When we turn to the relationship of the army to society, we will look at how British and Irish civilians (to use a modern but not contemporary term)[1] viewed the professional military. The picture painted will for many readers be unfamiliar, not least because it questions two established narratives relating to our subject. The message of many older accounts is that constitutional limitations on the army imposed effective control over it; as we will see, that view needs modification. Similarly, the evidence presented below of positive interactions qualifies the usual emphasis on British and Irish civilians' hostility to the army.

Ireland's inclusion may need some justification. England, Wales and Scotland formed a united polity throughout the period considered in this study, following the Anglo-Scottish union of 1707. But Ireland was different on many levels. It had its own system of government, including its own Parliament, based on English originals. But if the Irish legislature modelled itself on Westminster, the basis of its authority was much narrower than the British Parliament's; 80 per cent of Ireland's population was Catholic and so formally excluded from political involvement. Irish Protestants, who monopolized domestic political power, sometimes compared their country's situation to that of the colonies in North America, but argued on other occasions that Ireland was a sister-kingdom, sharing the same monarch but otherwise separate from Britain. Politicians in London faced their own definitional dilemma. They regarded Ireland as a subordinate jurisdiction, its local legislation subject to review by the English Privy Council, much like other dependent parts of the empire; yet at the same time they seem to have assumed that Ireland's geographical proximity and the close connections between British and Irish landed elites differentiated it from the colonies across the Atlantic. We should also recognize that Ireland, unlike the colonies in North America, had a British military garrison (known as the Irish establishment) for the whole of our period and many Irishmen served in the army, some in Ireland itself but many more abroad. While acknowledging Ireland's distinctiveness (confirmed, of course, by its formal separation from Britain in the twentieth century), it therefore seems acceptable, for our current purposes, to consider Ireland as an old and established internal colony, partially integrated into a British whole, rather than as part of the overseas empire.

The concentration on Britain and Ireland is not meant to suggest that the relationship between the army and civil authority and the army and society in the home islands was in all respects qualitatively different from the army's relationship with civil authority and society in other settings. In the American colonies, at least before the War of Independence, British soldiers were expected to defer to the civil power – particularly local magistrates – in the same way as they did in England and Wales, Scotland and Ireland. Famously, when soldiers of the 29th Foot fired on a crowd in Boston in March 1770, their commander, Captain Thomas Preston, faced a murder charge and trial before a local jury.[2] In all areas where the army operated, we can see the same negative and positive features of its relationship with local society, the same threats and the same opportunities. This was true whether we consider the Low Countries and western Germany, the Mediterranean garrisons of Gibraltar and Minorca, the West Indian islands, the mainland colonies of North America and even the West African forts and trading stations and the territory controlled by the East India Company in South Asia. But it was in England that the legal restraints on the army originated and were most rigorously policed and it was in the British Isles that the army had its most substantial continuous presence throughout the period that we are considering.

The Army and the State

We begin with the army's relationship with the state or rather the apparatus of the state, its governing institutions. As we will see, there were two fundamental principles of the English (and then British and Irish) constitution relative to the army: first, that it should be subordinated to civil authority; and second, that it should be placed under Parliamentary control. The thinking behind these constitutional safeguards was clear: subornation to civil authority would prevent the army from acting as a political force in its own right, with generals setting themselves up as rulers of the people; subordination to Parliament would avoid the army becoming an instrument at the command of a malignly-intended monarch and ministers. We will also see, however, that the checks imposed on the army were not as great or as universally successful in practice, as might be imagined.

Britons prided themselves that their army, unlike some armies in other parts of Europe, was not a state within a state. It became a much-repeated platitude and cause for complacent self-congratulation that the army was subject to the civil power and Parliamentary oversight. Local magistrates, appointed by the county lord lieutenant, had to certify the validity of military enlistments, as a safeguard against coercive practices of recruitment that infringed the liberty of the subject. The surviving notebook of William Hunt, a Wiltshire JP, records his swearing 'three recruits into his Majesty's service' in January and February 1745.[3] Hampshire magistrate Thomas Woods Knollis appears to have been much more active in the early stages of the American war, reporting in June 1776 that he had 'attested near 100 [enlisted men] since last Christmas'.[4] It was Parliament, however, not the local magistracy, that exercised the most important checks on the military. The Glorious Revolution of 1688–9, which increased Parliamentary involvement in the system of government generally, inaugurating a partnership between the legislature and the crown and its ministers, gave MPs significant tools to manage the army and prevent its acting independently of their control.

Parliamentary oversight owed much to seventeenth-century experience of what could happen if an army acted as an instrument of coercion in the hands of an arbitrary ruler who wanted to impose his will on reluctant subjects. Anxiety about an unchecked military derived partly from developments across the Channel, where Louis XIV of France, the first monarch to create a substantial standing army (or permanent military force), had no hesitation in employing his troops to coerce his people into obedience to his absolutist regime. Louis deployed troops to help collect unpopular taxes, to put down local disaffection and to force Protestants to convert to Catholicism. The

French army garrisoned major towns and cities, often in purpose-built barracks, at least partly to overawe the local population. To punish communities that incurred the king's displeasure, soldiers became uninvited guests in private homes, at the expense of the residents, who were exposed to all the demands we associate with armies of occupation.[5]

England's recent past also pointed to the need to avoid an army becoming a threat to its own people. The rule of Cromwell's major generals in the 1650s, when senior officers in the New Model Army had acted as local governors with sweeping powers, was a reminder of what could happen if the military operated beyond effective civil control. In its essentials, one historian has commented, England became a 'military dictatorship'.[6] After the restoration of the Stuart monarchy in 1660, Charles II had used his limited military forces to support his own authority within England. Between 1679 and 1681 there was a political crisis over the succession to the throne on Charles's death. Those who supported the claims of Charles's brother, James, despite his Catholicism, came to be known as Tories; those who insisted on a Protestant successor and James's exclusion were called Whigs. In 1681, as the Exclusion Crisis came to a head, Charles summoned Parliament to meet in Oxford, where he brought a significant force of his own troops to make clear his refusal to concede to Whig attempts to deny the throne to his brother. Even more instructive, in the minds of many English politicians, was the way in which James, when he became king in 1685, built up a strong army to support his allegedly absolutist intentions. James's Catholicism and his well-known admiration for Louis XIV added to contemporary fears that he was intent on using his army in the same coercive way as Louis used the French military. James's keenness to deploy troops in the City of London, where opposition to him in the Corporation was particularly strong, appeared to many of his reluctant subjects as evidence that he was as despotically inclined as his French mentor.[7]

Both foreign and domestic example, then, led the English Parliament to impose significant limitations on the army's independence once William of Orange took the throne in 1689. From that year, the very existence of the army now required legislative sanction. The ability of the army's officers to discipline their men and hold courts martial relied from 1689 on the annual passage of a Mutiny Act. The preamble to the first Mutiny Act announced unambiguously that 'the raising or keeping of a Standing Army within this

Kingdome in time of Peace unlesse it be with the Consent of Parlyment is against Law'.[8] The next year's Mutiny Act extended the provisions of the legislation to include the regulation of the impressment of carriages and accommodation of troops on the march, enabling them to be put up in 'public houses' – that is, inns and taverns – but 'in no private houses whatever'.[9] To avoid the appearance of military interference in elections and reassure his new subjects of his benign intentions, William ordered that army units withdrew from places holding a vote for their representatives in the House of Commons. This became established practice thereafter. Most importantly, perhaps, the army's pay was also dependent upon the Secretary at War (the minister responsible for the land forces) presenting to the House of Commons estimates of the size and cost of the army, for approval by MPs. Parliamentarians, in other words, expected that the power of the purse could be used to ensure that the military behaved in ways that Parliament found acceptable. A similar process occurred in the Parliament at Dublin, which had to approve the Estimates for the army based in Ireland and pay for it from Irish revenues.

We should note, however, that the subordination of the army to the civil power might be suspended in exceptional circumstances. An important, though rarely used, limit to civil control was the doctrine that, in cases of dire necessity, such as rebellion, martial or military law could become the means of administering justice for civilians as well as soldiers. The Duke of Cumberland had no hesitation in acting in this spirit when he dealt with Jacobite prisoners during the 1745 rebellion (intended to restore the deposed Stuart dynasty). At Carlisle, he ordered the summary execution of members of the Jacobite Manchester Regiment, captured during and after the siege of the town's castle. While he did send some Jacobites for later formal trial for treason, Cumberland's logic in administering summary justice on others was clear; in his eyes, these men were not legitimate enemies in the army of another state, but rebels. His treatment of prisoners at Carlisle was a small foretaste of what was to come; after the Battle of Culloden in April 1746, Cumberland's troops killed many rebels and destroyed much property supposedly associated with those involved in the uprising, without worrying about bringing alleged rebels before civil courts.[10]

However, the use of martial law as a system of administration of justice for civilians occurred for the longest period not in the British Isles themselves but in the rebel colonies in North America. Martial law, declared by the local commander-in-chief and governor of Massachusetts in June 1775 after the initial clashes between British regulars and New England militiamen at Lexington and Concord, remained in force in most of the areas occupied by the British Army until the end of the War of Independence (1775–83). Some commentators doubted the wisdom of suspending the local civilian courts for so long, arguing that it was a gift to the rebels, who had long portrayed the British state as set on establishing an authoritarian regime in North America, a claim that the maintenance of martial law made appear more credible.[11] While this state of affairs lasted, civilians, as well as soldiers, appeared before courts martial. To give just one example, Peter Waglum, an inhabitant of British-occupied Staten Island, in New York, found himself, 'with all other Prison[rs]' appearing before a brigade court martial in July 1782.[12]

We should also note that in Ireland and Scotland, even in more usual times, the government used the army to subordinate people that it believed to be a threat to the established order. In England, politicians and public regarded barracks as redolent of Continental-style despotism; but in both Ireland and Scotland barrack-building was thought acceptable – indeed, desirable. In Ireland, a barrack board oversaw the construction work; the intention was clearly to facilitate the rapid deployment of troops to overawe the Catholic population. In the Highlands of Scotland, after both the 1715 and 1745 Jacobite rebellions, striking major new fortifications, in Continental European style (including barracks), proclaimed the willingness of the British state to impose its authority by military force. In both the Scottish and Irish cases, the need for Parliamentary approval offered no safeguard against the military's coercing the crown's subjects. English and Lowland Scottish MPs had few qualms about supporting these architectural embodiments of state power in the Highlands and the Protestant Irish landowners who dominated the Dublin Parliament happily provided the money for the construction of barracks designed to help secure the passivity of the Catholic majority in their country (and which might provide profitable business for local tradesmen).[13]

Even in England, controls on the army were not necessarily as robust as they appeared in theory. Magistrates might see their role as facilitating the army's recruitment efforts (and earning official approval as a result), rather than protecting the subject. Some – such as Thomas Woods Knollis, whom we met earlier – had military experience themselves and were perhaps especially 'attentive for the good of His Majesty's service'.[14] Others, keen to rid their communities of troublesome individuals, drew the attention of the Secretary at War to men whom they believed should be enlisted; in July 1776, for instance, a Shropshire magistrate contacted the War Office about a Ludlow man who was 'drunken, abusive, quarrelsome and a common Disturber of the Peace – in all respects, a fit Object of military Discipline and Government'.[15] Recent scholarship has shown that, despite the withdrawal of military units from places holding elections, the army was often deployed with political considerations very much in mind. In the long period dominated by Sir Robert Walpole, effective prime minister in the 1720s and 1730s, the army tended to be quartered in areas hostile to his government, suggesting that it was intended to overawe (and perhaps win over by the more positive aspects of its presence) political opponents.[16] And of course in an era when voting was open rather than secret, the withdrawal of troops offered little security against intimidation. The troops might disappear during the election, but they would then return. Their presence before and after the voting must, for some electors at least, have inhibited free choice.

Secretaries at War, furthermore, came to realize that they could secure the smooth passage of the Army Estimates through Parliament if they deliberately understated the true costs. At the end of the financial year, the minister would then return to the House of Commons and ask for approval of the army's 'extraordinaries' – that is, overspends or costs incurred in excess of the original Estimates (and without Parliamentary permission). Presented with a fait accompli, MPs might fulminate at the size of the 'extraordinaries', especially during wars that divided political opinion, such as the War of American Independence; but very few of them seriously engaged with the accounts presented to them. A few MPs did go to some trouble – Sir Francis Dashwood, for instance, kept detailed notes on military expenditure in the Seven Years War – but most lacked the determination, stamina and financial skills to sift through complex and often rather opaque accounts.[17] For the most part, they preferred to make general points and complain about the process. After much sound and fury, the extraordinaries would almost always be supported, sometimes without a formal division.

In practice, contrary to the intentions of the architects of the constitutional settlement of 1689, the Treasury, the department of government ever conscious of the need for parsimony, probably exerted more control over army spending than did Parliament. It was the Treasury – not the House of Commons – that instituted an enquiry into the seemingly uncontrolled expenditure on army supplies at the end of the Seven Years War.[18] The Commission on the Public Accounts, established by Lord North's ministry in the later stages of the American war (in the hope that it would present a positive message about the government's handling of war expenditure), surprised everyone by taking its task seriously. The Commission's seventh report, published in June 1782, found that more than £19 million of army extraordinaries had been approved by the House of Commons since the beginning of 1776.[19] While this report stood as a rebuke to government for its seeming extravagance, it also highlighted the ineffectiveness of Parliament as a check on military spending.

Perhaps it was no coincidence that many opposition politicians remained worried about the army. Anti-standing army sentiment had many supporters in Parliament, amongst both Tory and dissident Whig MPs, who regularly spoke against increases in the size of the army and pressed for a reformed (and locally controlled) militia as an alternative.[20] Opposition to the army was at its strongest in the first half of the eighteenth century, before the reform and revitalization of the militia at the beginning of the Seven Years War in 1756. But in some circles the army continued to be viewed with suspicion and dislike long after that. The new militia soon disappointed its advocates. Militia service proved unpopular – resistance took the form of rioting in some counties – which undermined the faith of its support-ers in the public's enthusiasm for a system of defence based on bodies of patriotically-motivated citizens. Perhaps worse still, the new militia con-stituted in 1756 soon became an extension of, rather than an alternative to, the standing army. By the time of the American war, advocates of popular arming wanted a different kind of militia, based on strict rotation, to avoid the same men serving for long periods and becoming indistinguishable from professionals; or they promoted volunteer corps, with elected officers, as the best safeguard for a free people.[21]

Anxieties about the army owed something to continuing concern that it might act as a coercive instrument to compel obedience to a malignly-intentioned government, in much the same way as James II and Louis XIV were assumed to have used their militaries. But after 1689, when Parliament became an entrenched institution rather than an occasional event, a perhaps more persistent worry emerged. With Parliament more powerful, ministers had an obvious interest in devising ways to manage it. One of the methods that they used was patronage. Offices in government pay rewarded MPs who consistently supported the government's measures in Parliament – and won over MPs who might be inclined to oppose the ministry but would welcome the money associated with public office. Those who valued the role of Parliament as a check on the conduct of ministers worried that if the House of Commons contained too many MPs who were financially dependent upon the government, it would become a mere rubber stamp for ministerial decisions. Government errors would go unchecked, because a significant number of MPs had an interest in supporting ministers. One of the most conspicuous groups of MPs in government pay were army officers, of whom there were 182 in the Commons between 1715 and 1754 and 208 between 1754 and 1790.[22]

Edward Southwell, MP for Bristol, was one of many parliamentarians who worried that the expansion of the army in wartime gave a great boost to government power and threatened 'the security of our constitution'. He was unusual only in arguing that the expansion of the navy posed a similar threat; most MPs viewed the navy benignly and reserved their constitutional anxieties for use in their diatribes against the standing army.[23] As Lord Talbot told the House of Lords in December 1740, 'That the army is instrumental in extending the influence of the ministry in parliament, cannot be denied'.[24] The claim was not without foundation. Even though army officers in Parliament did not act as a professional grouping and consistently vote together, we have some evidence that governments saw military MPs as reliable lobby fodder. In 1780, when Lord North's ministry was under pressure in the House of Commons, John Robinson, the Secretary to the Treasury, wrote to the Secretary at War to ask him to ensure that all army officer MPs attended the House for a crucial vote: 'we want every one I assure you, that it is possible to get. Not a man must be spared.'[25] There were occasions when officer MPs paid a military price for opposing the government – General Henry Seymour Conway lost his colonelcy of the 1st Dragoons in February 1764 after he voted against the Grenville ministry on the issue the use of general arrest warrants to detain everyone involved in the publication of material that the government found objectionable. Such episodes, however, precisely because they were so unusual, probably had the effect of reinforcing the belief that most army officers in Parliament were too beholden to government to risk voting regularly against it.

The Army and Society

To summarize the army's relationship with society in the home territories is no easy matter. A leading military historian has stated emphatically that 'Civilians generally hated soldiers'.[26] There is indeed abundant evidence to support the well-established view that the British Army, like all armies, was deeply unpopular. Yet by no means all the available sources point to this conclusion. Some present a very different picture – a picture of attraction and benefit. Opinions on the army, we can reasonably assume, varied from individual to individual, from place to place and from time to time. The same person might even be negative about the army on some occasions and more positive about it on others. To negotiate our way through the tangle of conflicting views, we will consider first the evidence of unpopularity and then go on to see the other side of the story. That other side may be more important than many historians acknowledge.

We should start by acknowledging that civilians' fears about the army owed much to the belief that it was an institution separate from the rest of society – an outside imposition, whose soldiers ('they') posed a threat to the local community ('us'). Members of the army sometimes played the part assigned to them in inhabitants' worst nightmares. A good example of the rank and file behaving as a group cut off from the norms of civil society, and even hostile to them, is the practice of rescuing fellow soldiers who had been held by local magistrates. In 1773, an officer in the 42nd Highlanders told his father of a serious incident at Longford in Ireland, when grenadiers in the 5th Foot attempted to free from prison one of their comrades held for killing a local civilian.[27]

Unsurprisingly, we have plentiful evidence that British soldiers were disliked by Irish Catholics, who ever since the creation of the Irish establishment in 1691 had seen the redcoats in their midst as an army of occupation propping up a Protestant regime that denied them opportunities to participate in public life. As Lieutenant Colonel Matthew Sewell wrote from Kinsale in August 1752, 'If Roman Catholicks were permitted to be on Grand Jurys, They would present the whole English army as a nuisance.'[28] Catholic resentment continued to be palpable even at the end of our period. In 1776, the order-book of a British regiment based in Waterford warned its soldiers not to leave their quarters except in groups of four or five.[29] Those who were incautious enough to ignore similar warnings might be attacked and maimed, even on the streets of Dublin.[30] Equally unsurprisingly, Highland Scots did not warm to the British troops who garrisoned their country in the aftermath of the 1745 rebellion. The testimony of members of the British forces in the Highlands makes clear their hostility to the local population. But the feeling seems to have been mutual. As an officer based at Fort William remarked in 1750, the inhabitants of the region displayed a bitter 'hatred of the English' and made life very difficult for his men.[31]

In England and Wales, the army, though less obviously an occupying force, could still appear as an external threat, the presence of which would bring untold ills to local communities. Smugglers, and those who benefited from their illegal trade, had an obvious reason to dislike soldiers; detachments of the army regularly supported the customs service in the enforcement of the trade laws. Protesters – whether against the militia ballot or trading practices deemed unjust or poor labour conditions and pay rates – also had cause to look on soldiers with a wary eye. Troops called to aid the civil power could, as a last resort, open fire on crowds that would not disperse. While officers and men might sympathize with rioters (James Wolfe clearly felt for the West Country textile workers he encountered in 1756),[32] from the perspective of those confronted by redcoats it must have seemed that the army was supporting authority and acting against them.

Even amongst those unconnected with smuggling and uninvolved in popular protests, the army could inspire fear. In popular imagination, soldiers were morally corrupting; their swearing, gambling, drunkenness and womanizing regarded as posing a challenge to order and decency. As the Rev. Joseph Greene wrote to his brother from Stratford-upon-Avon in March 1739, the local community ran 'some risque of having more Whores and Bastards' if 'our Pacifick Forces alias Review-Warriors continue to quarter upon us'.[33] Local court records suggest that these fears had some substance or at least led to a propensity to prosecute. In Leicester, for instance, Andrew Anderson, a corporal in General Bragge's Regiment of Foot, was ordered in October 1745 to appear before the borough magistrates to 'to answer charges *re* the bastard child of Sarah Hickling, widow'; in October 1757, the same borough's magistrates convicted Corporal James Ridgeway, of Bland's

Regiment, 'for swearing 1 profane oath'.[34] Perhaps most tellingly, the army's own records tell a similar story of disruption to the settled patterns of civilian life. The commanders of the garrison of Plymouth Citadel urged their men in July 1776 to stop spending all their money 'in a most Scandalous Manner' in the town and then returning to their quarters after 'Drinking to Excess'.[35]

Innkeepers may have profited from soldiers' drunkenness, but they – as well as merchants and manufacturers – complained bitterly to the War Office of officers who had failed to honour debts incurred on their own account or on behalf of their military units.[36] Innkeepers had a further grievance: the quartering of troops could lead to a fall in normal custom and exposure to all manner of inconveniences; they regularly complained of the burden.[37] As an army surgeon wrote of his experiences, every innkeeper looked upon soldiers 'not only as a nuisance but also a great drawback to the profits of his business'.[38] The wider community, meanwhile, might find itself paying more for necessaries due to the increased demand created by the military; a number of commentators noted the inflation common in garrison towns and in the proximity of large encampments.[39] The requisitioning of horses, carts and carriages could lead to local shortages and disrupt the movement of goods needed by the civilian population and thereby add to inflationary pressures.

To many property holders, large and small, soldiers in the vicinity meant loss – of fruit from orchards, fish from ponds, chickens and other poultry from farmyards and even cattle and sheep from the fields. In 1780, Sir Francis Buller, a Cornish MP, complained that a party of the 50th Foot stationed near his estates was 'an intolerable Grievance to the Country . . . Hardly a Night passes that some Felony is not committed by them.' Buller explained that 'they have broken open several Houses, committed Highway Robberies, stolen four sheep from one man & three from another, stripped a third of all his poultry, & robbed Orchards & Gardens without End & to a considerable Value'.[40] Southern England, where troops were deployed to counter invasion in the wars of our period, perhaps suffered particularly badly. Henry Penton of Winchester had to give up part of his estate for a military encampment in the American war. He, along with other landowners in a similar position, received payment for use of his land, but this did not cover the expense caused by the occupying troops. Penton calculated that his losses – through fences destroyed, crops trampled and other causes – came to more than £862.[41]

Local communities might also fear soldiers as bringers of disease. Troops on the march could convey illness from one settlement to another; their mobility made them agents of contagion. But even when soldiers were stationary, they posed a threat to local health, especially when they were under canvas with only the most basic systems of sanitation. The camps not only became places of high mortality themselves, but spread the problem to neighbouring communities through the regular visits to the camps of curious (or profit-seeking) outsiders. In the American war, the burial registers for St Mary the Virgin in Great Warley, close to the camp on Warley Common in Essex, record an average number of burials of 14.7 a year for 1775–7, before the camp was established, but 76 in 1779, when the camp had been in being for a year.[42] These acute problems were specific to particular communities, of course; they affected only places where troops were concentrated or where large numbers of them were nearby.

But if death from disease caught from the army tended to be a very localized problem, dislocation caused by the army's need for recruits created much more widespread difficulties. The wives and children of the men enlisted might become a charge on the local poor rate, much to the displeasure of the property owners who paid the rates. Employers of labour might lament the loss of skilled men. The army secured some of its manpower from what contemporaries regarded as the most expendable parts of society – paupers, vagrants, criminals and the unemployed – but, as we will see later, in wartime, when the military's need for soldiers was at its highest, it took significant numbers of men with craft skills. Legislation designed to shield apprentices from military service seems to have offered little protection.[43] In the Seven Years War, Isaac Fletcher, a Cumberland tradesman, was vexed to discover that one of his apprentices had apparently 'gone away with the souldiers'.[44] Other employers were similarly troubled. George Wansey, a Wiltshire clothier, complained that his 'workfolks are grown scarce', with the result that wages had risen.[45] A related worry was that some of these men would never return. Death and disability may mean that they were lost permanently to their employers. Perhaps worse, in the minds of some masters, was the fear that their workers might be discharged from the army in Continental Europe, where they had been serving, rather than in Britain itself. In these circumstances, skilled manpower was not only lost to their employer, but gained by foreign competitors. In 1748, at the end of the War of the Austrian Succession, worried employers in the 'cloathing Towns' lobbied the Secretary at War to agree to disband men at home rather than in the Low Countries.[46]

Look again, however, and we see a very different picture. Catholic dislike of the army in Ireland did not stop Catholics from volunteering to serve in its ranks. From the Seven Years War (1756–63), prohibitions on the recruitment of Catholics, always fitfully enforced, were relaxed to allow considerable numbers to be recruited.[47] The Highlands of Scotland, from the same time, became equally important as a recruiting ground for the British Army; the Seven Years War and the War of American Independence both saw the creation of specifically Highland regiments, often raised by the same landed families as had supported the Jacobite rebellion in 1745.[48] The end of the Jacobite alternative (effectively in 1746, with the defeat of the rebels at Culloden and certainly by 1766, when even the Pope gave up on the Stuarts) changed official British attitudes to both Irish Catholics and Highland Scots; but it had no less an important impact on attitudes in Catholic Ireland and Highland Scotland. Before the Seven Years War, many Catholic Irishmen seeking a military career had found it in the army of a Catholic state on the Continent, some of which had Irish regiments on their establishments. Highland Scots has similarly served in the Scots Brigade attached to the Dutch army. After the war, these overseas alternatives attracted fewer Irish and Scots recruits. The Irish Brigade in the French army and the Scots Brigade in Dutch service filled their ranks more and more with men from the Austrian Netherlands (modern-day Belgium), the Dutch Republic and the German states. Irish Catholics and Highland Scots increasingly saw their military futures as in the British Army.[49]

In England, meanwhile, local communities might be fearful of a military presence, but they might just as often see it as having a more positive side. The army provided business opportunities for a multitude of people. The camps that we have considered as hotbeds of disease also constituted a significant market for those able to supply them with their wants. Their military population was often the equivalent of the number of inhabitants in a sizeable town.[50] In the summer and autumn of 1778, Warley Common, near Brentwood in Essex, was the temporary home to some 11,000 regular soldiers and militiamen, plus assorted camp followers. Brentwood – more a village than a town – found itself in close proximity to a military population as numerous as were the inhabitants of contemporary Hull or Coventry. Coxheath camp, established at the same time near Maidstone in Kent, was even larger; its 17,000 military occupants put it on a par with the Leeds of its day.[51] Like a town, a camp consumed a great range of necessities. 'A General Estimate of the Quantities of Bread, Straw, Wood and Forage, to be furnished . . . at the several Encampments of the Troops in South Britain 1778', probably drawn up by Treasury officials, gives us a flavour of the scale of what was required. The authors reckoned on the need for 59,377½lbs of bread a day, 31,668lbs of straw every three weeks and for the same period 2,493,855lbs of wood and at least 215,670 rations of forage for the horses, each comprising 18lbs of hay and a peck of oats.[52] The opportunities were even greater than these mind-boggling figures suggest. Although contractors, often based in London, agreed with government for the provision of standard rations for the soldiers,[53] fresh food was sold to the military by local people and vast quantities of beer were made available in stalls set up on the fringes of the camps. The military authorities tried to regulate the number of local people selling their men food and drink, but they had no wish to discourage them altogether, as supplements to the standard ration boosted the troops' morale, reduced desertion and took away one of the incentives for soldiers to steal.

A camp, furthermore, acted as an important public attraction, drawing vast crowds of sightseers, many of whom would have spent money getting there and still more during their time in or near the tented settlement itself. Within a few weeks of its formation in the American war, Warley camp was drawing large crowds; up to 20,000 on one Sunday, according to a press report, many probably coming from London.[54] In the early autumn of 1741, an officer based at the Colchester encampment reckoned (perhaps with a touch of exaggeration) that a review of the 'Whole line . . . together in Front of the Camp', drew an audience of '40 or fifty thousand spectators'.[55] Inns in the vicinity of the camps did a roaring trade ('a fine Harvest', in the words of one commentator in 1756),[56] providing dinners for officers and sleeping space for sightseers who had travelled too far to return home on the same day. In July 1778, an officer based at Coxheath reported that 'The accommodations immediately about the Camp are . . . always crowded' and that the inns in Maidstone, four miles away, were 'from the great resort of people to this camp . . . generally full'.[57] Another report suggests that Maidstone's inns could not cope with the increased demand and beds were being hired in private homes.[58] Even the owners of roads near the camps were able to benefit from the increased traffic generated by so many visitors; turnpike trusts might waive the tolls for officers travelling to and from the camps, but they were careful not to extend this patriotic dispensation to civilians.[59] As a visitor to Salisbury camp noted on 1 October 1778, 'It was . . . a glorious day for the Turnpike, as I believe the Cavalcade of Coaches, Chaises Waggons, Carts, Horses &c extended near 2 Miles'.[60]

The army, whether in camps, quarters or on the march, offered civilians manifold opportunities for profit. We can start with perhaps the least important way in which money might be made. Non-military labour was vital to enable the army to function – especially to carry its baggage, munitions and food supplies. No uniformed in-house transport corps existed until the 1790s and in its absence, civilians had to be employed. Infantry regiments on the march had legal sanction to impress carts without payment. The owners seem to have received recompense from their local authority; Nottingham's records reveal frequent settlement of bills submitted by the owners of horse-drawn vehicles impressed by various regiments moving through the borough.[61] Whether the army itself had to remunerate the drivers is unclear, but they certainly received payment.[62] We know that the Board of Ordnance, responsible for the artillery, hired civilian drivers for each year's campaign to move its guns, powder and ammunition. In 1755, just to transport the artillery train at home, fifty-two civilian drivers were taken onto the payroll; two years later, more were required 'for sundry Services in England . . . , exclusive of those contracted for'.[63]

The supply of goods offered much better prospects for significant profit than the supply of labour. The military, as we have seen, consumed vast quantities of foodstuffs, to the benefit of not just wealthy contractors but also farmers and other producers. Even British troops serving abroad – in the colonies or on the Continent – might provide business opportunities. In the Seven Years War, when local sources proved inadequate for feeding the army in western Germany, English farmers, provision merchants and shippers benefited. We know from the letter book of Commissary Lawrence Dundas that he personally ordered oats from England to help feed the horses in his wagon train.[64] Other evidence in the papers of members of the commissariat suggests that ships regularly crossed the North Sea to bring cargoes of British wheat, barley and oats for use of the army. Daniel Weir, the commissary at Bremen, recorded, for instance, the arrival of a convoy of no less than sixty ships from England on 24 June 1762.[65] An affidavit relating to one such ship, the *Wakefield*, from Wisbech, in Cambridgeshire, gives us an indication of the range of people who had a stake in this trade. Not only were the master, Charles Low, and his crew paid for transporting the cargo, but the shipowner, Robert Standige of London, also benefited from the freight charges. Walton and Stone, the London merchants who were selling the oats and barley on board, were advantaged to the tune of nine pence per quarter of the cereals carried or more than £500 (the equivalent of nearly £86,500 in modern values).[66] The profits of the producers of the barley and oats, presumably from Wisbech's East Anglian hinterland, are not known, but we must assume that the prices they were offered were competitive enough for the farmers to agree to sell their cereals to Walton and Stone or their local agent. Nor should we forget Ireland's contribution. One German contractor's tender suggest that large quantities of Irish butter found their way to the troops in Westphalia.[67] In the American war, the British soldiers campaigning in the rebel colonies relied on even large quantities of foodstuffs conveyed over a 3,000-mile supply line, as local sources were much less reliable that in the previous conflict. Amongst the beneficiaries were the Irish merchants and farmers that specialised in 'wet provisions', that is, meat and dairy products. East Anglia, meanwhile, provided vast quantities of bread, oats and peas and other 'dry provisions'.[68]

But soldiers needed more than full stomachs; they had to be clothed and equipped. Even in peacetime, money could be made from supplying the army with such necessaries; in 1736, Thomas Hoggart, a Dublin clothier, won a contract to provide uniforms for an infantry regiment on the Irish establishment. War led to greater opportunities, as the army grew in size and its requirements increased proportionately. Further demand for uniforms gladdened the hearts of woollen manufacturers, boosting their profits; John Brearley of Wakefield wrote contentedly in 1760 of the 'good trade for soldiers cloaths'.[69] Retailers shared in the bonanza: John Hetherington, a London tradesman, received £1,237 in May 1781 for the clothing he supplied to the newly-raised 22nd Light Dragoons.[70] Even military buttons, as we can see from the business records of Boulton & Fothergill, metal-ware manufacturers of Birmingham, made money for those who could supply them.[71] Demand for weapons – swords, bayonets and muskets, as well as artillery pieces – provided orders for iron works. Samuel Walker's Rotherham establishment doubled its capital in the course of the American war, largely due to profits from the manufacture of artillery pieces for the Board of Ordnance.[72]

It would be reasonable to assume that the purchasing power of the army often put it in a strong position to secure a good deal, much as a modern supermarket chain is able to dictate terms to its suppliers. There is some evidence that those doing the purchasing did indeed have the whip hand; in some cases, they were dominant enough to secure reduced prices on the renewal of contracts.[73] Nevertheless, there were times when civilians were able to take advantage of the army's desperate need. In 1745, as regular troops were moving north to engage with the Jacobite forces, the government instructed the Earl of Cholmondely, Lord Lieutenant of Cheshire and governor of Chester Castle, to provide essential items for the soldiers who would pass through his area. Cholmondeley was worried that the local farmers would combine to push up prices and soon found that his concerns about cartels were justified. Local shoemakers, sensing an opportunity, insisted on a higher rate per pair than they had originally agreed.[74]

If the army generated money, it also provided social opportunities. We know that officers, in particular, mixed amicably with local people in the places where military detachments quartered. Lord Francis Napier told his cousin Mary Hamilton of his playing cards in the homes of the well-to-do in Worcester, while there on the recruiting service in 1781. In an account meant to amuse her, he complained that the good people of the town 'are inhuman enough to turn you out of their Houses at Nine O'Clock *supperless*'.[75] That same year, Thomas Hawkins, a young officer in the 10th Dragoons, recorded in his diary a breakfast given by his regiment to about a hundred inhabitants of York, the grandstand on the racecourse being used for the purpose. Hawkins was especially keen to note his social calls on the leading families of the area, making a careful list of the names of the eligible daughters.[76]

It seems that the attraction was often two-way. Women's fascination with soldiers even appeared as a theme in contemporary literature; in John Dobson's *Robin: A Pastoral Elegy* (1746) the eponymous central character sees his beloved Susan fall for a soldier, recently returned from Flanders to combat the Jacobite invasion ('He came from Flanders with the red-coated crew, To fight with rebels and he conquered you').[77] The disruptions and uncertainties of wartime probably had the effect, overall, of delaying marriage; this is certainly the impression conveyed by the records of Edinburgh for the middle years of the eighteenth century.[78] But, where soldiers were concentrated, the pattern was somewhat different. In Exeter, for instance, the number of marriages seems to have risen sharply during the mid-century conflicts, especially in the War of the Austrian Succession. The proportion of marriages involving military personnel also increased, which suggests that local women benefited from a more favourable marriage market created by the availability of more men.[79] For all the sense that the army was an institution separate from the rest of society, these marriages and liaisons remind us of the intimate connections between the two.

Nor should we forget that opposition to the army, both in Parliament and beyond, lost some of its strength from the middle of the century. Anti-professional army sentiment did not disappear; in 1760, one pamphleteer lamented what he saw as the militarization of British society and the paradoxical threat of French-style government embedding itself even as Britain fought against France.[80] But such laments were now competing with more upbeat assessments of the army. An important part of the explanation for this softening of sentiment was the army's association with the great triumphs of the Seven Years War. Local communities marked British victories on land with much enthusiasm. In September 1758, for instance, when news arrived of the British capture of the French fortress of Louisbourg on Cape Breton, the vicar of the Berkshire village of East Hendred noted that 'nothing was heard almost the whole night long, but hazzas, firing of guns and ringing of bells'.[81] When a year later, the inhabitants of London learned of the victory of British and allied troops over the French at Minden in Germany, 'Our Citty', in the words of a Quaker observer, 'was Illuminated from One End to ye Other'.[82] The war, just as importantly, produced military heroes to match naval ones. James Wolfe, who died at the moment of triumph when capturing Quebec from the French in 1759, rapidly acquired a reputation that eclipsed even that of Marlborough in his glory days in the War of the Spanish Succession (1702–13).[83] The Marquis of Granby, who commanded British forces in Germany in the Seven Years War, owed his celebrity less to military success than to his paternalistic care for his men.

Edward Penny's depiction of him offering help to a sick soldier, painted sometime after 1765, no doubt contributed to Granby's reputation; but the number of inns and taverns named after him stands as eloquent testimony to his popular appeal.

Chapter 2

The Military Background

While this book focuses on the British Army as an institution – on its inner life – to understand that how that institution worked we need to be familiar with the essentials of its scale, organization and distribution. This chapter accordingly looks first at the fluctuating size of the army, in peacetime decidedly small by European standards; even in war, no more than medium-sized. We then examine its structure and particularly the importance of the regiment. Attention is finally turned to the army's deployments, considering its peacetime service and campaigning in various locations from 1714, the end of the War of the Spanish Succession, to 1783, the close of the War of American Independence. With this military background in place, we can go on to examine other aspects of the army in subsequent chapters.

Numbers

To calculate the size of the army might seem an unproblematic endeavour. In truth, it poses considerable challenges. We know how many troops Parliament at Westminster was prepared to support financially, as 'Estimates' of the size the land forces had to be presented for Parliamentary approval every year by the minister responsible for the army, the Secretary at War. Care needs to be taken, however, to distinguish spending on the regular regiments of foot and horse, plus the artillery (which had a separate set of Estimates) from payments for British military forces more generally. As explained earlier, this book focuses on the regular army; but from the Seven Years War, militia regiments were included in the army estimates and in all of the wars of our period considerable sums were expended on foreign troops, whose costs accounted for 23 per cent of the Westminster Parliament's total military spending in the War of the Austrian Succession and 30 per cent in the Seven Years War.[1]

But if we need to take account of these deductions, we must also recognize that the Parliament in London did not pay for all of the army. The

Irish establishment was funded by taxes raised in Ireland by the Dublin Parliament. Until 1769, the Irish establishment was fixed at 12,000 troops, when it was increased to 15,000, as part of a constitutional settlement that allowed the Irish electorate to vote for a new Parliament at least every eight years.[2]

The paper strength of the army, however, both in Ireland and in Britain, is only a very rough guide to its actual strength. In peacetime, the Dublin Parliament covered the costs of the army based in Ireland; but in wartime Irish infantry regiments were often the first to be sent abroad, at which point they left the Irish establishment and became part of the British establishment and therefore funded by the Westminster Parliament. In wartime, then, the Irish garrison was rarely at its full paper strength. At the beginning of the War of American Independence, the Irish Parliament agreed to release 4,000 troops for campaigning in the rebel colonies, without any replacements. Even before that, however, the army in Ireland was seriously below its establishment size. In August 1775, three months before the Dublin Parliament agreed to the release of the 4,000 men for American service, the regiments in Ireland could muster only 10,545 effectives or just 70 per cent of the 15,000 troops supposed to be on the Irish establishment.[3]

Most of the time, regiments in both Britain and Ireland struggled to reach their establishment strength, particularly in wartime – because recruitment was difficult or a unit had suffered losses through desertion or discharge or death in action or by disease.[4] In November 1760, in the later stages of the Seven Years War, Lord Ligonier wrote with alarm that the British regiments in Germany had been greatly reduced in numbers; the Royal Welch Fusiliers, Ligonier believed, was no more than 300 strong.[5] Just a few weeks before, General Jeffery Amherst had expressed similar concerns about the army in North America, which he reckoned to be 'near Seven thousand men' short of its establishment strength.[6] Countless other examples could be given of the impact of years of hard campaigning and still more of the effect of disease.[7]

Remedying shortfalls in regiments on campaign often relied on taking the men from units that were not actively employed – a form of robbing Peter to pay Paul known as drafting. Regiments about to embark abroad often filled their ranks with men taken (or drafted) from other regiments, which left those regiments that had provided the top-up depleted in numbers. Usually, the numbers taken from a regiment were quite small – all the regiments remaining on the British or Irish establishments would be expected to contribute, which made the loss for any of them manageable. It seems entirely possible that some officers welcomed drafting as an opportunity to purge their units of troublesome or inefficient soldiers. But at least a few regiments suffered serious inroads from drafting, which meant that it took from them good and valued members of the rank and file as well as the bad and indifferent they were happy to lose. In 1762, Samuel Bagshawe, colonel of the 93rd Foot, complained bitterly that in the last year '218 Men were culled and taken' from his regiment to reinforce under-strength units destined for foreign service.[8] To devote great efforts to recruiting only to see your regiment hollowed out to fill the ranks of others must have been very frustrating.

John Houlding, who has done heroic work comparing actual with establishment strengths for the British Army between 1750 and 1793, reckons that the cavalry was best able to approach its establishment totals, especially in peacetime, when it probably reached about 95 per cent of what either the Westminster or Dublin Parliaments had financed. The infantry, however, fell significantly behind, achieving only 80 per cent of its target strength in the War of American Independence.[9] At other times, when regiments moved from a wartime establishment to a smaller peacetime strength, the opposite problem occurred: large numbers of men had to be discharged, as they were no longer required for military service; too many men were on the books, not too few.

The principal variant explaining the strength of the army was indeed whether Britain was at war or at peace. As Britain's eighteenth-century wars became more and more demanding, the size of the army increased. The Army Estimates for 1748, the last year of the War of the Austrian Succession, envisaged paying for 76,516 officers and men. At the end of the Seven Years War, Parliament agreed to fund 117,633 troops for 1762.[10] The Westminster legislature voted money for about the same number in 1783, the last year of the War of American Independence.[11] Compare these wartime strengths with the size of the army that the Westminster Parliament was prepared to fund in peaceful years. In 1714, just after Britain had withdrawn from the War of the Spanish Succession, the army on the British establishment may have been no more than 16,400 strong.[12] In 1738, the year before the outbreak of fighting with Spain that merged into the War of the Austrian Succession, the Westminster Parliament agreed to give financial support for an army of only 26,891 officers and men. In 1755, just before the Seven Years War began in earnest, Parliament voted to pay an army of just 31,422 troops of all ranks.[13]

In wartime, the demands of increasingly global armed conflicts inevitably produced pressure for a larger army; but in peacetime, the pressure pushed in the opposite direction. Once hostilities ended, parliamentarians sought, above all, to reduce wartime levels of taxation and pressed for reductions in the size of the armed forces and the revenue services to make the savings needed to pay for tax cuts. Governments, mindful of the need to win (or keep) the favour of backbench MPs, were generally happy to oblige. The army, which was much less well-regarded than the navy for most of the period we are considering and barely more popular than the Customs and Excise, unsurprisingly struggled to find Parliamentary advocates willing to oppose a determined post-war drive for economy. After the War of the Austrian Succession and the Seven Years War, admittedly, the army was numerically stronger than it had been at the end of previous conflicts; governments recognized that another war with France (and probably with Spain too) was more-or-less inevitable and tried to avoid paring the army back to the bone. Even so, the army became a shadow of its wartime self. Not only was the number of regiments reduced, but the number of soldiers in each of those regiments that survived dropped also, down from a wartime establishment to a much slimmer peacetime strength. At the height of the War of American Independence, for instance, a company of infantry contained seventy private soldiers; in the years immediately following the conflict, when retrenchment was the order of the day, this number was cut to forty-two.[14]

Some European benchmarks underline the modest size of the British Army by contemporary standards, even in wartime, when it was at its largest. The official strength of the British Army, calculated by the number of troops Parliament agreed to pay, stood in 1740, at the start of the War of the Austrian Succession and after a year of conflict with Spain, at 40,800 officers and men. By comparison, the army of Prussia in that year was 77,000 strong, Austria's 108,000 and France's 201,000. Towards the end of the Seven Years War, France fielded 347,000 troops, Austria 201,000, Prussia 130,000 and Britain 99,000. In peacetime, all armies diminished in size, but Britain's strikingly so. In 1730, when the British Army was no more than 23,800 officers and men, France still had a military 205,000 strong, Austria had 130,000 men in its army and Prussia 66,900. Forty years later, in 1770, the British peacetime army remained small – 31,000 soldiers, compared with 160,000 in France, 151,000 in Austria and 160,000 in Prussia.[15]

Comparing like with like, admittedly, is very difficult, but these figures are accurate enough to give us a clear sense of the disparity between the size of Britain's army and those of the other major European powers. This disparity no doubt owed much to the constitutional concerns about the army that we considered earlier. But it was also based on a rational strategic choice. Britain, as an island, had an extensive coastline to defend, but no land boundary with any other power. It made sense, therefore, for its navy to take priority and to be the favoured service when it came to the allocation of public money. In every decade from 1714 to 1763, spending on the navy outstripped spending on the army; usually the navy commanded around 60 per cent of total military expenditure, sometimes more.[16] The Continental states, by contrast, had long land borders to protect, which made their armies much more important.

Structure

If the army was in theory under civilian control, it usually had its own military leader, sometimes known as the captain-general, on other occasions called the commander-in-chief, who worked in parallel with the Secretary at War, the civilian minister responsible for the army. A captain-general or commander-in-chief who had good political connections, such as the Duke of Cumberland, George II's second and favourite son, could exert considerable influence, often eclipsing the Secretary at War, at least in the eyes of the army's officers. The captain-general or commander-in-chief was assisted by the adjutant-general, who looked after communications and gathered information to assist the commander-in-chief, acting rather like a regimental adjutant for the whole army.

Also available to support the head of the army was the board of general officers, an advisory body, composed by rotation of the general officers on the British establishment. It oversaw the provision of uniforms for the army, though it delegated most of the routine work to a subordinate clothing board. More importantly, great faith was placed by captains-general and commanders-in-chief in its accumulated wisdom and experience; the board of general officers acted as a problem-solving body when awkward issues arose. It in turn was advised by the judge-advocate general, the army's chief legal officer, who attended board meetings when legal questions required determination.[17] The judge-advocate general also oversaw all general courts martial, receiving records of them from his deputies and gave advice on jurisdiction and procedures both to his deputies and to local commanding officers.[18]

Beneath this governing structure was a collection of regiments, which formed the army's basic unit of organization. Regiments, as we will see later, did not always form the primary unit of identification for the officer or common soldier, which, according to circumstances, might be a smaller unit, such as a company or squadron or troop or a composite unit, formed on campaign, from the flank companies (grenadiers and light infantry) of different regiments.[19] But, in structural terms, the regiment was the main denomination of currency in the army. It was the regiment, furthermore, that was familiar to the politicians who agreed to raise the taxes to fund the army – it appeared as a collection of regiments in the annual Army Estimates presented to Parliament. Generals, who often commanded their own regiments, understood the army in the same way.

Those regiments raised in wartime might be disbanded in time of peace and new ones formed at the start of the next hostilities, but a core number of regiments always remained in existence, in peace as well as in war. Regiments varied by function; mounted soldiers were meant to break through enemy ranks and pursue a retreating foe, turning their defeat into a rout, while infantry were valued for their firepower, which, by the use of disciplined musketry, produced a deadly hail of lead in a concentrated area. Regiments differed greatly in size; infantry regiments (usually the equivalent of a battalion, though in a few cases comprising more than one battalion) were around twice or three times the size of cavalry regiments. In both arms, furthermore, there were variations by type. The cavalry comprised regiments of horse, dragoons (originally mounted infantrymen), dragoon guards and, from the Seven Years War onwards, light dragoons. The infantry divided into the marching regiments of foot, including a few regiments of fusiliers (whose function was no longer distinct from the rest, but were distinguished by different headgear) and the three regiments of foot guards.

In the cavalry, the regiment would be divided into squadrons or troops; in the infantry into companies. The captains who commanded squadrons, troops and companies (who had often purchased their commissions) still tended to regard their unit as a species of private property, for them to run as they saw fit. We can see this in the way in which contemporaries described these units. In the modern British Army, they are usually identified by a distinguishing letter – A Company, B Company and so on – but this was not the practice in the eighteenth century. A roll of infantry, drawn up in about 1750, listing their age, size and nationality, identified them as soldiers in 'the Right Hon^bl Lord Balgonies Company', as though it were his personal possession.[20] We can see faint reminders in our period of the ancient status of captains as proprietors; some new regiments formed during wartime brought together independent companies, raised by their captains. But, by the time we are considering, many of the symbols of captains' autonomy had disappeared and many of their privileges.

Colonels, like the squadron, troop and company commanders, gave their name to their units. Captain Lord Balgonie led a company in Lieutenant-General Roger Handasyde's regiment, which was routinely described in just those terms – as Handasysde's Regiment.[21] But, unlike captains, colonels at the beginning of our period enjoyed additional privileges which underlined their independent status. In some cases, they even incorporated their own coats of arms into the regimental flags or colours. Concerns about the implications of such private symbols of ownership led to pressure, under the Hanoverian monarchs, to bring the army under greater central management and make it into more of an integrated and state-controlled whole, rather than a loose confederation of individual regiments. Admittedly, reform had its limits; the financial perquisites enjoyed by colonels remained largely intact at the end of the time we are considering. We might be tempted to think that no Hanoverian monarch, nor any British government, was willing to take on such a powerful vested interest as the army's colonels. A more likely explanation is that ministers condoned perquisites because they allowed colonels to be well remunerated without having to raise their official salaries, which Parliament would have had to approve.[22]

Nevertheless, in important ways the state did intervene to clip the wings of the colonels and assert itself as the master. Regiments had been given a number to indicate their seniority by date of formation from the creation of a unified English and Scottish army in 1707. But the 1742 clothing regulations were the first to use numbers only, without reference to the colonel's name, as had been customary. The 1747 regulations went further; they banned the use of the colonel's arms or crest on any regimental clothing or flags. A royal warrant of 1751 repeated this prohibition on the use of personal insignia and insisted that henceforth regiments would be denoted by their numbers only. In practice, unsurprisingly, the personal and numerical identifiers tended to be used alongside each other long after 1751, even in some official documents. But now the number was always used, with the colonel's name usually serving as a supplementary descriptor only, as in the copies of returns in the papers of Charles Jenkinson, Secretary at War in the second half of the War of American Independence.[23]

At the end of our period, in 1782, a step was taken that at first glance might seem to have put the trend towards centralization in reverse – the army's infantry regiments were given county affiliations, with the 6th Foot becoming the Warwickshire Regiment, the 10th Foot the North Lincoln Regiment and so on. The logic seems to have been that local loyalties might encourage enlistment more readily than national identification. It would be easy to see a sense of local belonging as an antidote or alternative to national consciousness. But we should not conclude that county naming represented a slackening of official efforts to impose more central control; it was, in truth, a means to further it, for the counties were seen as vital building blocks to help construct in military and civilian minds a sense of the wider nation that the army was there to serve. Local loyalties, in short, were not incompatible with national allegiance; the first was meant to act as a stepping stone to the second.[24]

On campaign, a regiment might be brigaded with others; usually three or four regiments formed a brigade. But these were temporary formations, which lasted for the duration of a campaign and usually no longer. An army might comprise several brigades – at the Battle of Long Island in August 1776, for instance, most of the British regiments were grouped in six brigades, each bearing a number, though some remained un-brigaded[25] – but even at the end of our period these brigades were not brought together in divisions. When contemporaries used the term 'corps' to refer to a body of troops, they did not mean it in the modern sense of an army corps – a large assembly of units, bringing together several divisions – but simply as an alternative term for the regiment (as when the commander of the 47th Foot referred to the regiment as 'the Corps' when reprimanding his men for ill-conduct in 1777).[26] For all the attempts to mould the army into a state-controlled whole, there was still some way to go to its becoming like the army of the Napoleonic Wars, let alone the army of the twentieth or twenty-first centuries.

Deployments

In peacetime, most of the army was based in the home territories. In 1726, six regiments of foot and two of horse garrisoned Scotland. In England, fourteen regiments of foot served alongside twelve regiments of horse, not counting the Guards and Household cavalry, who remained in London for most of the period covered in this study. Ireland's establishment consisted of eighteen regiments of foot and ten of horse. Just one infantry regiment was in North America and another in the West Indies. The Mediterranean garrisons of Minorca and Gibraltar contained four and three regiments of foot, respectively. In other words, all twenty-four of the cavalry units and thirty-eight of the forty-seven infantry regiments (just under 81 per cent), plus all the Household troops, remained in Britain and Ireland. In terms of the army as a whole, of the seventy-one regiments of foot and horse, just nine (13 per cent) were stationed abroad.[27]

The number of regiments deployed overseas increased in later decades of peace. In 1752, for instance, North America, the West Indies and the Mediterranean garrisons accounted for thirteen of the army's seventy-nine regiments or just over 16 per cent of the whole. After the Seven Years War, the government decided to keep a peacetime army in North America, ostensibly to defend the colonies themselves, but in reality as a mobile reserve (much like the infantry on the Irish establishment) for rapid deployment in the western hemisphere in what was assumed to be the likely event of another war with France and its ally Spain. The presence of a significant number of regiments in the mainland colonies (and more also in the West Indian islands) altered the pre-war distribution of the army quite radically. In 1767, the overall proportion of the army's regiments deployed abroad had risen to 31 per cent, thanks largely to the great increase in units based in North America.[28]

In theory, regiments moved by rotation from one place of duty to another. In 1726, one regiment of foot left Ireland for Minorca, where it relieved another infantry regiment that returned to England. More movement occurred in 1752, when one regiment of horse and two of foot exchanged duty in Scotland and England and each of the Mediterranean garrisons received a new regiment of infantry from England and sent one back. In 1767, the process of rotation led to a much greater turnover of troops: Scotland received from England a regiment of foot and two of horse, but sent back one of foot and one of horse; North America returned a regiment to England and four to Ireland, while receiving in return six regiments of infantry from Ireland.

But rotation did not prevent some regiments remaining in the same station for many years. Cavalry regiments did not stir outside the British Isles in peacetime; nor did the Household troops – both the Guards infantry and the cavalry. These units and their officers in particular, who could socialise with local elites and spend time with their families or on their estates, could consider themselves fortunate. Others had less reason to count their blessings. The 40th Foot languished in Nova Scotia from its foundation in 1717 until it was finally sent to Ireland in 1765. More unlucky still was the 38th Foot, condemned to serve in the disease-ridden West Indian islands from 1716 until 1765, when it, like the 40th, sailed for Ireland, leaving behind hundreds – probably thousands – of men who had died in the meantime.[29] Even regiments that remained in the same country for less time than the 40th or the 38th could find themselves becoming part of the local furniture. John Shy has written of a process of 'Americanization' of the British regiments that were stationed for many years in the mainland colonies after 1763. The regiments recruited more and more men locally, marriages between soldiers and local women became more common and officers acquired land in North America.[30]

War increased mobility. In the period we are considering, domestic and imperial rebellions led to the redeployment of many regiments. In 1715–16, an uprising by supporters of the deposed Stuart claimant to the throne required the concentration of troops in Scotland and northern England to put down the rebellion. The next Jacobite rebellion, in 1719, was a small affair and required only modest military effort to suppress; the government forces at the Battle of Glenshiel numbered only just over 1,000 men. The much larger 1745–6 Jacobite uprising, which started in Scotland and spread to northern England, brought forth a major movement of British regiments, not only from southern England, where they were deployed to resist a French invasion, but also from Flanders, where the army was serving alongside its Dutch and Austrian allies and German auxiliaries, in the War of the Austrian

Succession. By the time of the final defeat of the rebels at Culloden in the spring of 1746, a significant proportion of the army – 9,000 troops – under the command of the Duke of Cumberland, George II's son, was employed against the Jacobite forces.

The American conflict, which began in 1775, became a world-wide war in 1778, when first the French, then the Spanish and finally the Dutch became allies of the United States. But before foreign intervention, it was a regarded by the British state as a rebellion, much like that of the Jacobites in 1715, 1719 and 1745, albeit on a larger scale and at a much greater distance from London. On this occasion, a major field army was assembled and dispatched across the Atlantic from Britain and Ireland, with regiments also sailing to North America from the West Indies and the Mediterranean garrisons, reinforced by a significant contingent of German auxiliary troops. In 1776, the army in the rebel colonies comprised forty-four regiments of British infantry and two of cavalry or nearly 43 per cent of all the army's foot and horse units.[31]

The major international conflicts of the period saw an equally striking pattern of redeployment, though on a much more geographically dispersed basis. A small war against Spain in 1718–20 saw a British expedition attack and capture Vigo and Portevedra in the north-west of the country. Further conflict with Spain in the late 1720s involved the navy but not, in any significant way, the army. The war with Spain that began in 1739 was quite different. It led to an ill-fated expedition to the Spanish empire in the West Indies and the mainland of Central and South America, which involved regiments sent from Britain and Ireland as well from North America, where forces were raised specifically for the purpose. The failure of the expedition led to the recall of the British regiments in 1742.

By this time, sixteen regiments of British foot and ten of horse had been dispatched to Flanders, to help protect the Low Countries from French invasion during the War of the Austrian Succession.[32] Flanders was the main theatre of operations for the British Army until the end of the war in 1748, though many British regiments came home in 1745–6, as we have seen, to help put down the Jacobite rebellion and in 1743 a British contingent served alongside Austrian, Hanoverian and Hessian troops in western Germany, contributing to the defeat of French forces at Dettingen that June. The British government planned an expedition to North America, to expel the French from Canada, in 1746, but the Jacobite uprising and continuing fear of French invasion, kept the force at home. The most it achieved was a destructive raid on Lorient, on the coast of Brittany, the depot of the French East India Company. India itself was the scene of military operations, but though Royal Navy ships supported the British East India Company's own forces, regular regiments did not go to South Asia.

The next international conflict – the Seven Years War – witnessed a much wider dispersal of British troops. Even before the conflict formally began, a British infantry regiment (the 39th Foot) and an artillery contingent left Ireland for India. Other British regiments of foot sailed from Ireland for North America; the two regiments defeated under Edward Braddock's command at the Monongahela River in July 1755 had both recently arrived from Cork. The British war effort in India largely depended upon locally raised troops in the service of the East India Company (though a regular regiment served on the expedition to capture Spanish Manila at the end of the war). In North America, meanwhile, doubts about the reliability of local provincial regiments led to an increasing commitment of British troops. By the summer of 1757, Lord Loudoun commanded sixteen British regiments, mustering just over 14,000 officers and men.[33] By that autumn, further reinforcements had boosted the British battalions to twenty-one and the number of troops to more than 20,000. When the 1758 campaign began, that figure had risen to 24,000.[34] The capture of Montreal and the surrender of the whole of New France in September 1760 enabled British troops in North America to be redeployed to the Caribbean, where they served first against the French islands and then, from 1762, against Spanish Cuba.

The Seven Years War was truly global; not for nothing is it often called the 'first world war'.[35] British troops, besides serving in North America, the West Indies, India and the Philippines, were engaged in the capture of French slave trading stations in West Africa. But, despite the wide dispersal of deployments, the conflict involved a very traditional commitment of forces to the European Continent. In the War of the Austrian Succession that had mainly been in the Low Countries (modern-day Belgium and Holland), with a brief focus in the summer of 1743 on western Germany. In the Seven Years War, north-west Germany was the principal area of British deployment. William Pitt, the leading British war minister, had made his political reputation as an opponent of a Continental commitment, which he had claimed benefited Hanover rather than Britain. The government of which he was a part financed a German subsidiary army to protect Hanover and to shield Frederick the Great of Prussia (a British ally) from French incursions on his western flank, but limited its own military involvement in Europe to raids on the French coast, which their advocates claimed (somewhat optimistically) would divert French troops from Germany. These raids, which relied on British naval superiority, played well with opponents of a Continental engagement, but their impact on the French war effort was probably negligible.[36] In 1758, however, after a British-paid German army, commanded by Ferdinand of Brunswick, defeated the French at Krefeld and while Frederick the Great was enjoying great popularity in Britain, Pitt committed a small British force to serve in Ferdinand's army. Initially just 8,000 strong, the British contingent received reinforcements to try to dislodge the French from Westphalia; by the closing stages of the war, nearly 25,000 British regulars were campaigning in Germany. By this stage another European theatre had opened. When Spain entered the conflict as an ally of France, its army mobilized to invade Portugal, a long-standing British ally. A British expeditionary force of nearly 7,000 troops arrived in the summer of 1762, where it served alongside the Portuguese army commanded by a German general, the Count of Schaumburg-Lippe.

The final major conflict of our period was the War of American Independence. As we have seen, the war was initially fought for and in North America; from the British perspective it was a rebellion. From 1778, however, the war globalized in much the same way as the earlier Seven Years War. The entry of first France, then Spain and finally the Dutch into the conflict on the side of the Americans led to the creation of many new battlefronts and a major redeployment of the British Army. Until that point, suppression of the American rebellion had been the priority; as we have seen, in 1776, the first year of major campaigning, some 43 per cent of the army's regiments were fighting in the American theatre. But at the end of 1777, when news arrived in London of the defeat of a British field army under General John Burgoyne at Saratoga, the government began to plan for a completely different war. It was assumed, even before the formal signing of the Franco-American alliance, that France was bound to intervene on behalf of the rebels (its government had already been clandestinely supporting them with munitions and money). British ministers were equally sure that Spain, France's ally, would sooner or later enter the war, too. Regiments in North America were ordered to make ready to attack the French islands in the West Indies in order to cut a major source of the wealth that British ministers believed fed the French war machine – the profits from sugar production. Further British regiments sailed to reinforce the garrison of Florida, a former Spanish possession thought to be in danger of attack. The government in London also ordered some of the regiments in North America to return home; a war against France, still more against France and Spain combined, posed a real threat of invasion.

North America continued to be a major theatre of operations right through to the surrender of a second British field army, led by Lord Cornwallis, at Yorktown, Virginia, in October 1781. But the withdrawal of a significant number of regular regiments meant that the British war effort in North America depended to a much greater extent on the German auxiliary troops and locally-raised loyalists, who fought in their own provincial corps. The government persisted with the war in North America partly out of a sense of obligation to those colonists who had demonstrated their loyalty and refused to renounce their allegiance to George III. But more important in British thinking was surely the West Indies, which needed North American supplies – foodstuffs such as rice and meat in particular – as the islands' planters had devoted most of their cultivatable acres to sugar and had little capacity to increase local food supplies to feed the enslaved labour force. Retaining at least the southernmost rebel colonies – Georgia and South Carolina, which produced large quantities of rice and other provisions – therefore became the most important consideration for ministers in London; hence the emphasis on a southern strategy from the end of 1778. From that point, the war in North America was pursued for essentially Caribbean purposes.[37]

The intervention of Britain's traditional Bourbon foes, however, meant that North America became just one theatre amongst many and not necessarily the most important. The West Indies themselves, besides the regiments sent from North America in late 1778, received a further sixteen infantry battalions before the end of the war in 1783. In November 1780, St Kitts, Antigua, Jamaica, Barbados and St Lucia accounted for fifteen British regiments between them.[38] India commanded British attention, not least because the British East India Company struggled to contain the threat posed by the French-backed rulers of Mysore. Eight British regular regiments arrived in India between 1779 and 1783. British forces were even dispatched to West Africa (in a rerun of the Seven Years War) and a small body of regular troops served in Central America against the Spanish, as part of an ambitious (but unachieved) scheme to take the war into the Pacific, attacking Spanish outposts along the western coast of the Americas and even venturing towards the Spanish Philippines.[39]

But, as in previous wars, Europe absorbed considerable military resources. Neither the Low Countries nor Germany became a theatre of operations (the French government, having learned the lessons of the previous war, was keen to avoid fighting a Continental and imperial struggle at the same time); but the Mediterranean garrisons of Gibraltar and Minorca both became exposed with Spanish entry into the American war. Gibraltar endured a long siege, while Minorca fell to a French and Spanish army. Defence of these outposts involved several British infantry regiments, as well as troops loaned by George III in his capacity as Elector of Hanover. Moreover, the danger of invasion of the home territories – Britain and Ireland – meant that a significant number of regular regiments had to be kept in the British Isles, where they could bolster the newly-raised militia in trying to resist an enemy landing. That danger became intense in 1779, when the French and Spanish fleets combined outgunned the Royal Navy. It returned in 1781, with the added challenge that Dutch entry into the war exposed not just the southern and western coasts of Britain and Ireland to attack, but also the long North Sea coast of England and Scotland. For all the bravado about the power of the Royal Navy, British fleets could not simultaneously protect such a great expanse of coastline from multiple enemies. The army had to be available to save the day if hostile troops landed. In August 1779, two regiments of foot were stationed in the Plymouth district, eight in the Kentish district, four in the Essex district and three in the English North-East.[40] In July 1781, there were still seven infantry regiments in southern England, plus another three in the Channel Islands, which had been attacked by the French that January.[41]

From the time of the Seven Years War, then, the British Army found itself increasingly contributing to imperial defence and security, primarily in North America and the West Indies, but also in India and West Africa. This new imperial role was a natural consequence of the expansion of empire that took place as a result of the conflict and its aftermath. In 1763, the British crown acquired new colonies in North America – Canada from France and Florida from Spain – and control over a vast inland wilderness across the Appalachian Mountains chain. The whole of the eastern half of North America was now under British jurisdiction, from Hudson's Bay in the north to the Gulf of Mexico in the south and from the Atlantic in the east to the Mississippi in the west. Further islands were added to British dominions in the West Indies; a new British territory established in West Africa; and, from 1765, the British East India Company became effective ruler of three populous Indian provinces, of which Bengal was the most important. Politicians at Whitehall and Westminster, in the decades following the Seven Years War, became increasingly preoccupied with imperial matters and this preoccupation influenced the army's deployment. Important assets and interests had to be protected and the army was expected to play its part in providing that protection.

Deployments are one thing; sentiments quite another. Even as the British Army's commitments became more imperial, its members – and particularly its officers – clung to the familiar. Traditional European battlegrounds continued to cast a spell. In 1743, when British troops campaigned in western Germany, one of their officers wrote that 'The fame of what our ancestors did in this Country [in 1704, at Blenheim] . . . is still talk'd of as a recent thing.'[42] But it was not just nostalgia that drew eighteenth-century British soldiers to Europe as their natural military home. Even James Wolfe, the posthumous victor at Quebec in 1759 and later great icon of empire, would have preferred to be on the Continent. 'If I had followed my own taste', he told a correspondent in late 1758, 'it would lead me to Germany.' His preference seems to have owed much to his belief that campaigning in Westphalia would give him the opportunity to 'serve in an army commanded by a great and able Prince', by which he meant Ferdinand of Brunswick.[43] After the Seven Years War, the Earl of Shelburne, a lieutenant general as well as a leading politician, recommended that Pitt's son, who wanted to pursue a career in the army, go to Germany rather than Canada, for it was in Germany, Shelburne argued, that the young man would come into contact with a military culture shaped by Frederick the Great and Ferdinand of Brunswick.[44]

Shelburne's advice tells us a lot about the character of the army, the essentials of which subsequent chapters in this book will seek to capture. Shelburne, in his political life, spent a great deal of time focused on imperial problems, in North America particularly; yet he never lost sight of the importance to British interests of the European balance of power.[45] There were obvious parallels in his military life. As a general, who had himself served in Germany during the Seven Years War (he had fought at Minden under Ferdinand's command), he had no doubt that the British Army was part of a European military system. Even as Britain's military commitments became more imperial, the British Army remained an essentially European institution.[46]

Chapter 3

Entering the Service

This chapter attempts to answer three questions related to entry into the army. First, how did men become soldiers? Second, who joined the army? Third, why did they pursue a military career? The mechanics of entry into the service, for officers and common soldiers, is the subject of the first section. The second section looks at the composition of the army, again considering both the officers and the men that they commanded. The final part of the chapter explores the motives of those who became soldiers, whether as officers or members of the rank and file. Motivation is, of course, very difficult to uncover. What people profess inspires them may not necessarily be what really drives their actions. We need, therefore, to recognize that the third section is inevitably more speculative than the preceding two; often, we have no choice but to infer motives from actions rather than words.

How?

For officers, the usual route into the army in years of peace was by purchase. Commissions, from the lowliest ensigncies, cornetcies and second-lieutenancies to the senior regimental posts, were bought and sold according to an official tariff, which was periodically revised.[1] The 1766 regulations fixed the purchase prices in marching regiments of foot on the British establishment at £400 for an ensigncy, £550 for a lieutenancy, £800 for a captain-lieutenancy (officers of this rank usually commanded the colonel's company), £1,500 for a captaincy, £2,600 for a majority and £3,500 for a lieutenant colonelcy.[2] But that tariff, like earlier ones, was in reality no more than a guide; the true prices charged varied according to supply and demand. In North America, in January 1778, according to Lieutenant Charles Campbell of the 71st Foot, a captaincy cost £2,000 and a majority £4,000.[3] A seller received the regulation price of his commission from the government and the buyer paid the government the same sum. The buyer would then pay the seller the difference between the market and regulation price. The system encouraged those that held a commission by purchase to regard it as a form of private property. When they wished to leave the army, they could sell their commission (usually one associated with a higher rank than that with which they had entered the army) and use the proceeds to fund their retirement.[4] The peacetime entrant into the officer ranks, then, usually had to wait for a vacancy to become available by purchase at the bottom of the officer hierarchy as a result of a series of sales and purchases further up the line of command. His situation was in that sense akin to that of a first-time buyer at the bottom of a chain in the modern housing market.

Purchase continued to be a method of entry during hostilities, especially in already established or 'old' regiments. Major wars, however, always led to the adding of new regiments to the army, often raised by large landowners or borough corporations keen to assert their loyalty, increase their local patronage and (in the case of the large landowners) make money from the perquisites of command.[5] In these new regiments, commissions for the first-appointed officers in each rank could be acquired by recruiting a stipulated number of soldiers without government levy money. Unsurprisingly, this was a much cheaper option than purchase – recruiting costs were considerably lower than the price of purchasing a commission. Senior commissioned ranks were usually given to officers already in the army, who transferred from an old regiment to a new in order to acquire a more senior rank at little cost – they simply recruited the stipulated number of new soldiers to qualify for their commission. For those wishing to enter the army as officers, the new regiments offered a cheap way into the profession. Thomas Fraser, for instance, had to provide just eighteen men in three months at the beginning of the American war to qualify for an ensigncy in the newly-raised 71st Foot or Fraser's Highlanders.[6] While Fraser would have had to lay out some money to recruit his quota, mostly in the form of levy money, it would have been considerably less than the minimum of £400 he would have been obliged to spend on an ensigncy in one of the existing infantry regiments. But there was a longer-term price to pay. While officers who bought their commissions in old regiments could usually expect to remain in the service at the end of a war and could sell their commission when they decided to retire, an officer who secured his rank by recruiting the required number of soldiers had no such security for the future. As he was likely to be serving in a new regiment, he would probably be disbanded with his corps at the end of the conflict. Unless he had secured promotion by purchase, he would have no commission to sell to fund his life outside the army. His only long-term prospect was half-pay, a form of retained retirement, in which the recipient would seek to re-enter the army at his previous rank when it expanded again at the start of the next war.[7]

There were other non-purchase routes into the officer ranks. If an officer died, his place became vacant. If the fatality were a senior officer, his immediate junior would replace him, with all other officers moving one step up the seniority ladder, creating an opportunity for a new entrant at the bottom. So, if the major died, the senior captain would succeed him and all other captains would move one step closer to a majority. The senior lieutenant would become a captain and so on, down the chain of command. At the very bottom, a vacancy would be created for the 'youngest' or most junior ensigncy (or cornetcy in the cavalry). The regimental colonel recommended a suitable candidate for this post, who had to be approved by the government. The colonel might favour the appointment of a gentleman volunteer. Often the sons of impecunious officers, gentlemen volunteers served in the ranks, hoping to win favour and be appointed to the first available subaltern vacancy. As they tended to be included with the officers for social purposes, they had plenty of opportunities to build up a favourable reputation. Even so, gentlemen volunteers usually relied on the support of a powerful patron to be successful in securing the first step on the commissioned officer ladder. Walter Cliffe, the son of an officer killed at the Battle of Minden in 1759, came recommended to the colonel of the 46th Foot by the Lord Lieutenant of Ireland's chief secretary, Sir John Blacquiere. As Blacquiere explained, Cliffe 'will be content to do the Duties of a Soldier and with the greatest Chearfulness, in hopes that by demeaning himself to the Satisfaction of his Officers, he may hereafter obtain your Countenance & Protection'.[8]

In wartime, when experience mattered particularly, the colonel might prefer to promote a long-serving and distinguished non-commissioned officer to an ensigncy or lieutenancy without the sergeant having to purchase his new rank. The colonel's recommendation might also enable a sergeant to become a subaltern in another regiment where a vacancy existed. One authority reckons that some 150–200 promotions from the ranks occurred in the War of the Austrian Succession.[9] It seems likely that there was a larger number in both the Seven Years War and the War of American Independence, which saw much bigger expansions of the army than in 1740–8 and therefore greater need for experienced sergeants to be elevated to junior officer rank.

Recruits for the rank and file might also enter the service by a variety of routes. A relatively small number of common soldiers found their way into the British Army after having been recruited in the German states by paid local recruiting agents. The newly-raised Royal American Regiment benefited from the efforts of such recruiting agents during the Seven Years War.[10] The regiment enlisted more Germans using the same methods in 1766.[11] When the American war broke out, several German military entrepreneurs offered their services in recruiting manpower for understrength British regiments. The most important, a lieutenant colonel in the Hanoverian army, provided nearly 2,000 men under the terms of a contract with the British treasury. He relied on a network of recruiting agents across Germany, though most of the men enlisted came from the western states.[12] His recruits were distributed among the British regiments in or destined for, North America, with the largest number – 244 – going to the Royal Americans, but the rest scattered in smaller parcels, ranging from seventy-five in the 8th and 47th Foot to a mere five in the 64th.[13] The army serving on the Continent in earlier wars also recruited foreigners to make up for the usual loss of men; this was certainly the case with the British regiments serving in Flanders in the War of the Austrian Succession and in Germany in the Seven Years War.[14]

In Britain and Ireland, some men had little choice but to join the army, at least in wartime. The 1744 Vagrancy Act empowered the Privy Council to order magistrates to round up wandering paupers and force them to enlist. Convicted criminals could secure a pardon in return for military service; magistrates might on their own initiative offer the newly convicted (or even those accused but not convicted) the opportunity to join the army in lieu of formal punishment. In the War of the Austrian Succession, the Seven Years War and the War of American Independence, Recruiting Acts authorized the forcible recruitment of men with no visible means of support. We should note, however, that the number of soldiers raised by these non-voluntary means seems to have been relatively small. In the American war, from 1775 to 1781, some 500 convicts in England and Wales received pardons conditional upon serving in the army; for another 200, joining the army was one of their choices. Local justices, for their part, seem to have offered criminals the option of military service on just a small number of occasions: in Warwickshire only five; in Hertfordshire and Cambridgeshire, three; in Shropshire, two; in the City of London, one.[15] In 1744–6, perhaps 7,500 impressed men joined the army, which during the War of Austrian Succession probably saw around 100,000 men serving in its ranks.[16] In the American war, the yield seems to have been even lower: halfway through the operation of the 1779 Act, fewer than 1,000 men had been added to the army and marines by impressment in England and Wales.[17] But to the government the value of the Recruiting Acts lay as much in the encouragement they gave to voluntary recruitment as to compulsion. The 1779 Act offered those who volunteered the opportunity to practise trades after the war, regardless of guild restrictions.[18]

Most men entering the army's rank and file joined the service more-or-less voluntarily. Some officers or aspiring officers (such as Patrick Campbell of Barcaldine) paid recruiting agents to bring in willing men wherever they could be found – in Campbell's case Newcastle, even though he was enlisting men for a Highland regiment.[19] Others called on the services of friends and family members to help. In 1761, George Drummond, excited at the thought that a new regiment was about to be raised in Scotland, wrote to a relative explaining that he hoped that 'our Friends among the Clergy, in the Custom house & the Excise Office must in every Parish we can think of be applied to for their Assistance for a man or two'.[20] But enlistees usually found their way into the army after being encouraged to enter by a recruiting party, typically led by a junior officer, sent to find potential soldiers.

Recruiting parties looked for possible enlistees wherever their officers thought likely to be productive. Francis Hutchinson, appointed to an ensigncy in the Royal Americans in 1756, raised forty-two men for the 3rd Battalion in New Jersey.[21] In 1779, a relative of the Duke of Gordon predicted that the raising of a corps of Highlanders would lead to 'a new *Swarm* of Recruiting Sergeants over the Duke's Estate'.[22] Young officers from landed backgrounds tended to imagine that they would have the best results in areas where they were well known – which usually meant near their ancestral homes. Even so, most recruiting parties headed for towns and cities, the great magnets for the footloose in the surrounding rural hinterland, where officers reckoned that young men in search of opportunity congregated in the largest numbers. In North America, Captain John Cosnan of the 45th Foot recruited in Boston early in 1758.[23] Captain James Campbell of the 39th Foot, on the recruiting service in Scotland later the same year, identified Edinburgh, Glasgow and Paisley as 'the most Populous Places in this Country'.[24] In Ireland, Dublin attracted recruiting parties; in England, they headed for Birmingham, Bristol, Leeds, Manchester and, of course, London, which Captain Anthony Haslam, an old and experienced officer, looking for men for a regiment on the Irish establishment, told the Secretary at War in 1776 was 'the best [place] to carry on the Recruiting Service'.[25]

Entry into the ranks might be facilitated in wartime by the recruiting parties' offering enhanced enlistment bounties or one-off payments, which were sometimes increased by local elites or borough corporations. But persuasion took many different forms. Recruiting parties might include musicians who played songs specially composed for the occasion, which emphasized patriotic duty, defence of loved ones and even the attraction of soldiers to women.[26] The passage of potential recruits into the army might be lubricated by copious quantities of alcohol to help overcome their doubts; taverns and inns seem to have been the favourite haunts of recruiting parties. In a further encouragement to enlistment (which was also intended to avoid having an overly large army when the fighting stopped), the government limited the period of wartime recruitment, generally to three years or the duration of the conflict.[27] In peacetime, recruitment offered no such hope of early release; it was for as long as the army needed the enlistee.

Would-be officers, hoping to win a commission in a regiment in the process of its being formed, sought recruits with particular fervour, as they were incentivized to do so. Recruiting for old regiments tended to be a slower process, not least because the officers on the recruiting service usually displayed much less commitment.[28] Indeed, for officers in established units, the recruiting service was usually deeply unpopular. Patrick Clerk, recruiting in Somerset in 1740, went so far as to describe it as 'a Slavery that is unexpressible'.[29] In 1751, Archibald Cuninghame, more temperately, regarded recruiting as 'by far the most disagreeable part of our Trade'.[30] These negative comments should come as no surprise. The recruiting service could involve considerable expense, especially if men deserted shortly after enlistment. As Henry Fletcher wrote from Bristol in 1755, 'I have lately lost Three Recruits out of Six, which is very unlucky, as the Loss falls on the Recruiting Officer, being allowed nothing for Diserters, but only for the Men that are produced to the Regiment'.[31] But perhaps more important to many junior officers in old regiments was that the recruiting service physically removed them from their units, which in wartime meant that they could be forgotten by their seniors and so passed over when opportunities arose for promotion.

Who?

The Act of Settlement of 1701 prohibited foreigners holding commissions, which meant that, in theory, only the Crown's British or Irish (or colonial) subjects could become officers in the army. Two exceptions to this rule should be noted, however. The first was that naturalization overcame the barrier. The officer ranks contained a noticeable number of men with French-sounding names, who were almost all Huguenots or French Protestants or of Huguenot descent. Isaac Barré, whose father had been part of the exodus of Protestants from France after 1685, when Louis XIV revoked the Edict of Nantes, which had granted them toleration, is a good example. So, too is John Carnac, a lieutenant in the 39th Foot before he joined the East India Company's service and became famous for his military exploits in the subcontinent. Carnac's father, like Barré's, had migrated to Ireland, where the Protestant population was particularly welcoming. His widowed mother continued to write to him from Dublin while Carnac campaigned in India.[32] A more spectacular example is Sir John Ligonier, who became a peer and commander-in-chief of the army. Though thoroughly anglicized, he was born Jean-Louis Ligonier, in a small town in the Massif Central, in 1680. But these officers, foreign-born or the descendants of those who were, cannot truly be counted as outsiders, as they had become subjects of the Crown. More obviously foreign were the German and Swiss Protestants who received special dispensation by Act of Parliament to serve as officers in the Royal Americans on its foundation in 1756. Amongst them were Augustine and Jacques-Marc Prévost, Henri Bouquet and François-Louis-Frédéric Haldimand. All of them went on to hold senior posts in the army and Haldimand became governor of Quebec.

Even in North America, however, the presence of these foreigners offered only the slightest of qualifications to the picture of an ethnically British and Irish officer class. In 1757, Lord Loudoun's army contained a mere forty-one foreign officers (or 6.5 per cent of the whole). Almost exactly the same number of Americans, not at this stage considered as foreigners, held commissions in the regulars – forty-two. The overwhelming bulk were English (or Welsh – returns of this period made no distinction) or Scots or Irish.

What is perhaps surprising, given that England was by far the most populous country of the British Isles, was that English and Welsh officers (24.5 per cent) were less numerous than Irish (31 per cent) and Scots (31.5 per cent).[33] These proportions might reflect the nature of the regiments that served in North America – the first to go there in 1754–5 were brought over from Ireland and Irish and Scottish Highland regiments were conspicuous in later reinforcements.

The army's common soldiers and non-commissioned officers were more likely to be from beyond the British Isles than were their officers. We have already seen that, in wartime, the army recruited where it was campaigning to help make up for losses through death, discharge and desertion. That was certainly true in Flanders in the War of the Austrian Succession and in Germany and North America in the Seven Years War. In the American case, local recruiting may well have continued after 1763, to enable the regiments retained in the colonies as a peacetime garrison to be brought up to strength when a new war threatened – as in 1770–1, when a conflict with Spain (and probably Spain's ally France) over the Falkland Islands looked likely.[34] We have seen, too, that in both the Seven Years War and the War of American Independence, German recruiting agents provided significant numbers of men for some British regiments serving across the Atlantic, particularly the Royal Americans. Inspections of Lord Loudoun's forces in North America in 1757 revealed that of 14,126 privates, corporals and sergeants, 1,410 (or 10 per cent) were described as foreigners recruited in Europe or the colonies and another 755 (5.5 per cent) as Americans. As with the officers, however, the vast majority came from the British Isles, though the English were more proportionately represented than amongst the officers, with 30 per cent. Even so, the Scots and Irish, each with 27.5 per cent, were still over-represented considering the population split within the British Isles.[35]

At home – in Britain and Ireland – the foreign (and American) presence in the army's regiments was much smaller than abroad. In most units it was statistically insignificant. The percentages of English and Welsh, Scots and Irish, however, displayed the same broad pattern as in the overseas postings. Scots were over-represented amongst officers wherever they served. A careful study concludes that they held about a quarter of the army's commissions between 1714 and 1763.[36] And, as abroad, the Scottish and Irish presence in the ranks was disproportionate. In the 15th Foot, inspected in Ireland in

July 1775, the split appears to have been 43 per cent English and Welsh, 23 per cent Scots and 34 per cent Irish.[37] For the 48th, inspected in England in October 1781, it was 40 per cent English and Welsh, 29 per cent Scots and 31 per cent Irish.[38]

In popular imagination and even some older scholarly accounts, the eighteenth-century British Army appears as composed of the least productive and most expendable elements of society. Its officers appear as the sons (often the younger sons) of the landed upper classes, aristocrats and gentry, with the common soldiers that they commanded coming from the poorest and most marginal elements of society. The image, like most caricatures, owes something to reality: many officers did come from the landed elite and criminals, vagrants and paupers, as we have seen, formed part of the rank and file. But many officers were not from the top drawer and many common soldiers were not from the very bottom of the pile.

Let us start with the officers, about whom we have the most detailed and reliable information. The aristocracy was certainly well represented, particularly in the senior ranks. The Earl of Stair commanded the British contingent in Flanders in 1742. From 1756 to 1758, as we have seen, the Earl of Loudoun, another Scottish peer, led the British forces in North America. From 1758 to 1762, command of the British troops in western Germany rested with a series of aristocrats – first the Duke of Marlborough, then Lord George Sackville (the third son of the Duke of Dorset) and finally the Marquis of Granby (heir of the Duke of Rutland). In North America during the War of Independence, William Howe, brother of a viscount, commanded from 1775 to 1778; he was succeeded by Sir Henry Clinton, grandson of the Earl of Lincoln and cousin of the Duke of Newcastle. These men, of course, had entered the army at the bottom of the officer hierarchy, long before they acquired senior command – Stair in 1702 and Clinton in 1745. At any given time, aristocrats could be found in the lower officer ranks. The Marquis of Lorne, eldest son of the Duke of Argyll, later a field marshal, was a mere second lieutenant in the Scots Fusiliers in 1739. Lord Frederick Cavendish, the third son of the Duke of Devonshire, who also reached the military pinnacle as a field marshal, entered the army as an ensign in the 1st Foot Guards in 1749. The Hon. Edward Finch, fifth son of the Earl of Aylesford, who later became a general, started his military career as cornet in the 20th Light Dragoons in 1778.

Many more officers, however, did not come from the titled aristocracy. A good number were members of lesser gentry families or from the professional or commercial middle classes. Typical of this group were the following: Jeremy Lister, an ensign in the 10th Foot from 1770, whose father had a small estate near Halifax in West Yorkshire;[39] Samuel Bradford, son of an Irish linen draper, who became an ensign in the 92nd Foot in the War of American Independence;[40] and Joseph Jefferys, a lieutenant in the artillery, described in 1747 as 'the son of a very considerable timber merchant in Birmingham'.[41] Lack of money was not necessarily an impediment to access to the officer ranks. At the beginning of the American war, Lord Barrington, the Secretary at War, noted that the volunteers commissioned after the very bloody Battle of Bunker Hill were 'all without a farthing'. But General Thomas Gage, the local commander-in-chief, had no hesitation in regarding them as suitable.[42] Nor should we forget that sergeants were given ensigncies and second-lieutenancies in wartime. Amongst those promoted from the ranks was James Wood of the Royal Artillery, who became a lieutenant-fireworker in India in 1755.[43] In the same category were Thomas Barnsley, sergeant-major in the 30th Foot, who obtained an ensigncy in the Royal Americans that same year,[44] and William Ralston, the son of a Glasgow Hosier, who, after service as a sergeant in the 71st Highlanders, became a lieutenant in the newly-raised 100th Foot in 1780.[45]

If we turn to the rank and file, the received image is again in need of modification. Some officers have left us with an unflattering picture of the men that they commanded. General Robert Cunninghame, commander-in-chief in Munster, anticipating the Duke of Wellington, described the Irish recruits he had seen as 'the very Scum of the Earth'.[46] Various army returns suggest that his bleak judgement probably reflected his prejudices as much as it captured reality. We can certainly say that the picture he painted does not hold good for the army as a whole. A small sign, perhaps, is literacy amongst recruits. In the middle of the eighteenth century, according to a modern estimate, about 40 per cent of unskilled men in England could read.[47] Yet when sixty-nine men in Lieutenant Colonel Sir Andrew Agnew's company of the Scots Fusiliers acknowledged receipt of their pay in February 1745, forty-one (59 per cent) could sign their name.[48] Literacy rates may well have been higher in Scotland than in England; even so, the rate of (admittedly basic) literacy amongst these common soldiers is striking.

It remains the case, however, that unskilled men were prominent in many units, which was probably the basis for General Cunninghame's unfavourable comment. In the British 52nd Foot, inspected in 1756, 47 per cent of the common soldiers appear to have been labourers.[49] The proportion varied in different British regiments, at least partly depending on the terminology used, but other recruiting returns underline the importance of labourers: they formed 70 per cent of the soldiers raised in Ireland for the 46th Foot in the winter of 1775–6,[50] and 52 per cent of the 96th Foot's enlistees between 1779 and 1782.[51]

But these same figures, of course, suggest the presence of very different men serving alongside the former labourers. Inspections and recruiting returns identify significant numbers of artisans or craftsmen. From shoemakers to weavers and from smiths to tailors and clockmakers, artisans comprised 38 per cent of the recruits for the 52nd Foot in 1756, 28 per cent of the men raised for the 46th in 1775–6 and 48 per cent of those joining the 96th between 1779 and 1782. Smaller samples suggest an even higher proportion of artisans in some units. A 'Description of Lord Rob[t] Berties Company Royal Fuziliers', penned in November 1772, identified twenty-five men (out of thirty-five with full descriptions) as having a trade or some 71 per cent.[52] Ensign Robert Johnstone of the 3rd Foot Guards enlisted twenty-two Scotsmen in late 1775 and early 1776, of whom thirteen (59 per cent) had trades of one type or another.[53] Of the twenty-five men that Lieutenant Allan Macdonald of the 76th Foot recruited in Glasgow in the last stages of the American war, a striking nineteen (76 per cent) were skilled craftsmen.[54]

Many recruiting returns, furthermore, identify men from more elevated backgrounds, such as merchants and teachers. If we move away from these impersonal lists, we can find, in at least a few cases, literary evidence that reveals the presence in the ranks of some soldiers who were very far removed from the image of the dregs of society. A chance reference to a young man recruited in New Jersey describes him as 'bred an Attorney'.[55] Walter Kirkam, a soldier in the 9th Foot, appears from papers relating to a property dispute to have owned land in Staffordshire. His son Edward served as a private in the Foot Guards.[56] Correspondence about recruits reveals that some came from comfortable backgrounds, such as Benjamin Addenbrooke, 'the Son of a reputable Clergyman' and the men 'of Condition & property, Sons of freeholders &[ca]' recruited by one officer in Wales during the American war.[57]

Why?

Valentine Rudd, a lieutenant languishing on half pay from 1763, claimed that his desire to re-join the army in the American war was motivated by nothing less than ideological commitment. He wrote of his willingness 'to Sacrifice his Life, for his King, Country and Protestant Religion'.[58] Rudd, in other words, explained his inspiration in terms of his loyalty to the British state and its religious constitution. We can surmise that many an officer, if questioned, would have come up with a similar explanation for their presence in the army. Perhaps they chose to make their case in this way simply because they believed that an effusion of patriotic zeal would help them to secure what they wanted. But even if we assume, for the moment, that Rudd and others who professed the same sentiments were genuinely inspired by a sense of duty, we should not regard such explanations as sufficient in themselves. Nearly always, other considerations played a part.

For a significant portion of those who entered the officer ranks, a military career was almost inevitable. The sons of serving officers, brought up in military families, they knew of no other occupation. They slipped almost unthinkingly into the army as the calling for which they had been long prepared and long expected to follow. It seems likely that this was true of John Bradstreet, who made his reputation in North America during the Seven Years War. Born in Nova Scotia in 1714, he was the son of a lieutenant in the regular army garrison and a local Acadian woman. The young Bradstreet served as a volunteer attached to the 40th Foot in Nova Scotia before obtaining a commission as an ensign in 1735.[59] Similarly, we can easily imagine that Matthew Pearson, made an ensign in Richbell's Regiment of Foot in 1749, was destined for a military life from an early age; his father was the regiment's lieutenant colonel.[60] Henry Stirke, who served as a volunteer with the 10th Foot before obtaining an ensigncy in the corps after the Battle of Bunker Hill in June 1775, was surely equally marked out for a military career from a tender age. Stirke, according to the officer who recommended him, was 'a Young Gent^m of good Character, His Brother a Captain in the Reg^t and His Father Serv'd the crown with reputation as an Officer for many years'.[61]

If we consider the army's officers by social background, we can speculate on what might have motivated them to join a profession in which their lives were at risk. For aristocrats and members of the wealthy upper gentry, military service probably seemed a particularly suitable option. The origins of noble landownership, after all, lay in the feudal obligation to provide military service for the Crown; to many members of the landed elite, serving in the army, the successor to the feudal levy, must have seemed thoroughly appropriate. To a younger son of an elite family, with little prospect of inheriting his father's estate, the army represented an acceptable way to earn money and establish an independent reputation. The church or the law were alternatives, but perhaps ones more likely to attract the intellectually inquisitive. The army, to be sure, appealed to some well-educated youths from the top echelons of society; some even acquired instruction at military academies or technically-inclined universities on the Continent and clearly took their careers seriously.[62] But many aristocratic and upper-gentry entrants were characterized less by their cerebral accomplishments and more by their muscular commitment to the outdoor life. Well-educated or not, they had been brought up to believe that leadership was their right as well as their duty. Rapid progress to a more lucrative senior rank seemed to be their entitlement. In 1751, Lord George Sackville politely chided the apparently insouciant Lord Balgonie, heir of the Earl of Leven, for not fulfilling his destiny more speedily: 'Your Lordship knows that a person of your rank in the world seldom fails of rising in the army when they show an attention to the service.'[63]

For officers from the lower gentry, the financial imperative was probably more pressing than for the aristocracy and upper gentry. Young men from well-respected but cash-strapped landowning families had little choice but to find some gainful means of employment; a career was not just desirable but essential. While junior officers could not expect to make much money (in fact, they often had to call on their parents or guardians for continuing financial support), if they obtained a captaincy, as we will see, they usually were able to make enough, in pay and perquisites, to become truly independent.[64] In the case of members of the professional and commercial middle classes, monetary considerations may have been less important than social ones. Officer rank for their sons offered the chance to realize the dream of social advancement, if not for the parents themselves, then at least for their sons and then later generations. Proximity to members of the landed elite and the acquisition of the status of a gentleman, both of which were possible as an officer in the army, would surely have proved attractive to the parents of middle-class families wishing to elevate the social standing of their offspring.

For experienced sergeants promoted to become junior officers during wars, we can guess that their new status was not usually actively sought or expected, but thrust upon them by the circumstances of the time.

If we turn to the rank and file, the reasons for entry into the army can be surmised by circumstantial as much as by direct evidence. Those compelled to serve – the convicts, paupers and vagrants – need not detain us here; their degree of choice was very limited, though we should note that a few convicts preferred to accept their ordained punishment rather than to join the army and rather more impressed paupers appear to have self-mutilated to make themselves unfit for military service.[65] Our focus is on the men who entered the army more-or-less voluntarily. To make sense of the various motives, we will group them under two broad headings, borrowed from studies of migration, pull and push factors – or, in other words, the factors that attracted men to join the army and the factors driving them away from their pre-military life.

Amongst the important pull factors was the inducement offered by those involved in the recruitment process. Landowners used their influence and local prestige to encourage men to join the colours. In particular, they might try to persuade their tenant farmers to provide sons for military service, promising all manner of preferential treatment to those who complied; there is abundant evidence, as mentioned earlier, of junior officers from landed backgrounds going back to their ancestral homes to recruit in the areas in which they believed that their family's influence was strongest. But landowners were understandably reluctant to see their estates drained of men and most regimental recruiting parties, as we have seen, tended to gravitate to large urban centres in search of more readily-available surplus manpower. Here, encouragement might take the form of additional cash, over and above the government levy money, provided through local subscriptions. Edinburgh's council agreed in September 1759 to give a bounty of two guineas, over and above ordinary recruiting money, to every townsman who joined the army.[66] In the same year, Liverpool's corporation offered additional bounties to men entering the Old Buffs 'now recruiting in Liverpool'.[67] Military recruiters, as noted earlier, provided lures of their own. They presented military service in the best possible light and encouraged would-be enlistees to reflect on the opportunities that awaited them if they took the king's shilling.

Recruiting parties seem to have laid much emphasis, at least in war-time, on young men having the chance to serve their king and country. A song composed to encourage enlistment in the newly-raised 22nd Light Dragoons, at a time when French invasion threatened during the American conflict, opened with an appeal to 'All you who have spirit your Country to save'.[68] But whether patriotism motivated enlistment is a moot point. Contemporary accounts suggest that British troops in war zones exhibited a high degree of commitment, which the authors attributed to loyalty to the state and especially the Crown. Thomas Sullivan, a soldier in the 49th Foot, whose diary has survived, stated emphatically that the rank and file of the army in Boston was enraged with the enemy after the very bloody Battle of Bunker Hill and determined to do their uttermost to put down the rebellion.[69] Two years later, in 1777, a chaplain attached to the Royal Highland Regiment argued that Highlanders, in particular, were always 'friends to King & Monarchy' and implacably opposed to rebellion.[70] Before we accept these claims at face value, however, we should consider their admissibility as evidence of motivation. If accurate, they tell us about the attitudes of soldiers in service, who had been inducted into the army's values, whose lives were in danger from a real enemy. They tell us nothing about the motives of those who were about to join the military. And, in both cases, the comments may simply reflect the author's desire to convey a positive impression to the reader, rather than capture the reality of what the ordinary soldiers thought.

That said, it seems reasonable to suppose that the young men who entered the army were not immune from the national enthusiasm that seems to have gripped the country in wartime. The American war, at least until 1778, when it was just a struggle in and for North America, perhaps provided the least clear incentives to fight out of a sense of patriotic duty. The conflict divided opinion at home and appeared, to many Britons, as a civil war in which Americans were contending for English liberties. As Major Francis Bushill Sill of the 63rd Foot explained, 'it is a harsh Service to fight against our fellow Subjects who are probably in the right'.[71] Wars against France, Britain's main enemy in the eighteenth century, were another matter. They seem to have excited much enthusiasm. 'The natural antipathy I believe we all have towards the French', Richard Laurence, a young Oxford undergraduate announced when the French entered the American war, 'has rous'd the Britain [i.e., Briton] in my soul.'[72] Again, caution is in order: Laurence was not a soldier. But he was commenting on a national mood (which other sources corroborate) and we should not assume that young men who joined the army were unaffected by it.

Another argument used by recruiting parties to attract would-be enlistees was that service in the army offered the chance for a life of glory, adventure and glamour. Returning soldiers, military songs claimed, would be greeted as heroes and held in high esteem – 'Laurels let your glory crown for your actions bold', proclaimed *The Marquis of Granby's March*, composed and performed in or shortly after the Seven Years War.[73] For those who led inconspicuous and unexciting civilian lives, the attraction of such an appeal can readily be imagined. The opportunity to travel to places where the newly recruited soldier would not be known must also have been a considerable pull for young men who lived a highly regulated life, constrained by the prying eyes and moral sanctions of face-to-face rural communities. Sexual adventure was perhaps the great unspoken (perhaps even unacknowledged) motive at work for more than a few recruits. It would surely have been encouraged by the claims, made by recruiters, that soldiers' uniforms accentuated their manly virtues and made them irresistibly attractive to young women. As we have seen, popular culture – in the form of ballads and songs – valorised the image of the handsome soldier, beloved by women wherever he goes.[74] It seems reasonable to suppose that this image had an impact on at least some impressionable male minds.

Would-be soldiers may well have been lured by the prospect of material advancement. Soldiers' pay was notoriously poor – it seems unlikely to have acted as a draw in itself, other than for those in truly desperate circumstances. But there were other ways in which the soldier could make money and these would have been made known to those who were considering entry into the army. Not only did the lump sum of bounty or levy money paid on enlistment provide a financial incentive (especially if augmented by locally-raised contributions), but recruits learned that military service offered them the chance to enrich themselves at the expense of their enemies. Wars against Spain, still assumed in popular imagination to be fabulously rich thanks to its vast Central and South American gold and silver resources, particularly encouraged this kind of thinking. But, whoever the enemy, loot, plunder and prize money featured in military songs as the soldier's expected perquisites.

As *The Grenadiers March*, which had become popular before the American war, put it: 'We'll search every room for to find rich treasure, And when we have got it we'll spend it at our leisure'.[75]

A better life, for many who joined the army, was not just about the ephemeral pleasure of more money; the opportunity to acquire land was perhaps a greater pull. Land could produce wealth but, more importantly, conferred enhanced status. With freehold possession of land came independence and political rights. In Britain itself, the prospect of owning land for most members of the population was no more than a dream. Ownership of land was concentrated in very few hands and becoming more and more so as the eighteenth century progressed. For those who aspired to own land, therefore, the colonies in North America offered the best way forward. There, land was plentiful and European cultivators few. The British state, keen to encourage more settlers, both to develop and defend the colonies better, offered all manner of inducements to encourage population growth, including to soldiers. At the end of the War of the Austrian Succession, the rank and file of the regiments due to return home from Nova Scotia, rather than be brought back at considerable expense to the government, were offered the chance to transfer to a unit remaining in the colony or to receive a land grant and settle there.[76] In 1763, shortly after the end of the Seven Years War, a royal proclamation offered troops who had been serving in North America land grants calibrated by rank – even private soldiers were entitled to 50 acres.[77] Knowledge of these opportunities offered at the end of previous wars may well have motivated recruitment, particularly in Highland regiments in the Seven Years War and the War of American Independence. Historians of Highland migration to North America have pointed to the importance of military service as one of the ways in which Scots made the journey across the Atlantic. For many would-be soldiers – and not just Highlanders – a spell in the army probably appeared as a price worth paying to become a landowner in the colonies.[78]

As we have already seen, pull factors operated most powerfully when they interacted with push factors. Now we will focus on some of the most important push factors themselves. For many young men, military service may have been the way out of difficult personal circumstances. A local study in one London parish suggests that recruitment provide an escape from unhappy marriages.[79] It may also have enabled unmarried men to avoid responsibility for unwanted children. James Swift, of the parish of Rowington in Warwickshire, held by local magistrates for fathering an illegitimate child, was discharged with the agreement of the parish authorities, which would have had to pick up the bill, after he 'enlisted in His Majesty's Service as a Soldier'.[80] It seems very likely that others took the same route as Swift before they were brought before local magistrates. Personal debt could similarly be evaded by joining the army, where the anonymity of a uniform (and physical distance from the person owed the money) might secure the debtor from prosecution or other forms of retribution. Men who had committed crimes might be no less inclined to see the army as a refuge, in which they could hide and remain undetected and unpunished.

More important for understanding the process of recruiting in general is the state of the economy, locally or nationally. The seasons had a particularly marked impact in rural areas; in an era before the mechanization of agriculture, labour was in great demand in the summer and particularly at harvest time (harvest wages were usually about 50 per cent higher than wages at other times of year).[81] Winter, by contrast, provided fewer opportunities for employment on the land and so represented a good time for recruiting parties to search for unemployed (or under-employed) farm labourers. Harsh winters increased the number of men in need of employment; the extremely hard winter of 1739–40 seems to have driven many Highlanders into military escape routes – some to time-honoured ways out for Scotsmen, namely the Scots Brigade in the Dutch Republic and the French army, but others into the British service.[82] Urban areas were affected by seasonal labour requirements, too, as it was to them that men gravitated from their rural hinterlands in search of opportunities, particularly in the winter months. Recruiting parties, as we have seen, flocked to towns and cities, confident in the knowledge that they would provide rich pickings. Of the twenty-five men whom Lieutenant Allan Macdonald enlisted for the 76th Foot in Glasgow in January and early February 1781, only one came from Glasgow itself.[83]

Non-seasonal economic disruptions and downtowns, affecting a particular trade or a particular region or even the whole country, also boosted recruitment. We can be reasonably confident that a high proportion of the skilled men who joined the army, especially in wartime, were recently unemployed or hit by a reduction in their income. The beginning of the Seven Years War saw an economic crisis, as trade contracted and poor harvests led to food shortages. In October 1756, James Wolfe told his mother of the willingness of the 'poor and . . . wretched' cloth workers of Gloucestershire to join the army 'through sheer necessity'.[84] In February 1757, recruiting appears to have gone well in Edinburgh, not least, in the view of one observer, because 'a prospect of scarcity of victual' made men more ready to agree to enlist.[85] In the American war, the entry of France in 1778 made accessing European markets much more difficult than in the first phase of the conflict, when the rebel colonies were the only enemy. In Birmingham, a public subscription was opened to help 'many of our industrious and deserving Artificers', who were out of work and with their families 'in great Distress'.[86] But if contemporaries lamented the 'the misery occasion'd by the loss of our trade',[87] for recruiting parties they were a blessing. That summer, with economic conditions grim in Ireland, James O'Neill of the 67th Foot secured in just a fortnight the number of men his commanding officer expected him to enlist.[88]

Chapter 4

Military Communities

What was the nature of the institution that these new entrants had joined? It was a community, with its own sense of who was a member and who was not; but it was made up of a set of sub-communities organized by hierarchy, structure and function. Privates formed one sub-community; non-commissioned officers, another; officers, another still. Not everyone in these sub-communities saw eye to eye, of course. Dedicated and serious-minded officers, for instance, bitterly criticized their insouciant and unprofessional colleagues.[1] But, whatever their divisions, officers all recognized that they formed a community that was very different from those of the common soldiers and the non-commissioned officers. The same was true of the privates, who would have been aware of what differentiated them from both non-commissioned and commissioned officers; and of the sergeants and corporals, who would have been very mindful of their separation from both those above and below them in the military hierarchy. Gun crews in the artillery and sections, platoons, companies, troops and squadrons in the infantry and cavalry, might be the bases for other distinct communities. So might regiments, which had identities shaped in part by their traditions and histories – particularly their roll call of battle honours – and also by the existence of their own distinctive flags or colours, reinforced by uniform particularities, such as the facing colours of the coats and the special arrangements of lace and buttons.

Beyond the regiment, soldiers might identify with other units in their arm of service – infantry, cavalry, artillery or with others sharing their skills, such as engineers. Beyond them, the army as an entity might form an imagined community in the minds of military men – imagined because no one could know everyone else in the army or even see it all gathered together, but soldiers might still feel that they belonged to it.[2] The army in its totality was not necessarily the outer boundary of a sense of soldierly community, however. Military men were able to see connections, and feel a sense of solidarity, with their counterparts in other armies, whether they were allies, auxiliaries or

even enemies. It might be tempting to conceptualize these different communities or sub-communities as organized concentrically, with the strongest at
the centre – the close bonds of section, platoon or troop – and the weakest
– international or transnational military connections – at the distant edge
of the circle. But it would be more appropriate to see these different senses
of belonging as coming to the forefront of military minds according to circumstances and stimuli. In Ireland, for instance, regiments often acted as
communities only in a weak sense, for the simple reason that many were
dispersed for long periods into smaller units scattered across the country in
aid of the civil power; they came together only to be inspected, when soldiers'
unfamiliarity with operating as a regimental whole became only too obvious.[3]
In the Seven Years War and the War of American Independence, regimental
identity was undermined still further on campaign by the practice of putting
the flank companies (the grenadiers and light infantry) of each regiment in
a particular army into composite battalions. We can readily imagine that
these battalions would have become the unit of association for most of the
soldiers in them, not their home regiments. We might go further and say
that the troops in these composite battalions probably had a stronger sense
of attachment to the army as a whole (through their working with other light
infantry or grenadier companies in it), than they had to their own regiments.

As with all professions or occupations, the army had its own ways of doing
things, its own language, customs, etiquette and values, largely unknown and
impenetrable to those on the outside. These distinctive features helped bond
soldiers together, creating a sense of comradeship that made them look out
for their fellow soldiers, seeking to protect or cover up for them when they
had done wrong and risking their own lives rather let down the men they
served alongside. While they were never a caste totally separate from the rest
of society (soldiers' connections with those outside the military made that
impossible), in some circumstances they had stronger links with soldiers in
other armies than with civilians in their own country. This chapter explores
the bonds that connected soldiers with their colleagues and also the idea of a
European military fraternity, uniting military men of different armies.[4]

Norms and Values

The new recruit, if he did not come from a military family, soon began to
appreciate that he had become part of an institution that spoke a different

language from the people with whom he had previously associated. Soldiers had to learn the technical argot of weapons and equipment, the arcane terminology of 'subsistence' and 'offreckonings' (the two segments into which their pay was divided, only the first of which they could be reasonably confident of seeing at least part) and the language of drill and military manoeuvre. Their non-commissioned officers played an important part in the induction process, but long-serving private soldiers no doubt helped too. Contemporaries reckoned that it took a year in the army for a recruit to become a fully-fledged soldier, able to be trusted to carry out all the functions required of him.[5] But as soon as the new men had acquired the rudiments of military knowledge, they were on their way to building barriers, constructed of special inside information, which separated them from the outside world. The army's customs and traditions, unknowable to anyone but insiders and gradually learned by the newcomer from the old hands, added to the height of the barriers.

Training, of course, even in seemingly endless routines of cleaning weapons and equipment, was meant ultimately to prepare soldiers for the core purpose of their occupation. Inculcating obedience to orders and drilling and manoeuvring on the parade ground aimed to make the soldier better able to fight effectively as part of his unit in the stressful conditions of the battlefield.[6] Active service made the bonds connecting soldiers to their colleagues stronger and their links to wider society more tenuous. The experience of combat – the shared danger and stomach-churning fear – naturally increased identification with other soldiers undergoing the same ordeal as friends and colleagues. But even in times of peace, when there was no foreign enemy or rebel against whom soldiers could unite in common effort, there were external 'others' who helped to bind military men together. The frequent hostility of the outside world – for much of our period, as we have seen, there were circumstances in which soldiers were distrusted and even feared by civilians – only served to reinforce a sense of soldierly solidarity.[7]

One of the symptoms of this 'us versus them' mentality was the tendency of soldiers to try to liberate colleagues that they thought had been unfairly treated by civilian courts. Prison rescues occurred particularly in Ireland, where many soldiers thought that the local population was especially hostile, but they were far from unknown in England. In the spring of 1779, for instance, a Wiltshire magistrate reported to the War Office that a trooper of the Enniskillen Dragoons, committed for assault and attempted rape, had been sprung from gaol by fellow soldiers.[8] Another sign of soldierly solidarity was the way in which sentries turned a blind eye when regimental or company colleagues returned to camp after clandestine visits to local towns and villages in search of drink and women or slunk in under the cover of darkness after a predatory raid on local farms in search of additional food. In Philadelphia, in February 1778, 'Sejeants & Sentries at the several Barriers' received orders to stop soldiers from passing without an officer with them; the implication was clearly that sentries were allowing their colleagues to slip in and out without questioning them.[9] We can see soldierly solidarity, too, on the battlefield, in the very willingness of members of the rank and file to stay besides their comrades in arms, even under the heaviest enemy fire, rather than break and run. Months or even years of repetitive drill and the threat of harsh punishment, including a capital sentence, no doubt played a part in overcoming the natural instinct to survive; but a deep reluctance not to let colleagues down, not to desert those with whom they stood shoulder to shoulder, may well have been more important.[10]

If the British Army's common soldiers bonded with the men in their own units, their feelings of military solidarity might extend much further. Members of other British regiments could be incorporated in the soldier's view of who constituted a colleague, especially those serving in the same arm, such as other infantrymen or other cavalry or fellow artillerymen. General courts martial records suggest that when more than one soldier was accused of a crime they usually came from the same regiment. In at least a few cases, however, we can see that soldiers worked with men in other units, which suggests that the regiment was not their universe. In December 1776, for instance, three soldiers from different corps – the 57th, 44th and 55th – were charged, but acquitted, of robbing the same boatman in New York. Despite their acquittal, there can be no doubt that these soldiers of different units had been together when the incident occurred.[11] Bonds with soldiers in different regiments are also apparent in some of the prison rescues mentioned earlier. On 12 September 1777, a party of about thirty soldiers from the garrison in Dublin rescued from gaol a soldier of the 66th Foot and another of the 68th, who were both due to be executed the following morning after having been found guilty of highway robbery.[12] Three years later, in 1780, soldiers of the 68th Regiment, quartered at Galway, freed from prison a deserter from the

67th Foot, who had been tried for murder. The rescuers, according to their colonel, had acted in angry response to the acquittal of a civilian who, in a separate incident, had attacked and maimed a private of the 68th.[13]

We can even see evidence that members of the British rank and file had a sense of occupational connection with soldiers in other armies. British soldiers shared their rations with Hanoverian troops after the hard-fought Battle of Fontenoy in 1745; a deeply symbolic gesture of inclusion. The year before, a senior British officer reported that the common soldiers were socializing with the Hanoverian rank and file despite the language barrier.[14] Feelings of military solidarity could even extend to enemies. Corporal William Todd, who kept a detailed – and invaluable – journal of his military life, recorded a very revealing incident in north-west Germany during the Seven Years War. He was frequently hungry, due to problems that the army's commissaries and contractors encountered in maintaining a regular supply of provisions and on 31 August 1761 he noted that he and his colleagues bought supplies from French sentries, from whom the British sentries were separated by 'only a small Ditch': 'they are very ready', Todd wrote, 'to Either Buy, sell or Exchange anything they have with [us] as Bread, Liquor etc.' As Todd explained, 'the Enemy seems very agreable'.[15]

Officers were perhaps even more inclined to see themselves as members of a military fraternity that transcended national boundaries or what we might describe, in a useful shorthand phrase, as 'military Europe'.[16] The rules of 'military Europe', well understood by the initiated but difficult for outsiders to understand, derived from a common etiquette – the knowledge of what to do in certain situations. The British Army shared with other European armies of the time a commitment to defending the regimental flags or colours; to allow these to fall into enemy hands was regarded as a disgrace and extraordinary efforts were made by officers in all militaries to defend the colours to the uttermost and, if all else failed, to destroy or hide them rather than permit them to be displayed as trophies by victorious foes.[17] British soldiers – like their Continental counterparts – were equally familiar with what was expected of both sides in a siege. The formalities of offering terms, turning them down and resisting until further defiance was hopeless, were followed even by armies fighting beyond Europe. Indeed, punctilious observance of the ornate choreography of siege warfare was perhaps still more obvious when Europeans were locked in conflict in America or Asia than when they fought each other in Europe itself. Walter Rutherford, a Scottish officer in the Royal American Regiment, related his attempts to persuade the French officer commanding at Fort Niagara to surrender in July 1759. Rutherford explained that the defences of the fort were weak, but the garrison was determined. 'I drank an excellent Bottle of Claret and a Glass of Liquer with the [French] Commandant', whom he described, breaking into French, as 'bon Soldat, et Homme d'Esprit'.[18]

The club's membership, then, might incorporate enemies as well as allies. The gentlemanly exchange between Rutherford and his French opponent in the North American wilderness is revealing of a willingness to put professional respect above national distinctions. But the boundaries of the transnational fraternity glimpsed at Fort Niagara were not limitless. Non-Europeans were rarely regarded as part of this professional association. Very occasionally, a particularly skilled native warrior might elicit professional respect; some British officers showed a grudging regard for the martial abilities of Tipu Sultan, the prince of Mysore who inflicted embarrassing defeats on British arms in India.[19] But not even Tipu, for all his military prowess, truly qualified as a member of the fraternity. Racial and cultural prejudice no doubt partly explains his exclusion; but it hardly accounts for the similar British reluctance to admit colonial Americans. They might in exceptional circumstances be viewed as associate members if they played by the rules – George Washington, the Virginian planter who could have passed for an English squire, is perhaps the most obvious example of such a special case – but usually colonists were denied access to the club on the grounds that they lacked the professional qualities required.[20] In the War of American Independence, the rebels' Continental Army was usually dismissed by British officers as a glorified militia ('they are the most paltry Enemy, that ever Soldiers had to deal with', wrote Captain Baldwin Leighton; 'one only dirties one's fingers' in dealing with them, was the haughty verdict of Captain Lord Rawdon).[21] American soldiers were routinely assumed to be ignorant of military etiquette, which made it impossible to regard them as equals. During the British siege of Charleston, South Carolina, in 1780, General Sir Henry Clinton despaired of his American counterpart, who seemed determined to continue resisting, even when the usual rules of European warfare required him to surrender. 'I begin to think these People will be Blockheads enough to wait the Assault', Clinton wrote with much exasperation; 'Je m'en lave les

Mains'.[22] Small wonder that British commanders, when obliged to surrender at Yorktown in 1781, tried to give their swords to the French auxiliaries of the Americans; to surrender to fellow-European professionals was one thing, to have to humiliate themselves in front of the amateurish Americans was quite another.[23]

Explanations

We have touched upon the reasons for soldiers' sense of solidarity with their immediate colleagues and how that feeling of connection could extend to other members of the British service. But how do we account for the apparent willingness of British soldiers, particularly officers, to regard members of other armies as part of a fraternity of arms that transcended political boundaries? After all, armies represented the nation and acted on behalf of monarchs, governments and peoples. They are not institutions that one would intuitively regard as cosmopolitan or transnational. Part of the explanation must surely be the shared experience of danger and fellow-feeling that could create for an enemy or an ally. Just as sailors of different nations felt respect for each other because they all had to contend with an untameable sea, so soldiers might feel a connection with their counterparts in other armies because they had in common the threat to life and limb inescapably involved in their occupation. But there were other reasons, connected to the nature of the British Army and its experiences of war that also helped to create feelings of military solidarity, regardless of nationality.

The fundamental similarity of the British Army to other European armies was surely an important factor. The hard school of war encouraged homogeneity, as armies emulated the best practice of others to avoid falling behind and exposing themselves to avoidable defeat. We can see this most clearly, paradoxically, when we look at the case of an army that had not kept up with the latest thinking. Colonel Charles Rainsford was unimpressed when he saw Danish troops drilling at Copenhagen in 1769. He noted that their approach 'is quite Old School Their Movements Slow & regular'.[24] The explanation for the seeming backwardness of the Danish army might well have been its not having fought in the Seven Years War. Those European armies that had been involved in recent conflicts quickly adapted their drill to reflect the practices of the leading military powers of the time – in 1769, after the testing experience of the Seven Years War, no one doubted that the trendsetter was Prussia's army, led with such distinction by Frederick the Great.

At a basic structural level, the British Army had much in common with other European armies. Even when it had a military officer serving as its nominal commander-in-chief, the monarch was its recognized head, just as he was in most Continental states. George I and George II took very seriously their role as warrior kings and were particularly committed to their army and solicitous about its welfare. George II had fought in the War of the Spanish Succession as a young man and in 1743 led his troops in person at the Battle of Dettingen.[25] But George III, despite his lack of military experience, was scarcely less proprietorial and just as committed to the minutiae of military affairs. His resistance to the creation of new regiments in the early stages of the War of American Independence demonstrates a commitment to preserving the army as an effective instrument and avoiding new corps acting as patronage vehicles of very limited military utility.[26] Royal command and control was symbolized by the granting of all officers' commissions in the king's name and the carrying of royal standards by each of the army's units.

The British Army's fundamental unit of organization, as we have seen, was the regiment, divided into battalions and companies for the infantry and into squadrons for the cavalry. While the number of men in such units might vary from army to army, they were to be found in all European militaries. Different types of soldier were replicated across Europe, too: each army had its standard infantrymen of the line and its handpicked grenadiers, who acted as shock troops; light infantry became a feature of more and more armies from the middle of the century. In the cavalry, regiments of horse and dragoons were again common to all European armies and light cavalry units came into vogue everywhere from the 1740s – such as hussars and light dragoons, who performed a similar scouting and reconnaissance function to the light infantry. Their model seems to have been the Hungarian light cavalry, who appeared in western Europe in the War of the Austrian Succession when Maria Theresa of Austria sought to maintain her family's hold on the Holy Roman Empire.

The rank system was remarkably similar across the European armies, too, which had the incidental benefit that it made easier the negotiation of exchanges of prisoners in wartime.[27] Every European army had private soldiers, non-commissioned officers – corporals and sergeants – and broadly similar officer ranks, from the lowly ensigns and lieutenants to the company and regimental commanders – the captains, majors, lieutenant colonels and colonels – and on to the major generals, lieutenant generals, full generals and finally field marshals. In all armies, furthermore, the proprietary rights of the company and regimental commanders were under pressure as governments sought to exercise more control over their armed forces and attempted to mould disparate military units into cohesive armies. Everywhere, state management increased and the captain's and colonel's proprietary rights diminished.[28]

Eighteenth-century armies even looked remarkably similar to each other. Many militaries, to be sure, had distinctively-dressed troops. Perhaps the most obvious example is the Russians, whose exotic Cossack and Tartar irregulars so startled one British observer at the end of the century that he described them as 'of a nature different from any which exists in any other Service'.[29] The alarming-looking Croatian Pandours attached to the Austrian military, who had learned their business on the Habsburg's military frontier with the Muslim world of the Ottoman Empire, attracted similar wonderment in earlier decades when they were deployed in western Europe.[30] But the same was true of the Scottish Highland regiments in the British Army, who appeared no less outlandish and noteworthy to those who were unfamiliar with their attire. In the Seven Years War, even American provincial troops found the appearance of the Highlanders a revelation.[31] Even so, the bulk of the infantry in every European army were dressed in a strikingly similar fashion. The colour of their coats might distinguish them from soldiers in other armies – red for the British, Hanoverians and Danes, white for the French, Austrians and Spanish, blue for the Prussians and many other German states, green for the Russians – but in every other respect their coats were very similar, usually with lapels and cuffs in a contrasting regimental colour and they wore very much the same form of breeches, gaiters and shoes, topped off with the seemingly ubiquitous tricorn hat.[32]

In their coercive or military role, European armies all used broadly similar weapons. The cavalry were armed with similar types of swords, pistols and short muskets or carbines. Amongst the infantry, the pike, originally intended to defend the musketeers from cavalry attack, was abandoned in the early years of the eighteenth century and the flintlock musket and socket bayonet were soon after nearly universal; only in the armies of Russia and the Ottoman Empire, which were both (to varying degrees) seen by many contemporaries as outside the European mainstream, did the older technology of the matchlock musket persist for longer.[33] The artillery also became an important arm in European armies more-or-less simultaneously. From the middle of the century, the Austrians formed a fully professionalized and fully militarized artillery corps, followed by the Russians, the Prussians, the French and the British. Artillery pieces were also increasingly similar in calibre and function, with most armies possessing 3 or 4-pounder guns to support the infantry, medium-weight 6 or 8-pounders for use in batteries and 12-pounders the heaviest battlefield cannon.[34]

Common weaponry partly explains common battlefield tactics. Armies deployed in lines to maximize the firepower of inaccurate muskets. Different armies, to be sure, had different tactical approaches; the number of ranks in the line might vary and the space between soldiers might differ. Some armies were more advanced than others in the development of light infantry, though any temptation to believe that they originated in North America and were exported to Europe should be resisted: light infantry emerged on the Continent before they were used extensively by European armies in North America.[35] American experience, admittedly, encouraged the adoption of looser formations; the British Army adapted to local conditions very rapidly in both the Seven Years War and the War of American Independence.[36] Indeed, even before hostilities broke out in the last conflict, British light infantrymen appear to have been trained to fight in 'irregular & Bush fighting'. Robert Honyman, a Virginian doctor visiting Boston in March 1775 noted that the light infantrymen, 'in one part of their Exercise . . . ly on their backs & charge their pieces & fire lying on their bellies'.[37] Even so, linear tactics were employed everywhere, including by the British Army serving in North America.

As we have seen, the drill used to train troops for battlefield conditions, preparing them to carry out manoeuvres under fire, from the middle of the century tended to follow Prussian example, for the simple reason that Frederick the Great's successes in first the War of the Austrian Succession and then the Seven Years War meant that Prussia set the tone that hitherto had been established by the French army.[38] As an officer in Dutch service noted in 1774, 'the Prussian exercise and discipline has been adopted more or less by almost every army in Europe'.[39] Nor was the British Army an exception to this general rule. One of the greatest admirers of the Prussian approach was David Dundas, British adjutant-general after the American war, who was particularly keen to ensure that his army's tactics conformed with the norms established by Frederick the Great.[40] Long before Dundas rose to prominence, however, Captain William Faucitt had translated *Regulations for the Prussian Cavalry* (1757), a publication funded by a subscription of army officers, which suggests much interest in following Prussian example.[41]

The social background of British Army officers was remarkably similar to that of their Continental counterparts. A comparison of titles might suggest otherwise. In many European armies, the officer corps was visibly dominated by the aristocracy, in the sense that titled officers abounded. Every single one of the 181 general officers employed in the French army in western Germany in 1758 was a nobleman.[42] In 1767, nearly 75 per cent of the infantry officers in Piedmont-Sardinia's army were aristocrats and 93 per cent of the cavalry officers. In the Prussian army in the year of Frederick the Great's death (1786), a mere 3 per cent of the officers ranked as major or above were commoners. By contrast, in 1780, only 30 per cent of regular British Army officers had titles.[43] But the British Army was not as out of step as these figures imply. On the Continent, titles were more liberally bestowed on younger members of aristocratic families, who in the British Isles had no outward signifier of nobility.[44] Many of those British and Irish officers whose plain and unadorned names in the *Army List* suggested they were commoners were in fact members of aristocratic families. Furthermore, a portion of the titled officers in Continental armies had acquired aristocratic status only *after* they joined the military. The French Minister of War introduced a *noblesse militaire* in 1750, but the hostility of the traditional nobility to this was so strong that restrictions on entry were imposed in 1758 and the famous four-quartering system of aristocratic exclusivity was eventually introduced in 1781.[45] But if in the French army ennoblement for military service was short-lived, it became the norm in the Austrian army, where, from 1757, officers with long and meritorious careers were able to apply for a patent of nobility.[46]

Military ennoblements and the opposition they provoked, reveal that middle-class penetration of the officer ranks was far from insignificant. Officers from middle-class backgrounds were a rarity in Guards regiments and the cavalry, but they were particularly well-represented in the technical branches, such as the artillery and engineers and to a lesser extent in line infantry regiments. European armies – including the British, as we have seen – even had a small number of officers who had been promoted from the ranks.[47] Not many made it beyond company command, but their presence and that of the more numerous middle-class officers, demonstrates that the officer corps was not an aristocratic preserve. That said, throughout Europe, officers from middle-class backgrounds, or who had been promoted from the ranks, were expected to subscribe to an essentially aristocratic honour code and behave like gentlemen.[48]

The common soldiers in all European armies also came from similar segments of society. Pardoned criminals, paupers and vagrants were present in Continental European armies, just as they were in the British regiments. At the other end of the scale, all armies had a sprinkling of socially superior men serving in their ranks – the sons of farmers or merchants or clergymen; students, teachers and even upper-class 'volunteers', acting as common soldiers while waiting for an officer vacancy.[49] But by far the most important social groups in the rank and file came from two broad occupational backgrounds; unskilled labourers and artisans. The number of skilled and semi-skilled men might have been smaller in some militaries than in the British Army; only a little over a quarter of the Austrian army's soldiers at the time of the Seven Years War 'declared a civilian trade upon being recruited'.[50] In the French army, however, the share of those with an artisan background was nearer to the British; in 1763 about 40 per cent of French soldiers were craftsmen or the sons of craftsmen.[51]

In many countries, furthermore, urban centres provided a disproportionately large share of recruits, as these were the places to which young men, in search of work and opportunities, tended to gravitate. In Britain, this tendency was perhaps more marked than elsewhere, as Britain was the most urbanized European country (apart from the Dutch Republic) and migration from countryside to town increased in the course of the eighteenth century.[52] As we have seen, Birmingham, Bristol, Glasgow, Leeds, Manchester, Dublin, Edinburgh, Glasgow and, most importantly, London were favourite haunts for recruiting officers.[53] But the tendency was discernible throughout western Europe.[54] Even in so rural a country as France, a disproportionate number of recruits came from urban centres, especially Paris: at a time when perhaps no more than a fifth of French people lived in towns and cities, something like a third of the French army's soldiers had urban backgrounds.[55] Nevertheless, the influence of large landowners was a major factor in recruitment everywhere in Europe, including Britain and Ireland, where leading noblemen played a key role in raising new regiments in all the wars of the period.[56]

The education of at least some British officers also fostered a European perspective. A small number of officers attended Continental universities or academies.[57] Lord Cornwallis, in command in the southern colonies during the War of American Independence, had attended Turin academy in the 1750s. But in the first half of the century, before Prussia established its military reputation, French academies attracted British students, many of whom were already young officers or were destined for a career in the army. Thus, Robert Carr, later a lieutenant colonel, attended Caen academy just after the War of the Austrian Succession.[58] From the mid-century onwards, while French academies continued to draw British students, such as Thomas Pelham who went to Caen in 1775,[59] Germany increasingly became the destination for ambitious British officers in search of training and connections. Brunswick academy attracted a steady flow of British students (Thomas Hawkins went there in 1777, before becoming a cornet in the 10th Dragoons); and Göttingen, in Hanover, had a fair number of military recruits from Britain and Ireland after the Seven Years War.[60] As one of Göttingen's British students put it, 'As I had resolved on being a soldier, a German education was the best suited to the profession I had chosen'.[61]

Even the small number of officers who enrolled at military academies at home might be exposed to Continental influence. The Royal Military Academy in London was run by Lewis Lochée, a native of Brussels, and schooled its students in 'the Modern Languages and all the Military Sciences'.[62] Larger numbers of British officers went on the Grand Tour, which sometimes involved temporary attendance at a Continental university or academy, but had a broader educative function. While travelling, they visited old battlefields, saw military manoeuvres and met officers of other armies, as well as learned or improved their competence in French, the international language of the age. For army officers, John Burgoyne urged learning French in a set of instruction he drew up for young officers when he commanded a regiment of light dragoons at the end of the Seven Years War. 'To those who do not understand French,' he wrote, 'I would recommend a serious and assiduous application till they attain it.' Not only did the language enable the officer to read the 'best modern books upon our profession', but 'in foreign service gentlemen will find themselves at the greatest loss if they do not both write and speak it readily'.[63]

Commonalities across the European armies almost certainly owed something to the movement of personnel between armies. British soldiers were involved in this military migration. Early in 1749, just after the end of the War of the Austrian Succession, a report from France suggested that 'some hundreds' of discharged British marines were crossing the Channel to join the Scots regiments in French service.[64] Nearly 30 years later, during the American war, a newly-raised Highland regiment probably secured some of its recruits from Scotsmen who had been soldiers in the Scots brigade in Dutch pay, a unit originally formed in the sixteenth century.[65] As usual, we know more about the officers. The Earl of Crawford, killed in action while leading British troops at the Battle of Dettingen in 1743, had earlier been an officer in the Austrian and Russian armies.[66] But the most important foreign military seminary for British officers was surely the Scots brigade in Dutch service. Even after the Seven Years War, when its rank and file became increasingly cosmopolitan, the brigade's officers continued to be overwhelmingly Scottish. In that same war, when the Dutch Republic remained neutral, significant numbers of Scots brigade officers applied to transfer into the British Army, partly perhaps from a sense of patriotic duty, but primarily, in all probablity, because they recognized that promotion was always easier in an army that was likely to see battle. The same process was repeated in the early stages of the American war, when the Dutch again adopted a neutral position.[67] A similar desire for professional advancement encouraged British officers, especially at the end of wars when the army was reduced in size, to seek their fortunes in foreign armies. The Portuguese service attracted a number of British officers at the end of the Seven Years War;[68] one of them, Francis McLean (who had earlier served in the Scots brigade), rose to become a general in Portuguese pay before rejoining the British Army in 1778.[69] At the end of the American war, at least one junior officer in a disbanded British regiment sought new employment in the Russian army.[70]

The traffic was two-way. The British Army provided a military home for Continental Europeans. As we saw earlier, the ordinary soldiers of the Royal Americans were drawn in significant numbers from Germany and the same was true, though to a much lesser extent, of other British regiments. The officer ranks were theoretically closed to foreigners; the Act of Settlement of 1701 stipulated that public office, civil and military, must be confined to the Crown's subjects. But at the end of the seventeenth century and the beginning of the eighteenth, large numbers of Huguenot, or French Protestant, refugees became officers in the British Army.[71] Their male descendants tended to follow in their footsteps; officers from Huguenot families continued to be well represented in the army for many decades after the main Huguenot migration. Special legislative dispensation was given for other Protestant foreigners to serve in the Royal Americans in 1756. German and Swiss Protestants dominated its officer ranks; they had often served in the Dutch or Piedmontese armies before they joined the British.[72]

The British Army not only contained Continental Europeans and British-born soldiers who had served in Continental armies, it also fought alongside European allies and auxiliaries. British troops campaigning in the Low Countries and western Germany in 1742–8 and 1758–62, did so as part of an allied force, brought together to resist French ambitions. In the Seven Years War, admittedly, when the Prussians were the British Army's main ally, direct contact between the two was very limited.[73] But British troops co-operated much more closely with the Austrians and the Dutch in the War of the Austrian Succession in the 1740s. Nor should we forget that in that same conflict and again in the Seven Years War and in the War of American Independence, British troops served alongside auxiliaries, mainly from the German states. Hanoverian units, from the other army of George II and George III, who were Electors of Hanover as well as Kings of Britain and Ireland, also acted as auxiliaries to the British Army. But the biggest contribution came from the soldiers of Hessen-Kassel, who formed the largest contingent of British auxiliaries in the North American campaigns of the War of Independence.[74]

Friction between British soldiers and troops in allied armies or auxiliary forces was a feature of all Britain's eighteenth-century wars. In the War of the Austrian Succession, for instance, Joseph Yorke, a staff officer at the British headquarters in the Low Countries, complained incessantly in his diary of the Austrian generals with whom the British Army worked.[75] The targets of British disdain often attributed it to national prejudice.[76] There was no doubt some of that, but British criticism was usually professional rather than national; it focused on allies' or auxiliaries' perceived military deficiencies, such as their being too slow to advance or too quick to retreat or not sufficiently committed to the common cause. This seems to have been the case with Yorke's irritation with the Austrian generals – it was their lack of energy and enthusiasm that angered him, not their foreignness. The Dutch military in the same war attracted even more critical comments from British officers and men, who regarded the republic's troops as deeply reluctant to engage with the enemy. 'If the Dutch had done their duty . . . we would certainly have won the day', was the judgement of an artillery matross after the Battle of Laufeld in 1747.[77] In the War of American Independence, British officers had no hesitation in blaming the German auxiliary troops attached to the army for the sufferings of the local inhabitants. Charles Cochrane condemned 'the Plundering Mercenary Irregular behaviour of the German Soldiery' and Charles O'Hara was still more scathing: 'As to the German Part of the Army . . . their Marauding, & Plunder is beyond belief – Cruel & Savage – they have without a doubt, done our Cause infinite prejudice.'[78] The surprise and total defeat of a Hessian detachment at Trenton, New Jersey, over the Christmas celebrations of 1776, also served as proof to hostile British observers that problems in suppressing the American rebellion owed much to the army's German auxiliaries.[79] When, on the other hand, allies or auxiliaries displayed military qualities, British soldiers tended to treat them as comrades and equals and were unstinting in their praise. Lieutenant Colonel Charles Russell lauded the bravery of the Austrian and Hanoverian troops who fought alongside the British at Dettingen in 1743.[80] In America, Major Henry Rooke approved heartily of the 'great steadiness and intrepidity' displayed by the Hessian soldiers involved in the capture of Fort Washington in 1776.[81] Both negative and positive British comments suggest that the army's officers (and perhaps even its rank and file) were thinking less as Britons and more as soldiers.

A sense of international military solidarity was also promoted by the Laws of War, part of what was then known as the Law of Nations or what we would now call international law. Based on the essentially European concepts of Christianity, chivalry and the more modern ideas of proportionality and rationality associated with the Enlightenment, these Laws laid down what was acceptable and unacceptable in the conduct of war. Needless to say, the practice of war was often very less controlled and limited than the ideal found in the lofty aspirations of contemporary treatises. Even so, the existence of a body of rules, which soldiers felt some moral obligation to obey, mattered to the way European military men conceived of their connections with their colleagues in other armies. Particular emphasis was placed by the public law writers on protecting non-combatants and restricting the business of fighting to professional armed forces. As Swiss jurisprudent Emerich de Vattel, one of the leading legal authorities of the age, explained, the use of violence in warfare was confined to regular soldiers in the armies of the belligerents; private persons who involved themselves in the fighting would not be entitled to the safeguards that operated for legitimate participants – professional military men carried arms; non-combatants should not do so.[82] By stressing the distinction between soldiers and civilians, the Laws of War encouraged military men in all European armies to think in terms of what united them in a professional comradeship that transcended national boundaries – and also what distinguished them from civilians of all countries, including their own.[83]

Yet the most fundamental explanation for the significant similarities and connections between European armies reminds us that armies are ultimately products of societies and not hermetically separated from them. European armies were similar in many ways for the simple reason that in pre-French Revolution Europe societies were themselves broadly similar. The Laws of War operated on the assumption that there was a European club of nations, sharing many values and norms, which all had an interest in promoting and preserving.[84] That assumption was sound. Despite their manifold local peculiarities, European states shared a great deal in terms of political structures and social organization and still more though their culture, religion and law.[85] As so often, the essence of what was becomes truly apparent only when it disappears. The French Revolution led Edmund Burke to lament the end, as he saw it, of 'the system of Europe, taking in manners, religion and politics, in which I delighted so much'.[86] Eighteenth-century Britain, whatever exceptionalist narratives might suggest, was essentially a European state, with many different connections with the nearby Continent. We should not be surprised, then, that its army displayed many of the characteristics to be found in other European armies of the time and that its officers and soldiers felt a bond of connection with the officers and soldiers of those other European armies.

The ruins of Ruthven Barracks, near Kingussie, in the Scottish Highlands. Built between 1719 and 1721, the barracks housed troops who were meant to deter further rebellions by the supporters of the deposed Stuart dynasty (known as Jacobites).

David Morier's portrait of the Duke of Cumberland, captain-general of the army, 1745–57. (Royal Collection Trust © Her Majesty Queen Elizabeth II 2020)

Soldier of the 29th Foot, 1742. This image is based on the clothing book of that year, which was the first to designate regiments by number rather than by the colonel's name.

David Morier's painting of the Battle of Culloden, 1746. The army fought against Jacobites in 1715, 1719 and in the rebellion of 1745, which Culloden brought to a bloody end.

Grenadiers of the 7th (Royal Fusiliers), 8th (King's Regiment) and 9th Foot, 1751, by David Morier. (Royal Collection Trust © Her Majesty Queen Elizabeth II 2020)

Trooper, 10th Dragoons, 1751, by David Morier. (Royal Collection Trust © Her Majesty Queen Elizabeth II 2020).

Grenadier of the 40th Foot, 1767. This modern depiction illustrates well the changes in clothing style introduced after the Seven Years War.

The King's Shilling, c.1770. This painting captures many characteristic features of recruiting: the distraught wife or sweetheart; the use of musicians in the recruiting party; the entry into a contract (signified by the handshake); the importance of the local inn. (National Army Museum: 1983-10-15-1)

Camp scene, c.1770. Note the mother and child at the centre of the painting, a reminder of the presence of women in an apparently masculine institution. (National Army Museum: 2001-12-35-1)

The BLOODY MASSACRE perpetrated in King—Street BOSTON on March 5th 1770 by a party of the 29th REGt

BUTCHER'S HALL

Engrav'd Printed & Sold by PAUL REVERE BOSTON

Unhappy Boston! see thy Sons deplore,
Thy hallow'd Walks besmear'd with guiltless Gore:
While faithless P—n and his savage Bands,
With murd'rous Rancour stretch their bloody Hands;
Like fierce Barbarians grinning o'er their Prey,
Approve the Carnage, and enjoy the Day.

If scalding drops from Rage from Anguish Wrung
If speechless Sorrows lab'ring for a Tongue,
Or if a weeping World can ought appease
The plaintive Ghosts of Victims such as these;
The Patriot's copious Tears for each are shed,
A glorious Tribute which embalms the Dead.

But know, Fate summons to that awful Goal,
Where Justice strips the Murd'rer of his Soul:
Should venal C—ts the scandal of the Land,
Snatch the relentless Villain from her Hand,
Keen Execrations on this Plate inscrib'd,
Shall reach a Judge who never can be brib'd.

The unhappy Sufferers were Messrs. Saml. Gray, Saml. Maverick, Jams. Caldwell, Crispus Attucks & Patk. Carr
Killed. Six wounded; two of them (Christr. Monk & John Clark) Mortally

Paul Revere's famous engraving of the Boston Massacre, 1770. A powerful piece of propaganda, Revere's image was almost certainly inaccurate. It seems that Captain Thomas Preston, here seen as ordering his men to fire, in fact tried to restrain them.

John Trumbull's painting of the Battle of Bunker Hill, 1775. Trumbull succeeded in bringing out the ambivalent feelings on both sides at the start of the American war. Note the British officer trying to restrain a grenadier about to bayonet the mortally-wounded American general, Joseph Warren.

Trumbull's representation of the surrender of the British army at Yorktown, Virginia, in 1781. The British commander, Lord Cornwallis, claimed to be too ill to surrender in person, leaving that humiliating task to his second-in-command, Charles O'Hara. O'Hara tried to offer his sword to the French commander-in-chief, but was eventually obliged to surrender, as Trumbull shows, to the American second-in-command, Benjamin Lincoln. O'Hara, like most British officers, saw the French as fellow professionals, with whom he had more in common than with the amateurish Americans.

John Singleton Copley's dramatic depiction of the heroic death of Major Francis Peirson, who was killed while leading resistance to a French invasion of Jersey in 1781. This painting was one of several that showed the army in a positive light after the Seven Years War, the successes of which seem to have boosted the reputation of professional soldiers, who until that time had widely been regarded with suspicion and often hostility.

Copley's equally dramatic painting of the repulse of the Franco-Spanish attack on Gibraltar, 1783. The successful defence of Gibraltar, which withstood a siege for nearly four years, lifted British morale at the end of an unsuccessful war in America, and helped to secure better peace terms than looked likely in the aftermath of Yorktown.

Chapter 5

Army Life

The subject of army life could be approached in a variety of ways. It would be reasonable to base an account on the army's different functions – as a fighting force, as a force used in aid of the civil power – or in peace and war or by looking at the way it operated in different geographical locations – at home, on the nearby Continent and in the farther-flung empire. This chapter seeks to capture elements of all of these different approaches, but focuses on the matters that occupied the minds of officers and common soldiers. It draws mainly on their own letters, diaries and memorials, supplemented by additional material from other contemporary sources. For officers, the evidence is relatively plentiful; as many of them were from landed families, who tended to keep their family papers over the generations, we have quite a bit to use. For members of the rank and file, the evidence is more limited; very few accounts penned by sergeants, corporals and private soldiers are available to us and those that are were probably produced by the most literate and educated, which means that they were almost certainly unrepresentative. We can supplement the small number of common soldiers' recorded thoughts with the views of their officers, which sometimes shed inferential light on their perceptions of the attitudes of the rank and file; but we should remember that officers did not always know what mattered to their men. Selectivity has been necessary; to cover everything that appears in the writings of officers and men would make this chapter unwieldy and not very helpful. Attention is concentrated on what appear to have been their main preoccupations.

What is very clear is that for officers promotion seems to have been a major concern. It features regularly in their correspondence with relatives and friends – as an object desired, as an ambition thwarted or as something towards which they were working or (more rarely) had achieved. Connected with promotion was money – both in the form of pay and perquisites. For officers, moving beyond the subaltern grade (ensign, cornet, lieutenant) to a captaincy was the way to acquire financial security. From the sources we have, the rank and file appear to have been less fixated on promotion, perhaps because it was an option only for a few and the soldiers themselves had very limited influence on the process of selection of non-commissioned officers – it was not something for which they applied; they were chosen. Pay mattered to common soldiers, but mainly in a negative sense – its inadequacy meant that many of them sought ways to make money from other sources. For the army's rank and file, a more consistent subject of concern seems to have been rations and the availability of food and drink more generally. The letters and diaries of both officers and common soldiers give us some interesting insights into the hardships that they experienced, most obviously in battle, but also in less dramatic settings – while marching or in camps or quarters – and due to extreme weather conditions. The writings of both officers and men reveal the long periods when they were not required for military duties. We learn much about how they filled their time and about their feelings of boredom. The promise of excitement and adventure used to encourage young men to join the army often turned out to be very far from the quotidian reality.

Promotion and Pay

Officers used up a lot of time – and emotional energy – in lobbying for promotion. In 1732, William Berry told the Duke of Dorset, the Lord Lieutenant of Ireland, that he was 'the oldest Lieu^t Colo^l in the Service', his commission for that rank dating back to June 1704. Berry staked his claim to a colonelcy not just on his seniority, however; he also emphasized that he had 'Serv'd faithfully and wthout blemish', adding that 'whatever your Grace shall think fitt to doe for me, I shall always remember it wth the utmost gratitude'.[1] Similar arguments to justify promotion – about seniority, long service, loyalty – and similar promises of undying gratitude appear in many other requests. Success seems to have come to those who had the backing of influential patrons – sometimes in the army, sometimes not – and in at least some cases to those whose credentials were at least as much political as military; officers who were also government-supporting MPs seem to have had an in-built advantage. Resentment at the failure to secure promotion is visible in many officers' letters and other written productions. It caused divisions within the officer class, with at least some disappointed English officers adopting the paranoid explanation that there was a Scots conspiracy to control the market.[2] Here, however, we are less concerned with the mechanisms of promotion or the resentment which it caused and more with why officers sought higher rank.

Enhanced status no doubt influenced their thinking. Rank and precedence mattered in *ancien regime* Europe, even more than they do now. Money, though, was never far from the minds of officers seeking promotion. Lieutenant Colonel Berry's keenness to acquire command of his own unit was unsurprising. In 1732, when he wrote to the lord lieutenant, regiments were still widely regarded as the personal property of the colonel, who ran it in ways intended to generate a healthy profit on the investment. While the salary attached to the command was not in itself substantial by contemporary standards – no more than the mid-range income of a landed gentleman, according to Joseph Massie's calculations in 1759, a modern authority tells us[3] – various perquisites boosted the value of a regiment considerably. Perhaps the most important of these perquisites related to the allowance the government gave to the colonel for the clothing, equipping and maintenance of his regiment. If he decided to wait another year to provide a replacement uniform for his troops or struck a good bargain with a clothier anxious for the business, the colonel could make a handsome profit by expending less on new clothing than his government allowance anticipated.[4]

If colonelcies offered the greatest rewards, subalterns, at the opposite end of the officer scale, usually craved promotion to company command. The full pay of a lieutenant in a regiment of foot was just four shillings and eight pence a day; an ensign's was a shilling less. Deductions reduced this paltry sum to a level that most subalterns thought to be utterly inadequate to their needs. Patrick Clerk lamented in a letter to his father in 1740 that he had just had to pay £40 to clothe and equip himself for service, 'a Sum that we subalterns are in no ways equal to, it is not possible that we can afford 40£ out of Sixty, which is the utmost of our yearly income'.[5] Ashton Shuttleworth, a lieutenant in the Royal Artillery, asked his uncle for 'New Shirts and Stockings' in July 1775, writing that 'I have no money to buy them with'. The following January, after explaining that he was forced to live on his rations, as he could not afford anything more, Shuttleworth requested his uncle to honour a bill of exchange drawn on him for £30; 'as my Pay is so trifling', he went on, there was no other way to afford more shirts and other necessary items of clothing.[6] Small wonder that subalterns seemed little short of obsessed with local prices, which they bemoaned in letters home ('everything most amazingly dear'; 'every Necessary of Life is so Extreem^ly dear there is no supporting it').[7] Many had little choice but to follow Shuttleworth's route and draw on supplementary cash from relatives and friends. Appealing for such help at the beginning of 1778, Ensign Hugh Campbell of the 35th Foot told his father that he had been 'obliged to Draw upon you for thirty Pounds Sterling'. Later that year, he asked his father to honour a bill for £40 more. 'I can assure you if it was consistent with nature to Keep up the Caracter of an Officer & a Gentleman, I do assure you I would not trouble you.' Campbell explained that 'Even the Article of Washing take[s] one third of My Pay so that you may judge how other things are in proportion'.[8]

Subalterns, then, had a strong incentive to escape penury and secure financial independence by gaining promotion to a captaincy, as we can see from the considerable effort they put into obtaining a company. John Jackson even lobbied the prime minister, Sir Robert Walpole, in 1736. He spared no rhetorical effort to make the case for promotion to a captaincy to which he believed his long and faithful service entitled him: 'if I had Justice', he concluded belligerently, 'I should have [had] a Company Twenty years ago'.[9] George Urquhart, a lieutenant in the 66th Foot in Ireland, augmented his meagre salary with an allowance from his family of £50 a year. Even this was not enough to cover his costs and he devoted a great deal of time and labour to assembling the money, borrowed from friends, to enable him to purchase the captaincy that would make his finances less precarious. It took several attempts before Urquhart achieved his objective, after more than two years of trying, in early 1782. 'I am very happy', he wrote in the aftermath of his final success.[10]

Urquhart's delight was no doubt informed by his appreciation that command of a company came with certain perquisites, which, while nowhere near as lucrative as those that accompanied a colonelcy, could transform the fortunes of a junior officer. George Vaughan Hart, a lieutenant in the 46th Foot in America, reckoned in 1778 that 'a company here is worth £300 a year'.[11] John Macpherson of the 17th Foot, apparently dependent upon his military salary, struggled as a lieutenant, but on obtaining his own company in August 1776 promised to send money home to restore his father's shaky finances.[12] Similarly, Edward Brabazon of the 22nd Foot, overdrawn with his regimental agent while he was a subaltern, registered healthy balances in his account on becoming a captain – once he had cleared the debts he had incurred in assembling the purchase money.[13] Urquhart himself was confident that, in his newly-improved financial state, he would be able to set aside £50 a year to help repay the money he had borrowed to secure his long-sought captaincy.[14]

Indebtedness appears to have been a common state for officers. For ensigns and lieutenants, as we have seen, it could be a consequence of borrowing to make up for the inadequacy of their official pay. Sometimes it was a result of gambling or another addiction; Earl Percy bailed out an artillery lieutenant in February 1775, who 'thro' Giddiness & inattention had run himself into Debt, & woud infallibly have been sent to Prison had I not done it'.[15] But the most usual cause of large-scale indebtedness seems to have been borrowing to fund the buying of commissions. James Dickson, an ensign in the 67th Foot, incurred unsupportable debts to purchase his commission (his father was a farmer, without the means to help). Friends loaned him money, as did Thomas Conolly, the Irish politician and local landowner; but his creditors could only be repaid (and then only in part) by Dickson's borrowing still more.[16] Robert Shawe, who purchased a lieutenancy in the 64th Foot in early 1770, borrowed the money for his promotion from the regiment's colonel and at least one of the captains. By that July, the original plan that Shawe would repay the captain by deductions of a shilling a day from his pay had been abandoned in favour of a more realistic six pence.[17] The family of Nisbet Balfour, the son of a minor Scottish laird, spent most of its money on purchasing commissions for Balfour and his four brothers. Even so, the family fortune was insufficient and in February 1778, by which time he had risen to be the lieutenant colonel of the Royal Welch Fusiliers, Balfour confessed to a friend that his promotions had caused him to go 'monstrously in debt'.[18]

Financial pressures encouraged some officers to try to supplement their pay, officially or unofficially. Certain regimental functions produced extra income, such as the quartermaster or adjutant. Financially-stretched junior officers often sought these roles, though colonels were just as likely to regard them as an appropriate reward for long-serving and trusted sergeants. Outside the regiment, a subaltern with the necessary training and aptitude could serve as an assistant engineer, which gave him five shillings a day on top of his regimental salary.[19] The impecunious Lieutenant John Blucke of the Royal Welch Fusiliers became an assistant deputy judge advocate, overseeing courts martial, but, still 'a little embarrassed' for money, sought the paymastership of the men from absent regiments at New York.[20] More senior officers might boost their salaries by taking on a role in the army's ancillary services; Lieutenant Colonel George Clerk, who served as barrackmaster-general in North America, received twenty shillings a day on top of his lieutenant colonel's salary, though this did not stop him from complaining that he was not paid enough.[21] At least a few officers, of all ranks, augmented their income by selling surplus rations; some may even have sold rations that they had claimed for non-existent servants.[22]

What of the army's rank and file? The records that they have left suggest that promotion was less of a preoccupation for them than for their officers. That does not mean, however, that advancement in the service was of no interest to common soldiers. Those few with connections in high places, however weak or tenuous, sought to use them to their advantage. Benjamin Dewhirst, who enlisted in Johnson's Regiment of Foot at Halifax, Yorkshire, in March 1746, described himself as the nephew of 'Dr Hargreaves late Dean of Chichester' in a letter to the Duke of Newcastle. Dewhirst, on the basis of the duke's having 'been a very great friend to my late Unkle', asked for Newcastle to use his 'Interest to prefer me in the military Way'.[23] The limit of the ambition of most common soldiers must have been to rise to non-commissioned officer rank. That status was open only to a portion of them, as one of the qualifications seems to have been literacy. Contemporary accounts suggest that good behaviour also mattered. We can be confident that corporals and sergeants had to show leadership qualities, as they were expected to play a vital role in the day-to-day management of the men under their command. They supervised the soldiers' messing arrangements and generally oversaw their conduct and listened to their concerns. Non-commissioned officers, it seems, could play an important role in defusing tensions between soldiers and between officers and men. It seems reasonable to suppose that older (and benignly inclined) non-commissioned officers acted as father figures for inexperienced recruits. We know that corporals and sergeants taught new soldiers how to clean and maintain their muskets and present themselves for duty 'clean in their dress their Arms & Accoutrements in Good order & their amunition Compleat'.[24] Their status is perhaps best captured by comparing them to a foreman in a factory – a vital intermediary between management and workforce. Important though they were to the functioning of the army, their position was often precarious; if they stepped out of line, they could be stripped of their rank and obliged to return to the status of a common soldier.

While most of those who became corporals and sergeants possessed the qualities of literacy and leadership that the roles demanded, we should not assume that only those from more elevated backgrounds – the Dewhirsts of the rank and file – could secure promotion to non-commissioned officer. An example of a sergeant with an unpromising provenance is Edward Kitson of the 46th Foot. He began his military career when Lieutenant John Ridout enlisted him in Shrewsbury gaol in August 1776. According to Ridout's report to the Secretary at War, Kitson and his fellow recruits were 'very fine Lads . . . confined . . . for petty offences'.[25] Kitson received an official pardon, conditional upon his joining the army, on 21 November of that year.[26] By 17 February 1777 he appears on the 46th Foot's muster lists in North America. Less than a year later, Kitson had been promoted to corporal. He held that rank until he became a sergeant on 25 August 1782 and he remained a sergeant until he left the army the following year.[27]

Non-commissioned officers received higher pay than privates, which was incentive enough to want promotion. The full pay of a corporal in a regiment of foot was one shilling a day; a sergeant's one shilling and sixpence. A private's daily full pay stood at just eight pence; on the Irish establishment, a penny less. Guards regiments and the horse and dragoons earned more, but none could be described as well paid by comparison with civilian labourers and artisans. In the mid-eighteenth century, labourers earned about a shilling a day in Lancashire, one shilling and two pence in Oxford and two shillings in London. By the 1780s, these figures had risen to one shilling and eight pence a day in Lancashire and one shilling and four pence in Oxford, while remaining about the same in London. For skilled workers, remuneration was higher; in the provinces, craftsmen could earn between two shillings a day and two shillings and sixpence; in London, three shillings seems to have been the norm.[28]

If the disparity between military and civilian wages were not bad enough, deductions for a variety of purposes – the paymaster-general, Chelsea Hospital (or Kilmainham in Ireland), the regiment's agent, paymaster and surgeon – cut deeply into the soldier's full pay. From 1771, troops at home were reimbursed some of these deductions half yearly. But these reimbursements, known collectively as the 'king's bounty', were not paid to soldiers serving abroad.[29] Troops based in North America also had a deduction made from their wages from 1763 to cover the cost of military rations. The introduction of this new stoppage caused widespread resentment, which manifested itself in serious mutinies in several regiments.[30] Concessions from the government – the original four pence deduction was reduced to two and a half pence – led to the subsiding of the mutinies in 1764, but unhappiness continued. In January 1775, a sympathetic lieutenant wrote that 'I shou'd imagine that 2½d can be of no great Consequence to Government, but of very great use to the Soldier'.[31]

Irregular payment added to the difficulties. Long periods of time could elapse between the settling of pay accounts. George Wade, in charge of the forces marching north to intercept the Jacobite advance from Scotland in the autumn of 1745, explained the likely consequences very succinctly: 'if the Troops are not regularly paid, they will of course plunder the Country.'[32] Abroad, the problem could be exacerbated by difficulties in securing cash locally and the need to bring it from Britain by ship. The commander of the British garrison at Savannah in Georgia warned in 1779 that 'some Corps have near ten Months [pay] due'.[33] But the fundamental difficulty was the inadequacy of what the soldier received when he was paid. Even in England, where the rank and file was better off than in North America, private soldiers saw little of their eight pence a day full pay. According to a contemporary calculation, they received just two shillings three pence and a farthing per week.[34]

Low pay led soldiers to seek ways to augment their official wage. As with impecunious officers, some members of the rank and file acquired additional regimental responsibilities, all of which provided the opportunity to make a bit more money. Sergeants might become regimental paymasters or adjutants. Others might serve as regimental or company clerks. Privates acted as servants to officers. Common soldiers could earn extra money by working on fortifications. In 1756, troops employed as labourers on the works at Albany received nine pence a day New York currency on top of their normal wage; artificers earned an extra fifteen pence local currency.[35] Those with craft skills also found employment in the army's ancillary services; an extra three shillings a day was the reward for a private in the 63rd Foot who worked as an armourer for the ordnance in South Carolina in 1780.[36]

Opportunities existed outside the army, too. Off-duty soldiers, particularly those with a trade, often sought work with local civilian employers. In many instances, their officers condoned the practice, as they recognized that without the ability to supplement their meagre army pay, soldiers were more likely to desert. Moonlighting, however, naturally provoked resentment from those who disliked competition for jobs. At Kinsale in 1752, the local grand jury complained of soldiers working in the local economy.[37] In Boston, Massachusetts, the 'Massacre' of March 1770, when troops opened fire on a hostile crowd, owed much to the townspeople's ire at soldiers' employment in the harbour-side rope-walks. At about the same time, rioting in New York seems to have been inspired by the same grievance of soldiers taking local jobs.[38]

Some soldiers resorted to truly desperate measures. William Harris, a private in the Royal Fusiliers, faced a regimental court martial in June 1744 for pawning his military shoes to a local blacksmith for a shilling and his shirts to a wagoner's wife for another shilling. Found guilty, Harris was condemned to 200 lashes.[39] He tried to dispose of his own footware and clothing; others stole goods from fellow soldiers or even their officers. Some of these items were retained for personal use of the soldiers or their families; but most of the ill-gotten gains were offered for sale, which suggests that a desire for money was a major cause of the crimes. Still more took valuables from the local inhabitants – everywhere that the army served, whether in North America and the West Indies or Europe and South Asia, soldiers stole from civilians. Again, the goods stolen seem primarily to have been taken for their value as objects for sale. An inventory of property seized by a soldier of the 15th Foot, executed for plundering on St Lucia in December 1778, included various items of men's and women's clothing and a 'Silver Punch ladle'.[40]

Food and Drink

William Todd, a corporal in the British Army campaigning in western Germany in the Seven Years War, wrote a detailed diary of his daily activities and reflections. On 16 June 1761, he described how he and a group of his regimental colleagues went in search of food. They came across a large house in the woods near their camp; most of the family who lived there had gone to church, leaving a daughter of the household to prepare a meal. The soldiers ate the dinner that she was cooking. Todd told the girl, according to his own account of the episode, that 'we had been in great wants of Victuals as we came out soon in the Morning, Otherwise we would not a taken theirs from her'. Food is a regular feature of the entries in his diary. Occasionally, he celebrated its availability ('We find parts roots here, as Pottatoes, Carrots etc which we are very Bussy in Cooking so that we think Ourselves much better of then in the Last Camp where we could get nothing'); but more often he lamented its absence.[41] The testimony of Lieutenant Colonel Robert Hall suggests that food shortages occurred from the moment the British troops began to campaign. In September 1758, Hall reported to his brother: 'now our Distresses were a little Serious . . . out of meer Necessity we Marauded the Country round, having no Bread'.[42]

Germany was far from unique in posing logistical challenges for the commissariat. In North America, the army during the War of Independence relied for long periods of time on salted provisions sent across the Atlantic from Britain and Ireland. Officers, however, believed that fresh food supplements were vital to the maintenance of morale. Unequal distribution of 'enemy' cattle and sheep, in the view of Captain John André, led to real discontent. He argued that the inadequate incentive given to surrender livestock to the commissaries for general use meant that some units consumed the animals themselves. Those units that handed over cattle and sheep to the commissaries therefore began to feel aggrieved and soldiers in those corps decided to right what they perceived as an injustice by seizing foodstuffs from the inhabitants, whether loyalist, rebel or neutral.[43] André was not alone in seeing a connection between shortages of fresh food – especially meat – and plundering. Orders issued to the small British army operating in North Carolina in 1781 sought to prevent thefts from the local population by assuring soldiers that fresh food would be provided for them.[44]

At times, desperation certainly caused soldiers to steal food. As we have seen, Lieutenant Colonel Hall had no hesitation in linking 'marauding' (plundering) in Germany in 1758 to shortages of bread issued to the army. The troops on the expedition from Canada that advanced into upper New York in 1777 under the leadership of General John Burgoyne soon ran into their own supply problems and resorted to stealing local vegetables. According to William Digby, a lieutenant in Burgoyne's army, the hungry soldiers dug up potatoes scarcely fit to eat 'without thinking in the least of the owner'.[45] Burgoyne himself was alarmed that, contrary to his express orders, 'Parties of thirty and Forty men att a time have gone out of Camp and taken away Every kind of Greens Which the Inhabitants had for the Sustenance of their Famillys'.[46]

Even away from active service on campaign, food was a preoccupation for many members of the army – officers as well as men. As one might expect, senior officers, with a larger disposable income, usually lived quite well in quarters or garrison; they could use their money to supplement their army rations, even arranging for foodstuffs to be sent to them from home. While he was based at Halifax, Nova Scotia, Colonel James Grant had shipped to him from Scotland 'a Cask of Eggs some Red Herrings and an additional number of Hams & Tongues'.[47] But for the junior officers dependent on their pay, local sources were the only option. Occasionally, probably because it was a rarity, plenty was a cause for comment. Ensign Richard Augustus Wyvill of the 38th Foot regarded Long Island, where he was cantoned in 1782, as a veritable 'Paradise'. His enthusiasm seems to have been based on the island's luscious fruits, especially peaches, which the local pigs feasted on, making 'their Flesh delicious'.[48] More often, however, junior officers complained about shortages or high prices that limited what they could afford to eat. If James Grant enjoyed his personal shipments of foodstuffs while in Halifax, Lieutenant Francis Laye of the Royal Artillery described the town as 'really a horrid place, every thing most amazingly dear'.[49]

Alcohol seems never to have been far from the minds of officers and men. A variety of sources suggest that, even in an age given to large-scale libation, the army contained more than its share of heavy drinkers. Lieutenant Colonel Samuel Bagshawe's accounts show that he bought substantial quantities of wine and brandy while serving in Ireland and then when he sailed for India in 1754. Some of these purchases were no doubt for his fellow officers in the 39th Foot; others we can assume were for his own use. In March 1755, for example, he purchased nine gallons of 'english Clarett' and seven gallons of 'Dry Rhenish'.[50] Martin Hunter, a lieutenant in the 52nd Foot when it advanced into New Jersey in late 1776, recalled George Hamilton, one of the captains of the regiment, insisting on taking as much Madeira as he could manage from the cellar of a house in which the light company stayed. 'The next morning when we marched,' Hunter wrote, 'Collins, the Captain's servant, who liked a drop as well as his master, had loaded the Captain's horses so much, that they could scarcely move off the ground.' Hamilton, Hunter explained, 'drank so hard that it was recommended to him to give up the Light Company, which he did'.[51]

If officers drank to excess, so did the rank and file. Official attitudes to alcohol consumption were ambiguous, to say the least. On the one hand, beer was supplied to the troops and rum when it was available; the standard ration, furthermore, might be increased to reward soldiers for success in battle or just to improve morale in trying circumstances. On the other hand, the army's commanders often had to take action to curb drunkenness. Sutlers and other peripatetic tradespeople, who sold drink to soldiers in camp, found their activities tightly regulated to avoid the troops having too easy access to large quantities of alcohol. General George Wade, commanding at Newbury camp in 1740, ordered that no alcohol should be sent to his men from neighbouring public houses and that sutlers who tried to sell spirits would have the liquor destroyed and they would be 'turn'd out of the Camp'.[52] Usually, however, local commanders adopted a less extreme position; they gave a limited number of the managers of 'dram shops' permission to establish temporary premises on the periphery of camps. Officers were well aware that their men spent as much of their money as they could on drink; hence the practice of paying them weekly 'pocket money' rather than allowing them to receive a lump sum when the regimental accounts were settled. Even so, payment days tended to be marked by much drunkenness.[53]

Inebriation inevitably impaired the ability of some soldiers to perform their duties. A private in the Royal Fusiliers, tried before a regimental court martial in June 1744 for 'being drunk & disorderly in his Quarters', acknowledged that 'When he is warn'd to go on Command, He gets drunk'. Found guilty by the court, he was sentenced to receive fifty lashes.[54] In May 1762, the members of the British contingent in Prince Ferdinand of Brunswick's army fighting in western Germany were threatened with punishment of 'the utmost Severity' if they were convicted of drunkenness.[55] In some places, the problem seems to have been general. Lieutenant Colonel Alexander Leslie of the 64th Foot reported (with remarkable candour) to the regiment's colonel from Halifax in July 1770 that 'we review in a couple of days, the men have got pretty sober and at least they are not seen in Liquor'.[56]

Maybe Halifax and the nearby New England colonies offered particular temptations; large quantities of rum were produced in Boston and Newport, Rhode Island. In September 1775, wounded troops from Boston who returned home to convalesce seem to have been in a state of alcoholic dependence. That at least is the impression conveyed by the lieutenant governor, who forbade the garrison of Plymouth citadel to give any liquor to the new arrivals and ordered none of the wounded men to try to go into the town.[57] But the problem was not confined to New England, with its plentiful supplies of strong rum. The agent for a government contractor reported from New York that the contingent of Foot Guards in the city 'are almost constantly drunk'.[58] In North Carolina, General Cornwallis threatened to curtail the normal rum ration if his troops continued to leave camp in search of more drink.[59]

Drink was undoubtedly responsible for many of the breaches of discipline in the army. While under the influence of alcohol, with their inhibitions removed, officers and men were more likely to engage in brawls. But drink played a more pervasive role as the motive for crime. The sale of clothing and equipment by soldiers often appears to have been motivated by a desire to increase drinking money: as a marine officer noted in Boston, some of the troops in the barracks 'sell the beds from under them to get this Cursed Rum'.[60] Thefts from local inhabitants sometimes had the same objective, as the historian of the British peacetime garrison in North America from 1763 has argued.[61] His view is confirmed by the experience of the War of Independence. A general court martial in Boston in 1775 found that two privates of the 35th Foot had stolen a quantity of flour from one storekeeper in the town and sold it to another, at whose shop they had been drinking before. The court learned that the men used the proceeds of their sale to buy cider and porter.[62] In New York, in September 1776, to give just one more example, a loyalist recalled seeing books plundered from local libraries offered as payment for drink by soldiers in a tavern on Long Island.[63] In short, it is difficult to dissent from the judgement of the Guards officer who claimed that 'Drunkenness & means of Purchasing Liquor . . . [were] the Cause of most of the Disorders, of which Soldiers are Guilty'.[64]

Hardships

We have considered the hardship caused by poor pay and shortages of food. Now we should look at the other trials that soldiers faced and which feature in their writings. Perhaps the most obvious danger that members of the army ran derived from the very nature of their occupation. In wartime, death in action was a real risk – or if not death, then severe injury. Pitched battles posed the greatest threat. Regrettably, from the historian's point of view, officers, who have left us the fullest accounts of military engagements, often provided few insights into the experience of battle itself. Perhaps from an understandable desire to protect relatives and friends from anxiety, many writers preferred to emphasize duty and service rather than go into gory details. After the action at Kirchdenkern (or Villinghausen), in western Germany, in the summer of 1761, Lieutenant Colonel John Maxwell simply commented sardonically to his friend John Dalrymple that 'there is no writing of a Battle without leting you Country Gentlemen Know what blood you have had for your money'.[65]

Sometimes, however, we get a sense of the awful reality of armed conflict. Philip Brown, describing the hard-fought Battle of Fontenoy in the spring of 1745, focused initially on 'true English Courage & Bravery' and the heroic efforts of the Hanoverian troops that had been alongside the British regiments. But, most revealingly, Brown noted that at the moment he wrote 'it is very uncertain whether I may yet live to see the Day out or the Sun rising the next Morning should the Enemy Determine to Harass us in our retreat'.[66] James Abercromby, commander of the army repulsed when it attacked the French defences at Fort Carilon (Ticonderoga) in upper New York in 1758, left a vivid account of the difficulties his soldiers faced. The ground approaching the French position, he wrote, was 'Cover'd with Trees, the Branches sharpen'd and pointed outwards and a vast Number of Pointed Stakes drove in to the Ground . . . Besides which, the Enemy were entrenched to the Teeth with a Breastwork of between 8 & 9 Feet high, from behind which they kept so hot and so successful a Fire on Our Troops'.[67] Abercromby's men, exposed as they were trapped in the tangled barriers prepared for them, suffered appalling casualties. The same was true of the British attacking force at Bunker Hill in June 1775. Francis Bushill Sill, the major of the 63rd Foot, was clearly deeply affected: 'this attack lost us the prime of our army, the Shocking Carnage that day never will be erased out of my mind 'till the day of my Death'.[68] On a few occasions we see the full horror. After the Battle of Long Island in August 1776, John McPherson of the 17th Foot told his father of the death of Captain Sir Alexander Murray, killed by a cannon ball ('I never saw a man so mangled').[69]

The danger of death was not limited, of course, to set-piece battles. In the War of American Independence, British troops often ran the risk of being attacked in isolated posts or while travelling. In New Jersey, in the first months of 1777, local militias harassed the soldiers in their winter quarters. On 14 January, Brigadier General Sir William Erskine wrote that 'the greatest danger is being fired at from behind trees and bushes, on the Road'.[70] A little under a month later, Captain Thomas Stanley of the 17th Light Dragoons sent the same message home: 'we Patrole the Roads & carry Letters & expresses from Post to Post, neither of which Dutys we can scarce perform without being Shot at.'[71] These attacks not only led to casualties; they also wore down the morale of the British forces, which were often subject to repeated encounters with a hidden enemy: 'fired upon by small sculking parties of the rebels', as one officer put it; 'almost daily molested', in the words of another.[72]

Surprisingly, perhaps, death at the hands of opponents was a less likely fate for the soldier than death by disease. Sickness was a common experience and it often appears as a cause for concern in contemporary accounts. In tropical stations, where Europeans faced unfamiliar microbes as well as extreme heat, disease often made deep inroads into units, reducing severely the number of men available for duty. Troops sent to the Caribbean always seemed to suffer high levels of sickness. The British forces dispatched to capture Havana at the end of the Seven Years War soon discovered that the strongest part of the Spanish defences was environmental; campaigning in the heat and humidity of a disease-ridden island took its toll. 'I have had Prickly heat ever since I saw you,' the commander-in-chief Lord Albemarle told his friend Robert Monckton, 'besides some half dozen fevers'.[73] At Gorée, in West Africa, captured by the British in the same war, a return of five companies of the 86th Foot on 24 August 1760 showed that of 482 privates in the detachment when it landed, just 316 were still alive.[74] In the next conflict, John Vaughan, in charge of the British forces in the Caribbean, reported to the Secretary of State in London that the high mortality rate among the troops under his command 'must effectively check all hopes of active operations – should it continue the army will be altogether inadequate to those of defence'.[75]

Sickness, however, was not a problem confined to the tropical zones. In Portugal, Thomas Woods Knollis reported to his wife on 28 July 1762 that though he was in perfect health himself, 'we have here very warm weather, We had 10 Men, 1 Woman and 3 Children kill'd by the heat & fatigue almost suddenly by one day's March & died in the Hedges and on the road'.[76] In Quebec, captured by the British in September 1759, the occupying forces suffered terribly in the months following the raising of the Union Flag over the city. By the spring, Malcolm Fraser, an officer in Fraser's Highlanders, wrote, scurvy had caused 'Great havock amongst the Garrison'. Since the British occupation had begun, 628 men had died and of the 5,653 troops surviving, 2,312 were sick.[77] Even in Flanders, illness left its mark. Cuthbert Ellison informed his brother in January 1744, while at Ghent, that 'our Men are very Sickly and have a very bad Sort of Feaver amongst us, that dayly lessens our Numbers'.[78] And, as we have already seen, the encampments in England itself often proved unhealthy places to be, spreading distempers to the surrounding settlements.[79] Illness, in short, was a feature of military life, irrespective of where soldiers served. Unsurprisingly, given the deaths that disease often caused, references to it appear in many of the letters, diaries and other papers of officers and men.

In more temperate climates, at least, disease in camps was often a product of insanitary living conditions, despite the efforts of senior officers to enforce good practices and promote cleanliness, though regular digging and filling in of latrines. But even the buildings in which troops quartered could prove detrimental to their health. Accommodation for the Highland battalion that landed at Charleston, South Carolina, on 3 September 1757 included 'a Half finished Church without Windows, . . . Damp Store-houses upon the Quay and . . . empty Houses, where most of the Men were obliged to ly upon the Ground without Straw or any sort of Covering'. Small wonder, then, that 500 of the Highlanders had fallen ill by the end of the month.[80] Barracks did not always prove any better. Lieutenant Colonel John Arabin of Bligh's Horse reported in the early 1750s that those at Phillipstown, County Louth, were 'in the most ruinous Condition possible'. The roof leaked so much, Arabin explained, that the previous occupants had been forced to drill holes in the floors of the upper rooms to 'Let out the Rain water, which falls from thence into the Stables'. The walls were so decayed, he continued, that 'if neglected for a while longer, may Endanger the Lives of the Men quartered in it'.[81]

Off Duty

At any given time, several of a regiment's officers would not be present, but away from their unit, whether it was based at home or abroad. In peacetime, recognizing that all officers were not required for the regiment to function, the military authorities allowed generous periods of leave. The muster of the 54th Foot taken at Gibraltar in January 1767, records eleven of the thirty-two officers (31 per cent) absent on leave.[82] For young officers, this might be to pursue their education. While on Minorca in the same year, 1767, Thomas Shairp received his commanding officer's permission to take eight or ten months' leave of absence 'to go to France, where he will recommend an Academy Militaire'.[83] Often, however, officers simply returned home to manage their estates or socialize with their local connections. On the outbreak of war, senior military commanders and the government adopted a different approach. Leave now had to be justified and was not automatically granted. It was still possible for young officers to be allowed time off for their education,[84] but in other respects the system became much more restrictive. In June 1775, with fighting having begun across the Atlantic, a lieutenant in the 45th Foot, who had been on sick leave, received instructions to embark at the first opportunity.[85]

Some officers continued to show a reluctance to join their regiments. Major William Saxton, also in the 45th, had already enjoyed two years' leave, to take the waters in France, when he incurred the displeasure of the Secretary at War in 1777. Saxton's leave, Lord Barrington reminded him, had been granted even though no field officers were present with 45th, 'the Lieutenant Colonel having a detached Command'. In February, Barrington asked Saxton to say whether he planned to go to America or preferred to sell out. The major continued to drag his feet, however, and in December Barrington wrote again, this time displaying considerable irritation at Saxton's conduct: 'After what passed between Us in the Month of February last, I am exceedingly surprised to find a Message sent me from Sir William Howe that you are still absent from your Duty.'[86] Seemingly impervious to criticism, Saxton remained in France for several months more, even after the signing of the Franco–American alliance made Britain and France effective enemies.[87]

Members of the rank and file were not usually so fortunate. If they secured leave, it was for exceptional reasons and usually of short duration, in peacetime and in war. A soldier might be allowed home for compassionate leave, for instance; or, if he possessed the right to vote, to go and participate in an election.[88] But there were some interesting exceptions to the general reluctance to allow members of the rank and file to leave their regiments for any length of time. Richard Slater, a private in the 31st Foot, seems to have received repeated furloughs of several months at a time and resided for long periods in his home village in Staffordshire. There, it seems, he was deeply unpopular, having joined the army only as an alternative to facing punishment for crimes he had committed in the locality. Everyone, according to a local magistrate, had been relieved to see him go off into the army. On this occasion, the temptation is to imagine that his officers were as pleased to see the back of him as his native parish was distressed to see him return home. Slater, it appears, was caught in a game of pass the parcel, in which no one wanted to be responsible for him when the music stopped.[89]

Those officers and men who remained with the regiment did not have to devote every waking moment to their duties. In peacetime, particularly, when they were not on guard duty or patrol or practising drill or undergoing inspection by a visiting general, they could fill their spare hours in a variety of ways. We have seen that soldiers worked for civilian employers during off-duty periods, to earn extra money. We have also seen that officers and men sought, and often established, intimate relationships with women near where they were based and often socialized with local men. But there is much that we have not considered. The letters that soldiers wrote and the diaries that they kept, on which this chapter has drawn extensively, were themselves a way of filling time, as well as recording experiences and thoughts for relatives and friends. For some officers, in particular, letter-writing seems to have become an important routine that helped to break up long and uneventful days. 'My only amusements', Lord Francis Napier wrote while on the recruiting service in Hertfordshire in December 1780, 'are Eating, Drinking, Sleeping, Drilling *Six* Men, Scolding my Sergeants, & letter scribbling.'[90] A few officers were more ambitious in their writing tasks and produced military treatises, some while serving in wartime. Major Robert Donkin of the Royal Welch Fusiliers published his *Military Collections and Remarks* at New York in 1777.

Donkin dedicated his work to Earl Percy, an officer who, while he wrote no treatise himself, showed great commitment to broadening his military education. In November 1774, while quartered in Boston, Massachusetts, Percy requested a copy of the *Memoires* of the French general the Marquis de Feuquières for his winter reading.[91] For his part, James Green, an ensign in the 62nd Foot who acted as a deputy judge advocate in America, felt it important to read Sir William Blackstone's famous *Commentaries on the Laws of England* to equip himself for his new legal role.[92] But we should not imagine that many officers filled their leisure hours so productively. George

Evelyn Boscawen, a junior officer in the same Boston garrison, was mocked by his regimental colleagues when he revealed an interest in reading military texts – they called him their '*Humphrey Bland*', the name of the general whose *Treatise of Military Discipline*, first published in 1727, became the bible of serious-minded military professionals.[93] By no means all officers, as Boscawen's treatment reminds us, could be categorized as serious-minded. William Cobbett, a non-commissioned officer who devoted many hours to reading and self-improvement while in the army after the American war, poured scorn on most of the officers he encountered in Nova Scotia. He regarded them as lacking any professional commitment and any intellectual curiosity.[94]

A more common time-filler for officers was gambling. At Philadelphia in the winter of 1777–8, according to a British lieutenant, betting on card games 'disordered the finances of several officers'. 'I am sorry to say', he went on, 'that the example of men high in rank seems to give a sanction to a vice so destructive to the Army and so fatal to individuals.' He believed that the problem's roots ran back to the 'extravagant rage for play, which prevailed at [New] York and [New] Brunswick last year'.[95] Heavy betting continued to occupy the time and money of many officers throughout the War of American Independence. At its end, Lieutenant Hew Buchan of the 31st Foot, according to his father, had run disastrously into debt as a result of the 'Scenes of Gambling Luxury & dissipation' he encountered while in America.[96] But in reality, gambling was a problem everywhere the army served – at home as well as abroad and in all overseas postings, not just North America. We can reasonably speculate that it owed something, as did drunkenness, which was equally ubiquitous, to an acute awareness among military men of the transience of life. But both gambling and drunkenness probably owed more to boredom.

Officers and men often found time weighing heavily on their hands. Their accounts leave us with many hints at their sense of having little to do. Jeremy Lister of the 10th Foot, on the recruiting service in England, found Gainsborough, where he was sent to find new soldiers, utterly depressing. From there he wrote in his journal at the beginning of 1783 that the forthcoming year, if he had to remain in the town, 'exhibits a prospect to me very dreary and gloomy'.[97] Minorca seems to have been widely regarded as a bad posting, thanks in part to its remoteness, high living costs and scorching summer heat, but also because it offered little in the way of interest to occupy the empty hours. Archibald Cuninghame, arriving in the spring of 1781, wrote to his mother that 'I can't say much about Minorca only that appearances are by no means in its favour'. A few weeks later, after having gone on a tour of the island, he told his sister that 'description is needless suffice it to say that it May justly be compared to the Isle of *Arran*'. The comparison, we can be confident, was not meant to be flattering. The best he could say for Minorca was that it was not as bad as Gibraltar.[98] It was from Minorca, as we have seen, that Thomas Shairp ventured to Grenoble academy in 1767, remaining in France for as long as he could and not returning to his regiment until 1769. Once back on Minorca, in August 1770 he complained of his inability, as a result of the searing heat, to go outdoors 'except when on duty', which must have made the experience still more tedious.[99] James Urquhart, based at Minorca in 1713, summed up many expressions of the way time dragged on the island by describing his posting there as 'a very Mellanchollic Confinement'.[100]

Chapter 6

Officers and Men

Why do large numbers of common soldiers follow the orders of small numbers of officers? Looked at from the outside, it seems a minor miracle that ordinary soldiers accepted the authority of their officers, even in the most dangerous of circumstances, when their lives were at risk. The usual assumption, in the case of the eighteenth-century British Army, is that fear secured obedience; soldiers, to put it bluntly, were more afraid of the harsh punishments inflicted on the orders of their officers than they were of the threat from the enemy. But violence and intimidation, while playing a part in maintaining the authority of the officers, was by no means the only means of winning obedience and probably not the most effective means either.

We have already touched on some of the possible reasons for soldiers' preparedness to obey their officers. The confidence of upper-class officers, who regarded it as their entitlement by upbringing and status to command, was no doubt of some importance in an era of great social deference. Sergeants, corporals and more experienced privates played a part, too; their induction of recruits into the ways of the army helped to ensure that obeying orders became the default position for most soldiers, unless very special circumstances arose. Officers also benefited incidentally from the sense of soldierly solidarity that led members of the rank and file to be unwilling to let down their comrades in arms. But to gain a better understanding of how the eighteenth-century British Army functioned – the purpose of this chapter – we need to borrow three concepts usually employed outside the military sphere: moral economy, contract and negotiated authority.

The idea of a moral economy, initially applied to the values of eighteenth-century English food rioters, is helpful as a means of illuminating the attitudes of common soldiers to their service.[1] Much like the rest of plebeian society, the rank and file inhabited a world of custom, precedent and rights. Officers who did not respect the soldiers' sense of a set of established entitlements were likely to find it hard to secure obedience. Related to the moral economy is contract, usually employed in political philosophy to describe the nature of the reciprocal relationship between ruler and the ruled. Eighteenth-century soldiers conceived of their service as a form of contract. The contract in question was implied rather than written; but if officers failed to live up to the terms of the tacit bargain struck at enlistment – a variation on the time-honoured governing compact of obedience in return for protection – then soldiers felt themselves no longer obliged to obey. Successful officers recognized the need to work within the boundaries of the soldiers' moral economy and to acknowledge the rank and file's contractual thinking. Indeed, the key to officers' effective exercise of power was to appreciate its limits and act accordingly. Here our final borrowed concept is useful. For historians of the eighteenth century, negotiated authority came into scholarly currency mainly as a means of capturing the political relationship between Britain and its American colonies in the decades preceding the Revolution.[2] But the give and take that it implies, the need for the nominal superior to secure the agreement or at least acquiesce of the nominal inferior, makes it applicable to the way in which eighteenth-century army officers were obliged to operate. Their authority was far from absolute; they could not take it for granted that their men would always obey. Only by keeping within the lines drawn by the military moral economy and their soldiers' contractual attitudes could officers run their units effectively.

Many historians of eighteenth-century American armed forces assume that these military dynamics were unique to their subjects of study. The provincial regiments that were raised in the colonies in the Seven Years War to fight against the French and their native allies and the Continental Army that fought under Washington during the War of Independence appear in many accounts as quite different from the British Army of the time. Americans, we are repeatedly told, would not unthinkingly obey. Soldiers in provincial regiments and the Continental Army had a strong sense of the contractual nature of their service. They had their own moral economy of rights and obligations. Their officers, faced with soldiers who were tenacious in defence of what they saw as their entitlements, were forced to rely less on physical punishment and its threat and more on appeals to reason, virtue and pride. To illustrate the supposed distinctiveness of this American military culture, historians of the colonial and revolutionary armed forces often draw a stark contrast with what they depict as a highly disciplined British Army, the product of a more hierarchical and authoritarian social order, commanded by officers whose control rested on brutal punishments that reduced the common soldiers to unquestioning automata.[3]

The contrast is greatly overdrawn. British redcoats were far from robot-like. Several scholars have demonstrated that members of the British rank and file had a well-developed sense of their rights and staunchly resisted any attempts to infringe them.[4] But these historians are mainly interested in the life of the common soldiers as an aspect of labour history; they say comparatively little about the various means – besides the lash and the noose – by which the British Army's officers sought to secure the obedience of their men.[5] This chapter builds upon earlier work on the British rank and file and provides some new evidence of their attitudes. But its main contribution perhaps comes in the parts that shed light on the officers and the ways in which their authority was negotiated.[6] Here the evidence is almost exclusively taken from the time of the War of American Independence, the period where my knowledge of the army is deepest and a comparison with the American military seems most apposite.

Moral Economy and Contract

James Wolfe, later immortalized by his early death at Quebec, wrote in October 1755 of British troops who had 'no idea of a free born English Soldier's marching, working or fighting, but when he thinks proper'.[7] Wolfe's depiction is a far cry from American historians' image of redcoats cowed by brutal discipline, but it accords with what we can glean of their attitudes from other sources. When they felt aggrieved at what they regarded as a breach of the military contract or behaviour by their officers that ran counter to their sense of fairness and the customs and traditions of the army, soldiers were likely to demonstrate their dissent. They might do this by leaving (desertion), by taking from the local inhabitants what they felt that they had been denied by their officers (plunder) or even by expressing their displeasure by refusing to obey orders (mutiny).

Each of these manifestations of dissent could, of course, have other causes than the soldier's perception that his officer had failed to fulfil obligations inherent in the bargain struck at the moment of recruitment. Desertion, for instance, might arise from a soldier's local attachments or his intention to profit by re-enlisting in a different corps or his overwhelming sense of fear or even his sickening of using violence against others.[8] Plunder might simply be a product of the soldier's desire to make money by selling stolen goods, often to buy alcohol.[9] Mutiny could stem from a lack of respect for inexperienced or unsuitable officers. But in many cases, desertion, plundering and mutiny seem to have been the consequences of the rank and file's belief that the military moral economy had been ignored or the implied military contract had not been honoured. The parallels with American thinking will be apparent if we look in turn at British soldiers' ideas on the legitimate exercise of authority, their length and location of service, their pay and their provisions.

Far from meekly accepting whatever their officers did, British soldiers showed their displeasure if they thought that a line had been crossed. They appear to have acknowledged that their officers could legitimately impose their own non-corporal penalties for minor infractions; confinement to quarters, extra duties and ordering offenders to wear their regimental jackets inside out, all recommended in military manuals, seem not to have caused ill-feeling amongst the rank and file.[10] Roger Lamb, a soldier in the 9th Foot, was later to praise his regimental commander, Major Mason Bolton, for employing such methods to bring erring members of the rank and file back into line.[11] But soldiers resented and resisted arbitrary physical penalties, imposed by officers acting without the sanction of a military court. The adjutant-general himself, perhaps recognizing the rank and file perspective, expressed uneasiness about officers' beating the soldiers on their own authority; the practice should be used as little as possible, he wrote in July 1775.[12]

At least a few members of the rank of file were so confident of their right to better treatment that they wrote to superior officers or even government ministers in London, to protest at company or regimental officers' abuse of their authority. An artilleryman penned his complaint to the commander-in-chief in 1779; too many troops in America, he wrote, were beaten 'like Dogs' without the authority of courts martial.[13] The following year an anonymous soldier similarly told the Secretary at War that in the 25th Foot 'no Man is Beat with a Cane or Stick at the pleasure of an Off' . . . but is legally tried by a Court Martiall And if by them found guilty, is punished accord[ing]ly'. The writer continued that soldiers so treated 'esteem *their officers* And in *Action* will *Stand by them*'; but added 'how different is the disposition of other Regiments!' His request was simply that 'in General orders you would please give it out that no off' *whatever*, he be, shall have it in his power to Beat the meanest of the *rank* and *file* without being tried by Court Martial'.[14]

Soldiers complained of other forms of ill-treatment that they believed to be unfair and they took other forms of action in response. Regimental or even company commanders who suspected a non-commissioned officer of wrongdoing might strip him of his rank. In December 1777, Colonel James Pattison of the Royal Artillery declared in daily orders that an undisciplined bombardier (the equivalent of a corporal in the infantry) was 'unworthy of Remaining a Non Commiss'd officer' and should be 'Reduced to a Gunner from this day from Rank and pay'.[15] Summary demotion of this kind could easily lead to as much resentment as did arbitrary physical punishment, if the rank and file thought that the officer had acted hastily and unjustly. Corporal Thomas Sullivan of the 49th Foot was reduced to a private by his regiment's lieutenant colonel in September 1777. Sullivan believed that his commanding officer took this drastic action simply because Sullivan could not explain the provenance of a piece of mutton roasting on a campfire. The discontented Sullivan continued to serve in the ranks until June of the following year, when he deserted. His decision to leave the army owed much, no doubt, to his marrying a 20-year-old Philadelphian woman in December 1777. When the army evacuated the city, Sullivan and his wife had to make an uncomfortable choice; she could follow him and his regiment or Sullivan could leave the army and stay in the city. But, by his own account, his decision to desert was also influenced by 'the ill usage I received (undeservedly,) when I was in the 49th Battalion', which seems to be a reference to the loss of his corporal's rank on the lieutenant colonel's command.[16]

British soldiers enlisted in peacetime were usually expected to serve for as long as the army needed them; but wartime recruits (the majority of men serving during conflicts) were in a different situation.[17] To encourage enlistment when soldiers were desperately needed, as we have seen, British governments offered new recruits the opportunity to serve for only three years or the duration of the war.[18] Men who were compelled to serve under the provisions of Parliamentary Recruiting Acts or volunteered to avoid being pressed, were enlisted on the same short-term basis. Soldiers who had joined up on the understanding that they would serve only for a set number of years naturally anticipated that they would be able to leave the army at the expiry of their term, just as did American provincials in the Seven Years

War and Continental Army soldiers in the War of Independence. While the evidence relating to British soldiers' sensitivity about the length of their service is not substantial, the few indications we have point unmistakably to the kind of contractual attitude usually associated with their American counterparts. In the spring of 1747, in the closing stages of the War of the Austrian Succession, soldiers pressed three years earlier demanded their discharge. From the point of view of their commanding officers, the timing could hardly have been worse. The army, together with its allies, was about to embark on that year's Flanders campaign against the French. The aggrieved soldiers were bought off only by the payment of a guinea per man and a promise of immediate release when the troops went into winter quarters.[19] The following September, regular troops in the Louisbourg garrison also argued that, having served three years, they were now entitled to their discharge; whether they were given an extra sum of money to continue serving is not clear.[20] In the spring of 1762, similar discontent emerged in the army in America. An officer's notebook records the 'unbecoming behaviour of some Soldiers who have lately demanded their Discharge aledging that their term of Service was expired'. On this occasion, a significant inducement was required to persuade the soldiers to continue with their regiments: 'each man whose time of Service is expired [will] be reinlisted for the War only and receive a gratuity of 3 Guineas and his discharge upon Application, at the expiration of it'.[21]

Soldiers might also hold their officers to promises about the location of their service. Those assured on enlistment that they would be dispatched to one theatre of war could become mutinous if they were then ordered to go somewhere quite different. As with length of service, the soldiers believed that a condition agreed when they were recruited had not been met and they were therefore free to refuse to comply with their officers' commands. The most spectacular rebellions occurred in Highland regiments in which the rank and file had expected to cross the Atlantic to North America, only to find that their corps was ordered instead to sail to India. Perhaps Highlanders were particularly prone to mutiny in such circumstances. Their regiments contained large numbers of men who had been recruited as a result of the influence of their landlords and might therefore have been especially disaffected if their expectations of paternal care were disappointed.[22] But probably more significant was the enthusiasm of many Highlanders to go to America.

They seem to have viewed military service there as a means of migration – assuming they survived the war, their regiment would be disbanded in America and the discharged soldiers might even be offered land grants in the colonies.[23] India, by contrast, was much less attractive as a destination, despite its reputed riches. Mortality rates were particularly high amongst the troops that went to Asia and good-quality land – the real draw for Highland recruits thinking of post-war possibilities – was not as readily available as in North America.[24] Even so, the virtues and disadvantages of the respective postings were probably less important for the soldiers than their sense of a broken contract. We can surmise that the mutineers justified their actions on the grounds that the bargain struck at enlistment had not been honoured. They were protesting at being recruited on the basis of their serving in one place and then being allocated, without their consent, to another. The mutiny in 1778 of Seaforth's 78th Highlanders owed much to rumours that the regiment was about to embark for service with the British East India Company. In 1783, two more regiments – the 77th and 83rd – similarly rebelled, again largely owing to their being ordered to sail for India.[25] Andrew Marshal, surgeon to the 83rd Foot, left a vivid account of the mutiny, with the men 'convening in small circles, talking to one another'. Senior officers at Portsmouth, from where the regiment was due to embark, tried on several occasions to quell the unrest by making concessions, including offering to replace the unpopular lieutenant colonel.[26]

British soldiers were also likely to mutiny if their pay was not forthcoming or was subject to new deductions. The most celebrated incident, affecting British troops in North America, occurred at the end of the Seven Years War in 1763.[27] Sir Jeffery Amherst, the British commander-in-chief, ordered money to be docked from the pay of his soldiers to cover part of the costs of their provisions. Amherst was responding to a new emphasis on economy encouraged by the government in London, which was trying to come to grips with a national debt that had grown enormously as a result of the war. But if he pleased his political masters, he alienated his own troops. The extensive nature of the mutiny – it spread rapidly across the British outposts in North America – revealed the soldiers' deep commitment to defending the pay to which they felt themselves entitled. Faced with such extensive resistance, Amherst had no choice but to stage a tactical retreat. A few weeks after bringing in the change, he offered concessions that lessened the monetary loss to the soldiers.[28] But even in this moderated version, Amherst's 'reform' of deductions left the rank and file worse off than they had been before. The mutiny subsided, though not in some garrisons until the spring of 1764, and resentment remained for years afterwards, not least amongst some of the junior officers, who were all too aware of the hardship inflicted on their soldiers.[29] Both the government and the military leadership should have anticipated that any attempt to alter the rank and file's remuneration would cause trouble. A similar mutiny had occurred at the end of the previous war, in 1747, when regular soldiers in the garrison of recently-captured Louisbourg objected to the introduction of new deductions.[30]

Much less conspicuous, but nonetheless important, was the smaller-scale mutinous behaviour, sparked by disputes about pay, which seems to have been as commonplace in the British Army as it was in the American Continental forces. A frequent cause of rank-and-file grievance was failure to pay additional money for extra work that they considered over and beyond their duty as military men. Amherst in 1759 tried to end disputes on this issue by stipulating the rates of pay to which soldiers were entitled if they served as artificers or labourers in the public service.[31] In December 1763, his successor, Thomas Gage, advised the Secretary at War that soldiers whose pay was now reduced by deductions for their provisions were even more likely to be sensitive about receiving proper remuneration 'for every piece of work' undertaken 'for the Publick'.[32] Late pay was even more contentious and much more difficult for officers to tackle. In 1777 more than fifty troops in different British regiments in North America refused to obey orders until their grievances – notably pay arrears – were redressed.[33] Nor was mutiny the only response of the soldiers to delays in receiving pay. As we have seen, in October 1745, George Wade, commander of the British forces assembled in northern England to resist the advance of the Jacobite forces from Scotland, told the government in London that he desperately needed more money to avoid his unpaid troops plundering the local inhabitants.[34]

British soldiers similarly showed their contractual mind-set when they protested at inadequate provisions. Troops at Oswego mutinied in the summer of 1755 when they regarded reduced rations as a violation of 'their Right'.[35] If their regular food rations were cut, they also had little compunction in stealing food from local inhabitants. At times, when on campaign, as we noted earlier, genuine food shortages could mean that soldiers purloined food because they were desperately hungry. As British troops on Burgoyne's expedition advanced into New York and ran short of food, they stole any foodstuffs they could get out without compunction.[36] But even when there was no absolute shortage of food, officers recognized that unless their soldiers were supplied with fresh produce, to supplement the salt rations sent from Britain and Ireland, trouble would ensue. Desertion might be justified by a lack of fresh food. Officers sometimes associated soldiers' plundering from the inhabitants with a shortage – or unfair distribution – of fresh meat.[37]

Court-martial records provide us with one of the few ways of glimpsing rank and file attitudes at first-hand, rather than through the refracted accounts left by their officers. Testimony given at courts martial suggests that soldiers saw any reduction in their rations as a breach of the implied military contract. Thomas Reedman, a private in the light infantry company of the 43rd Foot, accused with others in March 1779 of having killed and stolen an ox on Long Island, New York, argued that he had been 'forced to it' by the removal from his standard rations of the 'Small Species'. His fellow defendants, tried the next day, put forward the same defence.[38] On the face of it, their argument seems odd and unconvincing. The small species – items such as butter, cheese and peas – were missing from their rations, not the meat. Why should they steal meat to make up for a loss of the small species? But their action becomes more explicable if we think in contractual terms; the soldiers believed that their officers had failed to provide them with the full rations that were their entitlement, which meant that they were now free to find their own food supplies. Some support for this interpretation comes in the form of a letter written a few years earlier by an officer to his father, in which the officer explains that 'If the men chuse it, they may receive 7lb of fresh beef, instead of all the articles [in their standard ration] except flour'.[39] Reedman and his colleagues perhaps reasoned that as the small species had been removed from their rations, they were within their rights in seeking fresh meat as a replacement.

Negotiated Authority

American provincial soldiers who came into contact with the British regulars in the Seven Years War often commented on the extreme floggings and even capital penalties inflicted on disobedient soldiers. Capital punishment may have been far from unknown in colonial America, but the courts usually limited corporal penalties to the biblically sanctioned thirty-nine strokes of the whip.[40] To colonists accustomed to such a system, British military practice appeared shockingly inhumane. One anonymous American diarist, apparently from a New England provincial regiment, noted in October 1755 the death of a British soldier who had been flogged the day before; shortly afterwards, he recorded the severe flogging of two further regulars.[41] Another New Englander, part of the garrison of newly-conquered Louisbourg in October 1758, equally appalled by the penalties that could be inflicted under martial law, observed that 'ye regulars . . . are but little better than slaves to their Officers'.[42]

British general courts martial – the highest military tribunals – sentenced convicted men to 500 lashes as a matter of course; it was not unusual for them to stipulate 1,000 for more serious offences.[43] Very occasionally, offenders found themselves facing an even greater ordeal: five soldiers of the grenadier company of the 71st Highland Regiment, convicted of robbing a New York inhabitant in March 1779, were each sentenced to 1,500 lashes.[44] The most heinous crimes, or those that most detrimentally affected the army's discipline, attracted the death penalty.[45] Even brigade, garrison and regimental courts martial, dealing with lesser offences, could lay down punishments in excess of the upper limit of the number of lashes usually inflicted on soldiers in the Continental Army.[46] In June 1744, as we have seen, William Harris, a soldier in the Royal Regiment of Fusiliers, was sentenced by a regimental court martial in England to 200 lashes for selling his 'new Regim^t Shirt & Shoes'.[47] At Philadelphia, 33 years later, an artilleryman found guilty of 'being Absent seven Days without leave' was ordered by a brigade court martial 'to Receive *500* Lashes in the Usual Manner'.[48] Order-books, which contain copies of the commander-in-chief's instructions to the army as a whole or brigade or regimental commanders' orders to particular units, repeatedly threatened the common soldiers with extreme penalties if they transgressed even in the most minor way ('The Soldiers are once more forbidden to go into any Man's Field or Garden, to steal roots; any one detected will be severely punished').[49] On some occasions, senior officers promised summary execution for soldiers who stole from the local inhabitants.[50]

Rather than accept this brutally violent picture as all we need to know about how authority was exercised in the British Army, we might want to consider a different perspective; one that gives rather more active role to the soldiers themselves. Repeated orders promising dire penalties – up to and including death – might be interpreted not as sign of the power of officers, but of their weakness. Orders would not have had to be repeated if they were being obeyed; threats would not have had to be made time after time if soldiers were truly deterred by the possibility of the most awful retribution. General Howe, having told his troops shortly after they landed on Long Island in August 1776 that 'he is determined to Shew no mercy to any man found Guilty of Maurauding', found himself obliged to make the same claim a few days later: 'The General again repeats in Orders, that no Mercy will be shewn to any Man found Guilty, of Plundering.' The following week, the response had apparently been so unsatisfactory that he felt he had to up the level of threat: 'The Provost Martial [*sic*] has a Commission to Execute upon the Spot any Soldier he finds Guilty of Marauding.' For all Howe's attempts to sound tough, the impression that his men were not deterred is hard to avoid. We can even detect a trace of desperation in his orders.[51]

Once we appreciate the limits of officers' power, we can begin to discern the importance of negotiated authority. Officers could not take their men for granted and assume a robotic obedience; they were obliged to recognize that the rank and file had minds of their own, with which they had to engage in order to encourage the soldiers to do their duty. Major John Pitcairn, in charge of the marines in the Boston garrison just before the outbreak of the War of Independence, wrote of the way in which he treated his men 'with mildness' and sought 'to persuade them to behave well'.[52] Either through choice or necessity, officers like Pitcairn dealt with their soldiers as thinking beings, capable of responding to exercises of clemency, paternal care and appeals – personal, professional and political. Many of the methods British officers employed, in other words, bore a remarkable resemblance to those usually associated with the American Continental Army during the War of Independence.

Even though the British Army's courts martial sentenced soldiers to terrifying punishments, these were not always inflicted. Capital penalties were often remitted and general officers, who had to confirm general court martial decisions, sometimes chose to lessen the severity of corporal punishments.[53] Regimental commanders, for their part, exercised discretion over which men to send up to a general court martial and which to bring before their own lesser court martial, where they could control the level of penalty.[54] They could also use their power of clemency to pardon offenders brought before lower courts: Colonel Pattison of the Royal Artillery did so on numerous occasions while his unit was stationed in Philadelphia during the War of Independence.[55] Even junior officers might decide which offences to report to their superiors and which to overlook; Captain John Peebles of the 42nd Foot allowed his men some latitude when it came to stealing root vegetables and garden produce;[56] Captain Patrick Ferguson of the 70th drew the line at poultry and pigs, however.[57] Company officers might also provide character references for offenders brought before courts martial or plead mitigating circumstances to reduce their punishment. At a general court martial held in Boston in December 1775, Captain William Foster of the Marines testified that a soldier in his company accused of stealing wine 'was one of the last men he should have suspected to have been guilty of theft'.[58]

Discretion, some scholars argue in relation to the workings of the eighteenth-century English penal system, was merely a tool used to reinforce authority, a 'soft' accompaniment to the 'hard' approach of the extensive use of the capital penalty.[59] If we apply this view to the army and its punishment regime, we might see discretionary activity – whatever form it took – as doing little more than marginally tempering the violence of an essentially coercive system of control and at the same time strengthening its terrorizing impact by enhancing the impression that his officer had the final say over the soldier's fate. But, on the basis of the evidence available, we could just as easily argue that officers' use of discretion reflected their realization that terror alone could not induce their men to follow orders. Officers felt the need to cultivate their soldiers' loyalty and affection; discretion might even be conceived as a form of persuasion.

We can see paternalism in the same way. It no doubt reinforced officers' authority by making soldiers grateful, but it also suggests that officers recognized that their men had to be won over; their obedience could not be taken for granted. To encourage the troops and show them that the army's leaders cared, general officers ordered rewards to be given to the common soldiers at particular moments. Lord Cornwallis seems to have been particularly committed to this approach. In the spring and summer of 1781, he decided that his troops in North Carolina and Virginia should be given extra allowances of rum on numerous occasions.[60] Different sources reveal that regimental officers offered financial assistance when their men were in distress. A surviving notebook of Lieutenant Colonel Sir John Wrottesley of the Guards suggests that he lent impecunious soldiers money during the Pennsylvania campaign of 1777.[61] Ensign Daniel Gwynne of the 9th Foot wrote home to arrange for the pay of his sergeant to be transmitted to a needy relative ('The poor Man had no way of sending it to her but by applying to me', Gwynne told his father on 11 June 1778).[62] The journal of Captain Charles Napier of the 80th Foot shows that he decided to make financial provision for the widow and two children of one of his company sergeants who had died on the voyage from Scotland to New York in August 1779.[63] In each of these cases, we can view the officers' actions as having the likely result of increasing their hold over the rank and file; but we should also recognize that for the officers themselves the spur might well have been a sense that they had to demonstrate a commitment to their men if they were to expect their men to show a commitment to them.

British officers reasoned with their soldiers on many occasions. Orders appealed to the soldier's self-interest as often as they threatened dire retribution for disobedience. In March 1777, Howe informed the troops under his command that 'Several Lots of Ground being now inclos'd in Order to supply the Army . . . with Greens and Vegetables of all Kinds', he would therefore punish any soldiers 'guilty of breaking down any Fence or Inclosure'.[64] Soldiers often took down fences and other wooden structures to use for fuel; Howe was explaining that the removal of fences could have adverse effects on the soldiers' food supplies. Brigade orders for the British troops campaigning in Virginia in 1781 similarly treated soldiers as rational beings, capable of responding to appeals to their self-interest as well as to fear. On 1 June, the commander of the brigade ordered his men not to 'destroy the Bolting Cloths or any thing belonging to the Milns in the Country, as it is of great importance to the Army having them fit for use'. The next day's orders revealed that the appeal had not worked, but at the same time continued to rely on the soldier's sense of his interests to secure compliance. 'The reason the Troops can only be supplied with Indian meal instead of Flour is owing to some Soldiers having cut the Boulting Cloth at Prices Mill.' This explanation was followed by a threat of punishment for anyone 'detected in cutting or spoiling any thing belonging to a Mill'; but the incentive to good behaviour was increased by threatening that the offender's unit would 'receive Indian Meal or Flour with the Bean in it for the next Fortnight'.[65]

In this last example we see an appeal to self-interest supplemented by an appeal to unit solidarity – disobedience will disadvantage not just the individual involved but all of his comrades too. Officers often proceeded on the assumption that regimental pride could be used to secure good behaviour. An officer of the 47th Foot, when it was camped at Fort Edward, New York, during Burgoyne's descent from Quebec, told his troops that two 'hardened and atrocious wretches', who had robbed and threatened an inhabitant, were now in custody; 'a Circumstance which he doubts not, will give the highest satisfaction to all the men; who he is sensible, felt equally with himself, the insult that had been offered them and the Ignominy which was stamped upon the Corps'.[66] As the army marched across New Jersey in the summer of 1778, the commander of another unit attempted a similar appeal to group pride: as 'No Regiment having been formerly more Conspicuous for its Discipline than the Royal Fusiliers', the lieutenant colonel described himself as 'Mortified at Observing the great Irregularity and Excesses that have been Committed within these few days'.[67]

Officers also played on their men's sense of soldierly honour without referring to their regiment or corps. When Howe's troops were about to land on Staten Island in the summer of 1776, the general appealed to his soldiers' 'Superior Discipline' as he tried to persuade them not to ill-treat the local inhabitants.[68] The next year, troops of the 47th Foot were upbraided following a drunken brawl with German auxiliaries. Their officer conveyed the impression that the most shocking aspect of their indiscipline was that 'one of the greatest principals of military Order was so far forgot by some British Soldiers that a Guard was insulted'.[69] Cornwallis, for his part, spared no rhetorical effort to persuade his troops in North Carolina that without their help in detecting plunderers, 'the Blood of the Brave & Deserving Soldiers will be Shed in vain, & it will not be even in the power of Victory to give Success'.[70]

During the War of Independence, officers often appealed to their troops by referring to the need to win over the people or to protect loyal inhabitants who had already suffered at the hands of the rebels. The soldiers, in other words, were treated as though they understood that this was a struggle for American allegiance ('to gain the hearts & subdue the minds' of the people, as General Sir Henry Clinton put it) and not just a conventional conflict between two armies.[71] Before the main British army sailed from Halifax to New York to begin the 1776 campaign, Howe reminded his men that they were wrong if they imagined that 'the Crime of stealing is lessened' if the property they took belonged to 'persons ill affected to Government'. Rather than just require obedience, he explained why the troops should follow his order: pillaging not only eroded the army's discipline but also risked losing 'the affection of the people'.[72] When, later the same month, his soldiers arrived in New York harbour and were preparing to land, Howe also stressed the politics of the war, though this time he justified restraint on the grounds that the locals were friendly. 'As the Inhabitants of the Country are known to be well affected to Government & have suffer'd great depredations from the rebels', Howe 'recommends' that the troops offer 'protection [to] the Familys & properties of the people of the Country'.[73] Lieutenant Colonel Archibald Campbell issued similar orders to the soldiers under his command as they prepared to land in Georgia in late December 1778. He reminded the troops that the purpose of their expedition was 'the Relief and Protection of His Majesty's Loyal Inhabitants . . . who have long withstood the Savage Oppression of Congress'.[74]

Campbell, as we can see, assumed that his men were familiar with the political dimension of the war, that they were aware of the peculiar nature of the conflict. He was not alone. British officers – just like their American Continental Army counterparts – made direct appeals to the cause for which their troops were fighting. Perhaps we might interpret such appeals as attempts to inspire soldiers to extra effort, rather than persuade them to obey. But in practice the two are difficult – perhaps impossible – to disentangle. While we have little or no direct testimony to help us to understand officers' thinking, it seems reasonable to suppose that they believed that inspiration encouraged soldiers to follow orders that the uninspired might question or even refuse to accept. Inspiration, in other words, could be a form of persuasion, which officers used because they recognized that they could not be sure of the soldiers' obedience.

The soldier's patriotism was often invoked. Cornwallis flattered his troops by referring to his having 'seen so many proofs of their Zeal for the Service of their Country'.[75] A short while later, to deter soldiers from 'Stragling out of Camp in search of Whiskey', he appealed to them as individuals, claiming that each soldier possessed 'so much Honor & publick Spirit' that 'at a time when Britain has so many Enemies And his Country has so much Occasion for his Services', he would 'not run the hazard' of being captured by the enemy.[76] British officers also referred in more philosophical terms to the cause for which the army was fighting. Lieutenant Colonel Campbell, as part of his attempt to persuade his troops not to misbehave when they landed in Georgia, referred to his own pride at leading 'such gallant Troops, . . . employed on a service so essential to his Country, by which the Rights of Britons may be secured, legal Government established and the Insolence of usurped Authority annihilated'.[77]

Military Exceptionalisms

British officers and rank and file soldiers turn out, then, to have had much more in common with their American counterparts than many contemporary and historical accounts allow. But it was not just Americans who exaggerated – and, in many cases, still exaggerate – the distinctiveness of their military. Britons were (and are) no less inclined to identify their army as different from others. The point of comparison in the British case was Continental Europe and particularly the German states, where soldiers were thought to be poor benighted creatures, reduced to a robotic obedience by the most brutal discipline – an image remarkably similar to the one beloved by Americans describing the British Army.[78]

We have already seen that the British Army had much in common with other European armies. This was as true of the way soldiers conceived of their rights and officers exercised their authority as it was in other areas that we have compared. German troops had a strong sense of their customary entitlements and were likely to engage in forms of resistance if they felt those entitlements had been ignored or the military contract otherwise breached. Ansbach-Bayreuth auxiliary troops fighting alongside the British Army in North America displayed just such a keen sense of their entitlements. They mutinied over what they perceived as unfair treatment by their officers while the unit was in captivity in Maryland after the surrender of Lord Cornwallis's forces at Yorktown. While the background to the Ansbachers' resistance is unclear, the diary of one of the troops suggests that a dispute over pay was a factor. On this occasion, as all those involved were prisoners of war, we might reasonably conclude that the officers were in a less powerful position than normal, as their command over their men had already been undermined. Yet the same diarist recorded an Ansbach-Bayreuth soldier's speaking out about a grievance regarding his pay some years before.[79] A different source reveals that the Ansbach grenadiers collectively complained in 1777 when they were not paid what they felt was their fair share of 'the [prize] Money distributed amongst the Troops that were employed in the Jerseys'.[80]

German officers in North America, furthermore, like their counterparts in the British service, recognized that their authority could not be taken for granted – it was conditional, not absolute. The letters and journal of Major Carl von Baurmeister, the adjutant general of the Hessian forces, show the officers in his contingent had a keen awareness of their soldiers' sense of what was right and proper. In September 1776, Baurmeister reported back to the military authorities in Hessen-Kassel that when General Howe ordered German auxiliaries to help demolish the recently-captured Brooklyn lines on Long Island, General Leopold von Heister, the Hessian commander-in-chief, 'pointed out that the troops could not be expected to do this work, which would take four weeks, without remuneration'. Heister appreciated that his men's obedience could not be assumed; just as payment for extra work was a sensitive issue for British soldiers, so it was for the Hessian rank and file.[81]

The contrast, both between Americans and Britons and between Britons and Germans, was overdrawn in the eighteenth century and to a striking extent continues to be overdrawn now. To say this is not to attempt to deny that differences existed between armies, even in the way in which the military moral economy and contract were conceived and negotiated authority operated. But those differences were usually ones of degree, not of principle. Rather than think of contrasts and distinctiveness – of American or British military exceptionalism – we should recognize that common soldiers, European as well as American, conceived of a customary framework of rights and obligations and saw their service in contractual terms, while their officers (or at least the most effective and successful ones) recognized that their own power was negotiated rather than simply imposed.

Chapter 7

Women and the Army

The women of communities that experienced the military at close quarters, as we have seen, had special cause to be fearful of soldiers, who had a reputation as sexual predators. If this were true in Britain and Ireland, it was even more so abroad, where soldiers far from home had greater reason to feel that they had opportunities to behave badly without facing the consequences. The 50-year-old General John Mostyn, a living caricature of the unreflective officer, looked forward in 1759 to revisiting the German town where he was quartered in the previous war, primarily, it seems, because he wanted to relive his earlier sexual exploits.[1]

Women were most at risk, however, near the front line, where they might encounter military men flushed with victory. Soldiers in the process of occupying new territory tended to see sexual relations with local women as a reward for their military efforts and the dangers that they ran. When General William Howe's army landed on Staten Island in the summer of 1776, rape became a major cause of anxiety for local women. At least a few officers turned a blind eye to the offences committed by their men or showed no sympathy for the victims; Lord Rawdon, a captain in the 63rd Foot, merely commented that they were 'so little accustomed to these vigorous methods that they don't bear them with the proper resignation'.[2] Small wonder that when, a year later, British troops disembarked at Head of Elk, Maryland, they discovered, in the words of one of their officers, that the local women had 'fled to avoid barbarities, which they imagined must be the natural attendants of a British Army'.[3]

Yet women, as we have also seen, in less fraught contexts might welcome the opportunities that the presence of soldiers offered. For some women, newly-arrived military men increased the number of males available for matrimony and so increased their choice. For others, who were not looking for a marriage partner but engaged in selling goods, the purchases of officers and soldiers could generate useful profits and so lead to a positive view of the army, just as it did for men who were involved in trade with the military. In this chapter, however, the focus will not be on women in general, but on the women associated with the army, through service, marriage and patronage power.

The army, we might assume from all that has been said so far, was an exclusively male institution, its officers and common soldiers united by their masculinity, if not much else. The army embodied what eighteenth-century society regarded as distinctly male characteristics – its members were expected to show courage in the face of life-threatening danger, not to be squeamish about using violence, to possess physical strength and to bond in manly comradeship with their fellow soldiers. Women are conspicuous by their absence from this image of a profession or occupation not just dominated by men but where women were excluded. Yet women played more than a marginal role in how the army worked. A very few, as we will see, actually served (clandestinely) as soldiers. If in numerical terms they were insignificant, they played an important part symbolically, especially in wartime. Stories of women soldiers gained wide currency, not just for their novelty value, but because the inversion of roles their presence in red coats represented constituted an implied criticism of men for not offering their services at a time of need. This chapter will begin by considering these female soldiers and the way in which contemporaries used their image to inspire males to play their part by contributing to the war effort. It will then go on to examine the much more numerous group of women who were married to officers or common soldiers, but remained at home when their menfolk were on active service. Here the key theme is separation and how both husbands and wives sought to adapt to being apart for prolonged periods. We will see that correspondence with wives and sweethearts helped to sustain the morale of distant soldiers. The next section focuses on the women who accompanied the army – the wives and the assorted camp followers more loosely attached to the military. The presence of these women alongside their menfolk qualifies the exclusively masculine image of the army. When we look at what they did, it becomes apparent that their contribution to the functioning of the institution was far from negligible. The final part of the chapter examines the influence of upper-class women in the promotion process. Their patronage could be an invaluable aid to those seeking to enter as officers and rise within the service.

Female Soldiers

To modern eyes, there seems nothing outlandish about women serving in the army. Most militaries in our own age have women soldiers, often performing ancillary functions, but increasingly with some in front-line fighting roles. But the idea of women as directly engaged in war – women as fighters – is not just a feature of our own age; it has a long pedigree. Ancient Greek mythology identified the Amazons as a tribe of warrior women from Asia Minor.[4] In the eighteenth century, this tradition found expression in a military unit made up of the wives and daughters of Greek soldiers, which Prince Grigori Potemkin established in 1787 for Catherine the Great of Russia. While Potemkin's Amazons received military training and carried arms, their primary purpose seems to have been to impress the empress, who was at that time on a tour of the Crimea. These female warriors in fact never saw active service and their unit was disbanded as soon as Catherine's tour ended.[5] In eighteenth-century western Europe, however, even the idea of women in military service seems to have been widely regarded with a mixture of incredulity and downright hostility.[6] To most contemporaries – of both sexes – the mere thought of female warriors posed an unacceptable challenge to established gender norms. As a career in the army was open only to men, those few women who joined its ranks could therefore do so only secretly, by disguising their femininity and trying to pass as males.

Thomas Court, a mate on a British naval vessel during the Seven Years War, recorded in his diary on 20 April 1761 that while anchored in Yarmouth Roads, off the Isle of Wight, he 'discovered a marine of the name of William Pritchard who proved to be a Woman'. Court went on to explain that she was 'about 18 years old from Wales who had followed her lover'.[7] Court's discovery was clearly worthy of note in his diary and no doubt the talk of the ship's crew and probably those who came into contact with them on shore; but it does not seem to have entered the consciousness of the wider public. The same was not true of similar cases. Twenty-two months earlier, in June 1759, the *Scots Magazine* carried an item that began with what appears as a piece of rather unimportant news. Matthew Hudson, a young soldier in Colonel William Petitot's Regiment, had been admitted to the Edinburgh Infirmary with a sore throat. But, from that point, the report would surely have captured the attention of the reader. In the infirmary, those attending to Hudson discovered that 'he' was in fact 'she'. Hudson's real name was not Matthew, but Martha. She had been born in Northumberland, the report continued, and from an early age had liked dressing as a boy. She had served as a servant in Newcastle before enlisting in the army at Durham about two and a half years earlier. The report claimed that she had recently married a woman but managed to keep her true sex a secret from her military colleagues and officers. The author concluded that Hudson's story 'brings Hannah Snell to remembrance'.[8]

Hannah Snell was the most celebrated woman soldier of the age. Born in Worcester in 1723, she joined Guise's Regiment of Foot in 1745 after her desertion by her husband and the death of her infant daughter. She assumed the name of her brother-in-law, James Gray, and served in Cumberland's army against the Jacobite rebels in Scotland. Snell subsequently joined the Marines and travelled to India. On her return in 1750, she published an account of her military life under the title *The Female Soldier*. She received a pension from the Royal Hospital, Chelsea (presumably the first woman to do so) and in retirement ran a tavern in Wapping called, appropriately, 'The Female Warrior'. Snell's fame derived from the unusualness of a woman entering the army and serving in it, seemingly undetected, for several years. That she performed on stage after her military career was over, wearing army uniform, tells us that she attracted attention for her apparent freakishness.

The same was true of Lady Louisa Lennox. She was not a woman soldier, strictly defined, but she accompanied her husband, Lord George Lennox, colonel of the 25th Foot, when his regiment was sent to form part of the British garrison on Minorca. There Lady Louisa was captured on canvas, apparently in the early 1770s, by Giuseppe Chiesa, an Italian painter who spent most of his life on the island. The striking feature of the picture is that Lady Louisa is wearing clothing closely modelled on the uniform of her husband's regiment, the men of which, together with Lord George, surround her at a respectful distance, scattered in small groups, as if to symbolize her destabilising effect on military discipline.[9] When she returned to England, with her husband and his troops, Lady Louisa continued to wear her military attire. By doing so, she caused quite a stir. At Romsey, in Hampshire, the 25th's new posting, a visitor described the uniformed Lady Louisa as 'the principal feature of the Show, at the Evening Parades'.[10]

The image of the female warrior, however, did more than amuse and titillate; it also provided moral critics with ammunition to use against men who were reluctant to don a red coat. Perhaps it seemed particularly necessary to use that ammunition at a time of national anxiety. We can certainly see it surfacing during the crisis years of the American war, in 1778–9, when invasion by the Bourbon powers seemed a real possibility. A cartoon published at that time, 'An Officer of the Light Infantry driven by his Lady to Cox-Heath' depicts a woman in military clothing standing up, reins and whip in hand; her husband sits slumbering by her side.[11] No doubt meant to bring a smile to the face of its viewers, the cartoon also sought to convey a serious moral message: gender roles had been reversed, to the shame of inactive men. In broader terms, one historian has argued, such female encroachments into male spheres attracted criticism because they appeared as an 'unnatural' symptom of the all the ills that had befallen Britain in a long, demanding and deeply unsettling war, in which the main enemy was part of the extended national community.[12]

The Women Left Behind

Even though the figures are impossible to calculate, we can be confident that more women were married to soldiers than served as soldiers themselves. We can surmise that the majority of young recruits would have been single and we know that marriage received little encouragement from some regimental commanders, perhaps because they feared that it would reduce the willingness of their men to put their lives in danger.[13] Even so, a variety of sources suggest that a far from negligible number of officers and members of the rank and file were either already married when they joined the army or married while in military service. Of these military wives, a good number were left behind when their husbands went on active service. As Penuel Grant wrote to a kinsmen, who had enjoyed success in finding enlistees in Scotland in February 1757, 'I am afraid you would have not recruited so many without takeing some men from their poor wives and children'.[14]

Even for the female relatives of unmarried soldiers, parting could be painful. John Seaford, enlisting men for the Duke of Bedford's Regiment of Foot in 1745, reported that 'several of their Mothers & Sisters are overwhelmed in Tears and use all y^r endeavours thay can to diswade y^m from going'.[15] Perhaps in part these women were moved by the fear that the loss of a breadwinner would undermine family finances. We know that for the wives of members of the rank and file, cut off from their husbands and their meagre income, separation often led to dire financial hardship, even destitution. Lord Gower, who raised a regiment to help put down the Jacobite rebellion in 1745, committed 'all my pay & perquisites' to a subscription proposed 'for subsisting our Soldier's wives during the absence of their husbands'. Even so, his men mutinied at Chester, partly because they believed that 'their familys Starve in their absence'.[16]

Some insights into the circumstances of other women left behind can be gleaned from a variety of sources.[17] According to a report in a Dublin newspaper in June 1746, the city's Hospital for Poor Lying in Women, which was supported by charitable donations, included amongst its inmates several women who were the wives of soldiers, 'mostly abroad in his Majesty's Service'.[18] Local government records tell us rather more. In England, administration of the Poor Law, which provided a rudimentary safety net, centred on the parish, which was obliged to take responsibility for its own. Outsiders who could not support themselves would, after examination by a local magistrate, be sent back to their original parish of settlement. Settlement examinations, many of which survive today in preserved parish records, reveal numerous cases of struggling soldiers' wives whose husbands were on active service. Some took to the streets, from where they beseeched passers-by for money. At the beginning of May 1742, for example, Ann Frew was apprehended 'Wandering and begging' in St Margaret's parish, Westminster. She had with her three children. She was destitute, it seems, because her husband David was serving in Howard's Regiment (the Old Buffs) in Flanders.[19] About a year later, the 21-year-old Ann Wright, the wife of William Wright, a soldier in Skelton's Regiment, also serving on the Continent, was apprehended 'wandering and begging' at Boroughbridge, in Yorkshire.[20] She was returned to her native East Grinstead, in Sussex, where her parish was expected to support her through the poor rates, a local tax to which property owners were required to contribute. Every eighteenth-century war produced the same tragic stories.

For women such as Ann Frew and Ann Wright, financial desperation was the most obvious result of the absence of their soldier husbands. But for many wives of military men, separation's most painful aspect was emotional.[21] John Carnac's mother Andrienne told him a touching story of two sergeants' wives who had approached her in Dublin in 1760. The sergeants were both in Carnac's old regiment, the 39th Foot, which had left Ireland in 1754 and was then serving in India. Though Carnac himself was no longer with the 39th Foot (he had transferred to the East India Company's service in 1758), Mrs Carnac hoped that he might be able to help, given his connections with the regiment. She wrote that the two women had 'never heard from them [their husbands] since the Regiment came away, if you can give them any tiding of them, it will be a great charity for they seemed to be in great grief'.[22]

As always, the evidence is most plentiful for those at the top end of the social scale, which means, in this case, the officers' wives. Lieutenant Colonel Charles Russell's wife Mary worried greatly while he was away campaigning in Germany in 1743; 'how much I have been allarmed you can too well guess', she wrote to him after having received news of the Battle of Dettingen. 'I pray almighty God to have you in his Protection.'[23] For Martha Forde, writing in 1757, contemplating her husband Major Francis Forde of the 39th Foot remaining longer in India was too much to endure. She acknowledged that he might make more money by 'Staying abroad . . . but, I wou'd not undergoe, if had the Power to Prevent it, Such another Cruel Sepparation, for half India'.[24] In the late spring of 1758, the Duchess of Marlborough feared for her husband, who was in command of the expeditionary force assembled to attack the French coast. As the duke prepared to embark, she revealed her great worries for his safety: 'if you love me as you say, you will take care of your Dr Self when you reflect how absolutely necessary you are to my happiness. I confess I am very miserable about you.'[25] She seems to have continued to be prey to dark thoughts when, later that year, her husband led the British forces campaigning in Germany. This time we have the duke's perspective on the problems of separation. 'I must once again beg of you not to torment yourself unnecessarily', he wrote in September, 'tho' by your letters I have little hopes of your complying with this request.' Marlborough implored her to be more positive: 'the Campaign is very near over, & most probably there will be a peace in the winter, why will you always look on the black side[?]' He concluded, in a last (but not wholly convincing) attempt to lift her spirits, 'if I was to do so too I should not survive the reading of your letter, but I must & will think of the great probabillity, almost certainty, of my seeing you soon in peace & quiet'.[26]

Marlborough, it hardly needs to be said, was not the only absent military husband worried about his wife's state of mind. James Agnew wrote to his wife Elizabeth in May 1775 while he was at Cork, waiting to sail across the

Atlantic with his regiment to North America, begging her to be as positive
as she could be in the circumstances. 'I intreat my Love to be reasonable', he
began, 'and to meet this trial as will best lessen the ill of it, give yourself not
up to Grief or despair.' Faith, he argued, was a necessary preservative at such
times; without it, disaster could ensue: 'trust in Gods providence that you
will yet be happy, for without that hope your health will be impaired so soon
that the little Babes will loose their only support and make me the greatest
wretch on Earth.'[27] Family members provide us with further evidence of the
emotional problems created for military wives by their husbands' service
away from home. During the same war, Lady Lousia Conolly wrote that
General William Howe's wife (her sister-in-law), who did not accompany her
husband on his American command, was 'in such a miserable state of anxiety that I tremble for her continually'.[28] William Congreve of Shrewsbury,
the uncle of an artillery officer serving in America (also called William
Congreve), similarly made plain his concerns. He was anxious, he told his
nephew, 'for the bad health of y[r] Wife; and that she is affected on y[r] leaving
her; a Soldiers Wife like her Husband should aim at a necessary fortitude on
Such occasions'.[29]

For the men serving far from their wives, separation was perhaps not
always so dreadful. In this sense, Mary Russell perhaps had a point when
she differentiated between female and male reactions to being apart, though
her emphasis on 'the nature of Men & Women' may have been misplaced;[30]
a more obvious distinction was between the one who stayed at home and
the one who went away. Those who stayed behind remained in familiar sur-
roundings and had time to dwell on their absent partner, whose departure
disrupted domestic routine. Those who left, by contrast, found themselves
having to adapt to a new setting, which inevitably absorbed much of their
attention. Men had duties to perform and the challenges of a military life
acted as a distraction from feelings of homesickness. They also had something approaching a replacement family in the form of their comrades – for
the common soldiers, the other men in their platoon, company or troop, with
whom they ate and slept while on campaign or in quarters; for the officers,
their regimental colleagues and for staff officers, the general's other aides or,
as the staff of a senior officer was termed at the time, his 'family'. In a few
cases, the closeness of these bonds may have encouraged latent homosexual

feelings, though the evidence to uncover this is unsurprisingly difficult to find in an era when male same-sex liaisons were illegal and subject to capital punishment.[31] Rumours abounded about the married Lord George Sackville, the disgraced commander of the British cavalry at Minden, but these may well have been associated with the accusations of cowardice that were levelled against him.[32] Nor should we forget that some men found comfort with other women while away from their wives. General Howe could not shake off accusations that he had taken a mistress in America, Mrs Elizabeth Loring, who was responsible, in some minds, for his apparent reluctance to leave Philadelphia and campaign vigorously against Washington's forces. Francis Hopkinson, an American politician and ballad writer, memorably depicted Howe 'snug as a flea . . . In bed with Mrs Loring'.[33] Hopkinson was no friend of the British Army, but if the rumours against Howe were true, he was assuredly not the only soldier to find a local substitute for his wife. Yet, having said all this, separation must have been a painful affliction to bear for loving spouses, men as well as women.

Some, at least, found solace through writing and receiving letters, which helped to give wives a sense of purpose and helped to sustain distant husbands by reminding them of their homes and families. Countless officers' letters home enquired after relatives and friends, as if their authors believed that such news would bridge the gap between them and their loved ones. Officers also used correspondence with their wives to share feelings or express concerns which they might have been reluctant to reveal to their comrades in arms. Alexander MacDonald, a captain in the 22nd Foot serving in America, wrote regular and detailed letters to his wife in Scotland. He told her of his frustrations over promotion (resolved when he became a major in the 71st Highlanders). He gave her chapter and verse about his pay arrears and financial circumstances and about the attitudes of his junior colleagues; he even commented on politics and the course of military operations ('This country is now intirely conquered', he wrote, over-optimistically, after the fall of Charleston, South Carolina, in 1780).[34] It seems reasonable to suppose that MacDonald's letters to his wife acted as a safety valve, enabling him to unburden himself of some of his worries and so helped MacDonald – and perhaps his wife, who received these privileged insights into his life away from her – to endure their prolonged separation.

Women of the Regiment

Military wives (and women attached to soldiers more informally but still designated as wives in official accounts) did not always stay at home. A surprisingly large number accompanied their partners on campaign or garrison duties. If we start with the officers, we can see that some married or established equivalent relationships while abroad on campaign or in garrison. That seems to have been the case with Captain John Ridley of the 28th Regiment, who while serving in North America appears to have formed a long-running attachment to Elizabeth Fulton, who perhaps came from Halifax, Nova Scotia. Ridley and Fulton lived with each other for nine years until his death at the end of 1776; they had two children together.[35] Archibald Cuninghame of the 51st Foot, an officer based on Minorca just before it was besieged by the French and Spanish in the summer of 1781, told his sister that one of the captains in his regiment ('an exceedingly genteel kind of Man') was 'join'd to a Minorkeen Ladie about a fortnight ago'.[36]

A few officers' wives were even by their husband's side on the front line. Perhaps the most celebrated in the War of American Independence was Lady Harriet Acland, who kept a journal of her experiences while with her husband, Major John Dyke Acland, on campaign in Canada and upper New York in 1777. 'She loved him dearly', wrote the wife of a German senior officer.[37] Sir Francis Carr Clerke, an officer in the 3rd Foot Guards on the same campaign, noted with a bravado perhaps meant to reassure his friends at home (and perhaps himself) that 'One proof of the spirit of our army [is that] the Ladies do not mean to quit us'. He went on to extol the virtues of camp life with 'good Claret, good Musick and the Enemy near. I may venture to say all this, for a little fusillade during dinner does not discompose the Nerves of even our Ladies.'[38]

We can be confident, however, that the number of officers' wives accompanying their husbands on overseas postings was eclipsed by the number of women attached to the rank and file. When Matross James Wood embarked from Cork for Flanders in January 1747, he noted that 'In the company of artillery we lessened Ireland of the burden of 28 ladies'.[39] Fraser's Highlanders, when ready to sail from Halifax, Nova Scotia, in October 1757, had more than a hundred women on board their transport vessels.[40] It seems likely that not all of these women had come over with the regiment from Scotland. Some, in all probability, had met their military partners in North

America. Once they had arrived in distant garrisons or military theatres, soldiers unsurprisingly forged local attachments. A careful study of the marriage records in Boston, Massachusetts, reveals that some forty local women married British soldiers between the arrival of the army in 1768 and 1772. Given the reputed hostility of the town's population to its military garrison, this figure is striking. Even more so is the fact that half of the marriages took place after the notorious Boston Massacre in March 1770, which is usually assumed to have led to a marked deterioration in relations between soldiers and townspeople.[41] According to another modern account, some 500 local women followed the British Army back to New York when it evacuated Philadelphia in the summer of 1778.[42]

Whether they had come from Britain and Ireland or joined the army abroad, a significant number of women accompanied the common soldiers. A few examples from the American war give a sense of scale. A return of the troops victualled at New York on 17 May 1777 records the presence of 2,776 women, each of whom received a half ration, together with 1,904 children, on a quarter ration. Some of these women and children were attached to German auxiliary units or American loyalist provincial corps but the British regiments had their share; 70 women and 44 children are listed as with the 28th Foot's 327 soldiers and 119 woman and 83 children with the 1,274 men of the three battalions of the 71st Highlanders. At Philadelphia on 13 December, another return shows a total of 1,648 women and 539 children in receipt of rations, with the 17th, 23rd, 28th and 63rd Regiments each with more than 40 women on the ration list.[43] The commissary similarly provided half rations to around forty women attached to the 44th Foot between the end of May and early July 1778. The number victualled then dropped suddenly to fewer than ten until the end of August, but that was simply because the women of the regiment during July and August were returning to New York by ship, while their men marched through New Jersey.[44] At New York 'and the Out Posts' in August 1781, more than 2,173 women received victuals from the commissary, of whom at least 1,698 were attached to the British troops.[45]

The expense of maintaining such numbers of women and children inevitably concerned government, generals and commissaries. Shortly after the 31st Regiment embarked for Canada at the beginning of March 1776, Lord Barrington, the Secretary at War, complained to the colonel that 'One hundred & five Women have been allowed to embark, tho' only Sixty are permitted by His Majestys Order. There are also 47 Children.' Barrington went on to explain that 'The great number of Soldiers Wives & Children already in America, are very inconvenient to the Regiments there and more than the Number permitted by the Regulation, must be a burthen on every Corps that goes thither.'[46] If Barrington was less than explicit about the nature of the burden, others left no room for doubt. Daniel Weir, one of the commissaries in North America, wrote home to the Treasury from New York on 8 June 1777:

> From the conversation I have had with the General [Sir William Howe], respecting the great number of Women who follow the Army and are of course Victualled out of the Public Magazine, I find his Excellency has restrained them to six Women to each Company the remainder will be left here and Victualled with such Provisions as can be best spared and which will in some degree, reduce the Expense. [47]

The same concerns influenced official attitudes to women and children attached to the army in earlier wars. When a British expeditionary force sailed for the Caribbean in 1740, to attack the Spanish on Cuba, the Victualling Board, responsible for supplying the troops, refused to provide rations for more than three women per company of soldiers. The board's determination to save money meant that of twenty-one women accompanying three companies of Graham's Regiment on board the *Peter* and *Mary* transports, twelve received no official supply of provisions.[48]

Criticism of the presence of soldiers' wives and other womenfolk in distant postings was not just based on anxieties about escalating costs. Perhaps because their own food supply was so precarious, as many of them did not receive official rations, women attached to the army acquired a reputation for theft. In the War of American Independence, John Miller, an inhabitant of Germantown, near Philadelphia, noted in the autumn of 1777 that 'several of the Women belonging to the British Soldiery were catched last Night plundering Gardens'.[49] British sources during the same war tell a similar story. Captain Patrick Ferguson, in a report on the ill-treatment of civilians, probably written for the commander-in-chief in North America in 1779, argued that women and other camp followers 'distress and maltreat the inhabitants infinitely more than the whole army'.[50] In brigade orders for the Guards contingent serving in North Carolina in March 1781, General Charles O'Hara issued a more targeted rebuke, noting that women were 'Suppos'd to be the Source of the most infamous plunder[g]'.[51]

General courts martial records allow us some interesting insights into the world of soldiers' wives. The British garrison in Boston at the start of the American war provides a few choice examples. Women might appear before courts as witnesses, as with Mary Andrews and Mary Grant, each described as 'of the 4th or King's Own Regiment'. These two soldiers' wives testified in July 1775 that they had been sold shirts by Thomas Bell of the Marines. The women told the court that they had only bought the shirts because Bell had assured them that they were his own. Bell, it transpired, had stolen them from other soldiers in camp to make some money.[52] That September, Winifred McCowan, referred to in the court minutes as 'a Retainer to the Camp', appeared accused of stealing the town bull and killing it. She was found guilty and sentenced to be publicly flogged and then imprisoned for three months.[53] Three months later, in December 1775, a court martial tried three soldiers for breaking into a store in the town and taking money, rolls of fabric, thread, stockings, combs, shoes, tea and sugar. Two of the soldiers, who the court records say were married, kept part of the goods to give to their wives. The rest of their loot the two men conveyed to Thomas McMahon of the 43rd Foot, who, with his wife Isobella, arranged for them to be sold to another local trader, Catherine Thompson. The McMahons, it seems, had a well-established reputation in the garrison as handlers of stolen property, having the contacts to ensure that it could be disposed of speedily and profitably. The fact that the stolen items found their way to a woman trader perhaps indicates that Mrs McMahon was more an equal than a junior partner in this enterprise.[54]

These various accounts convey a far-from-flattering impression of the women who were associated with the army's common soldiers. Other sources, however, paint a more positive picture. Sir Francis Carr Clerke regaled his friend Lord Polwarth with the story of Mrs Middleton, the wife of a soldier in the 47th Foot, who captured six rebel troops single-handedly in Canada in 1776. According to Carr Clerke's account, she found the rebels in a house and berated them for 'fighting ag[st] your King and Countrymen' and demanded that they surrender their arms and become her prisoners. Rather fortunately, it seems, some British sailors happened to be at the nearby riverside and she called out for their help in securing the no-doubt surprised and bewildered rebel soldiers. To reassure his friend, Carr Clerke explained that Mrs Middleton was not the harridan that he might envisage, but 'a very modest, decent well looking Woman'.[55] Sergeant Roger Lamb of the 9th Foot later penned a moving passage in his published journal of the American war on the wife of a soldier 'who kept close to her husband's side' during fighting at Fort Ann, in upper New York, in 1777 and lost her life as a consequence.[56] Both of these accounts, for various reasons, may have exaggerated – Carr Clerke's because he was seeking to amuse his friend with a counter-intuitive story of female valour and Lamb's because he wanted to impress his readers (and boost his book sales) with sentimental scenes of battlefield bravery. Even so, we have no reason to doubt that they were based on the truth.

Not many women of the army distinguished themselves in this way, but we know that they carried out more mundanely useful tasks that helped to sustain the troops. Scraps of evidence point to their role as nurses and washers of clothing and as tailors, who helped repair uniforms. Captain Ridley's accounts, settled after his death in North America in December 1776, refer to a 'washing bill' owed to Margaret Green. Green is too common a name to be certain, but it seems very likely that she was a soldier's wife.[57] Some evidence suggests that the carrying out of these duties was not optional; the military authorities seem to have expected this work from soldiers' wives as a payback for their receiving official rations.[58] We also know that these women cooked for the soldiers, acted as servants to officers and even tended to sheep and cattle assembled to feed the army.[59]

Women and the Advancement of Men's Careers

Upper-class women played a part in the entry and progress of officers in the army. Modern accounts of the army rarely recognize that part, as the patronage power that eased the advancement of military careers is usually assumed to have been wielded by men. In general terms, that assumption accords with reality. The letters received by the Secretary at War or the Lord Lieutenant of Ireland, lobbying on behalf of a relative, friend or dependent for a first commission or promotion up the officer ranks, were nearly all written by men, in their capacity as fathers, brothers, uncles, guardians or patrons.

But in a few cases – how many is impossible to say – elite females exerted influence and sometimes their intervention proved important in securing the objective desired.

Influence might be direct or indirect. A good example of the latter can be seen in a letter written by Clementina Lockhart, the daughter of Scottish laird George Lockhart of Carnwarth. In the early stages of the Seven Years War (probably in January of 1757), she wrote to her friend Margaret Mercer, by marriage part of the ancient Mercer family of Aldie, to ask her help in securing recruits for a 'our friend Jock', who had the promise of a company in his uncle's battalion, if he could find the 100 men required for the commission, 'as fast as possible'. Lockhart asked for her friend's assistance in enlisting the men, 'either in picking up people round about you or by applying to any of your acquaintances'. She went on to stress the urgency of the matter: 'pray loose no time, the demand is so great that they list any Body & as I know you will if you can befriend Jock so I am certain he will be happy in having you Interested in his behalf.' Mercer's 'interest' – in other words, her influence – was here seen as a valuable asset, which Lockhart hoped would facilitate the recruiting of the 100 men that 'Jock' needed to qualify for a captaincy.[60]

Whether Margaret Mercer's 'interest' proved crucial in this case is unclear. The identity of 'Jock' remains a mystery, so we cannot tell whether or not he secured his company. Nor do we know whether her influence helped if he were successful. We do know, however, that some upper-class female attempts to smooth the way for male relatives failed to produce the intended outcome. Lord Barrington, the Secretary at War, wrote politely but firmly to the Dowager Lady Wallingford, the widow of William, Viscount Wallingford, when she tried to lobby for her nephew's promotion to the rank of major. As Barrington explained in January 1760, 'it is right I should acquaint your Ladyship that Lord Wallingford [her nephew] has not been long enough a Captain to ask for a Majority'. Undeterred, Lady Wallingford approached the Lord Lieutenant of Ireland, the Duke of Bedford, whose recommendation was vital in appointments in regiments under his political jurisdiction. Bedford replied very much along the same lines as Barrington, though with perhaps even greater politeness: 'I had it not in my power to obey your Ladyship's commands in recommending Lord Wallingford to the Majority in Major General Strode's Regiment'. He explained that 'as Lord

Wallingford had two Captains senior to him in the Regiment, I could not without doing great injustice to them, put him over their heads.'[61]

It might be tempting to assume that neither Barrington nor Bedford felt inclined to comply with the wishes of an overly solicitous – one might say pushy – dowager whose nephew (then in his early thirties) was old enough to fend for himself. But that would almost certainly be the wrong construction to put on this episode. Lady Wallingford failed to secure her nephew's promotion because she was trying to circumvent a system designed to ensure that the opportunity to purchase a promotion was offered in the first instance to the next officer by seniority. In this case, as Bedford explained, Lord Wallingford was the third in the queue; two other captains in the regiment had received their commissions earlier than him and therefore were entitled to be given the option of purchasing before he could even be considered. Lady Wallingford's failure, in other words, almost certainly owed little or nothing to her being a woman; a man attempting to jump the queue would, in most cases, have received a similar response.

By no means all female applications failed, even when they came from dowagers. In 1779, during the American war, Lady Glasgow, widow of John Boyle, the third Earl of Glasgow, used her influence to secure an ensigncy in a newly-raised Highland regiment for a young kinsman, William Boyle. The regiment's colonel, Lord John Murray, appears to have been persuaded to offer the commission to the young man 'in consequence of Lady Glasgow's applications'.[62] Perhaps one of the most spectacular success stories for a female patron occurred 20 years earlier, in 1759, when the eccentric Catherine Gordon, the Dowager Duchess of Gordon, lobbied on behalf of her husband, the American-born Staats Long Morris. Morris had married the duchess, who was 10 years his senior, in 1756, while a mere captain in a regiment of foot. In 1759, in order to advance his military career, she proposed to raise a new regiment in the Highlands, under Morris's command.

Her offer was accepted and Morris became the lieutenant colonel commandant of the newly-completed 89th Foot in October of that year. Morris had control of the distribution of commissions, which, unusually, came with the promise of half-pay if the regiment were to be disbanded at the end of the war. The duchess's local reputation, according to a contemporary account, helped to fill the ranks with remarkable speed. All did not go entirely to the duchess's liking, however: the regiment, much to her horror, received orders to sail to India. She probably feared for her tenants and other local connections, who ran a greater risk of an early grave in India than almost anywhere else the regiment might have been sent. She may well have feared for her own local influence, too; if the regiment lost large numbers of men, her role in recruiting them might be turned against her. But her assistance in 1759 gave her husband's career a boost at a vital moment (he leapt from captain to lieutenant colonel in one step) and paved the way for his ascending the ladder of more senior promotion thereafter. Morris accompanied the troops to India and received local rank as a brigadier in 1763. He went on to half pay in 1765, but rose steadily up the senior ranks, acquiring a colonelcy in 1772, becoming a major general in 1777, a lieutenant general in 1782 and a full general in 1796. He ended his life as governor of Quebec.[63]

Chapter 8

Leaving the Service

For common soldiers, three ways existed to depart from the army – death, desertion and discharge. Soldiers had little or no control over whether they lived or died; desertion involved at least an element of choice (stay or go); discharge usually involved no choice at all – once the army no longer needed the services of members of the rank and file, it released them back into civilian life, in a process analogous to modern-day redundancy. Death we have touched upon already, though we need to say more about it here; desertion and discharge, mentioned in passing before, merit fuller treatment, as they were important means by which members of the rank and file left the service and the circumstances that led to them require explanation. Just as death caused acute problems for the army at particular times (after a major and bloody battle) and still more so in particular settings (the disease-ridden tropics), desertion had its own peaks and troughs, also associated with time and place. Discharge, though far from unusual in wartime, tended to be concentrated at the end of conflicts, when the army slimmed down to a peacetime strength.

Death, of course, was the great leveller; it affected all ranks, both officers and men. But for officers there were more ways of leaving the army than existed for the ordinary soldiers. Some officers had no choice about leaving. A few – very few – experienced the humiliation of cashiering – removal with dishonour for a serious breach of discipline; rather more who had fallen foul of the military authorities probably slipped away without such disgrace, by jumping before they were pushed. A much more significant number had to depart because their newly-raised regiment was 'broke' or disbanded at the end of a war or their old regiment reduced its establishment strength, requiring fewer officers. For these reluctant departees, their military future was usually on the half-pay list, a kind of paid reserve, where they waited for the opportunity to renew active service when the army expanded again at the beginning of a new conflict. Other officers left voluntarily, by resignation, usually for personal reasons, but on occasion because they could not face overseas service or disagreed with the political reasons that lay behind a war. Many of them had a commission to sell, which could help fund their new life.

This chapter will examine the different means by which members of the army's rank and file and their officers left the service and the circumstances that led to their departure. It will also seek to explore what happened to both officers and men when they were no longer in the army. The chapter begins by looking at the experience of the ordinary soldiers and their non-commissioned officers, then goes on to consider the officers. The final section offers brief remarks on life after military service.

Rank and File

On a spring day in 1782, Dr William White, a York physician, noted in his diary that he had just seen 'ye remains of ye 90th reg^t of Foot (Col^l Tottenham's) being in all about 100 men, ye rest being destroyed at St Lucia [from] hence they lately arrived'.[1] St Lucia, as other accounts tell us, was one of the sickliest islands in the West Indies (it 'has almost destroyed the few troops that came from America and the recruits of new Corps [such as the 90th] are fast following them').[2] The sight of severely depleted regiments returning as shells from overseas service would have been a familiar one in many parts of Britain at that time and in the closing stages of every war of the period. But awareness of the casualties of conflict would not have been confined to the end of wars. In the summer of 1761, the Rev. James Newton, an Oxfordshire clergyman, recorded in his diary meeting 'a Lad whose Uncle went into Germany with eight Hundred men about a Year past & they are now reduc'd to about 135'. Newton described this news as 'A Melancholy Consideration', adding 'what makes it more dreadfull is that only about 10 of them were kill'd, but the rest perish'd through the Hardships of the Campaign'.[3]

Newton's comments accord with what we have already seen of mortality amongst soldiers – death in action was rarer than death by disease and other forms of ill-health. What neither White nor Newton mentioned was that the army also lost the services of a significant number of men by other means. A relatively small number died as a result of punishments inflicted on them for breaches of discipline; general courts martial could pass capital sentences for crimes they deemed heinous and they and lesser brigade, regimental or garrison courts martial imposed corporal penalties that could result in death. An American observer of the punishments inflicted on regular troops on

24 October 1755 noted that one of the men was flogged so severely the day before 'that he Died to day'.[4] Soldiers convicted of capital offences sometimes received a pardon, if their character or the circumstances of their crimes, seemed to justify mercy. But some men undoubtedly faced execution and the number, however small, represented loss of manpower to a regiment.

In terms of the number of men unavailable to their units, desertion was much more important. The extent of desertion depended, of course, on the nature of the service on which a particular regiment was employed; weekly returns of the Royal Fusiliers, based in Gibraltar during the Seven Years War, suggest that it lost a mere ten men to desertion in the months March to December 1756, four of whom returned to the regiment in the same period.[5] But Gibraltar was an encircled outpost, surrounded by people who spoke a different language from the garrison; desertion, in short, would have been very difficult. Elsewhere, where the opportunities to slip away were greater, the rate of desertion was much higher. In Ireland, as a number of contemporaries noted, the Catholic population often aided and abetted the process by offering shelter to runaway soldiers.[6] According to one estimate, the British Army in Ireland lost about a sixth of the men it raised to desertion.[7]

Shortly after enlistment appears to have been a peak time for desertion, when the reality of what he had agreed to do dawned on the new recruit. Lieutenant Nicholas Delacherois of the 9th Foot, who tried to enlist men in the south-western counties of England between May and August 1770, secured a mere nine recruits, four of whom deserted very quickly.[8] Delacherois's experience, as we have seen, was far from unusual.[9] For a few new soldiers, in the view of their officers, desertion was a business. They took the enlistment money, departed and then joined another regiment, pocketing the enlistment money before they left that too. James Wolfe complained of such a man who joined his unit: 'his Trade is to take money from recruiting Officers'.[10] But most of these early departures, we can be confident, had no so such mercenary motives; the soldiers just realized that they had made a dreadful mistake and could think of no other way to rectify it than by running. In the case of impressed men, obliged to serve under the provisions of the various wartime recruiting acts, the absence of choice made departure at the first opportunity still more likely. Adam Williamson, the deputy lieutenant of the Tower of London, recorded the escape in April 1744 of nine impressed men 'at once

[who] slipt downe the wall by a rope and the counter Scarp wall being broke, they got up and ran for it'.[11]

For established soldiers, desertion could be a way out of all sorts of scrapes. Quite a few men brought before general courts martial for desertion had fled from their regiments after having stolen goods from colleagues, their officers or the local inhabitants. James Kairns, a private in the 22nd Foot, faced trial in April 1778 at Newport, Rhode Island, for having left his post as a sentry, broken into a shop and then deserted. The court judged that there was 'not sufficient proof' that Kairns had entered the store, but found him guilty of leaving his post and deserting. If he did steal goods from the shop opportunistically, it seems reasonable to suppose that, having succumbed to the temptation to break in, he panicked and decided to desert rather than stay and face the consequences.[12] The following year, another soldier in the 22nd Foot, Bartholomew Gilmore, appeared before a general court martial charged with stealing from another private in the regiment and then deserting. In this case, the officers of the court had no doubt that the defendant was guilty on all counts. It seems reasonable to conjecture that, having robbed his colleague, Gilmore had no wish to stay in the regiment and have his crime discovered. He took what seemed at the time to be the easiest way out, though in this instance it proved to be a grave miscalculation; the court sentenced him to death.[13]

The rhythms of military service influenced rates of desertion. We have already seen that a cut in rations or a failure to provide expected fresh supplements could lead to desertion (as well as theft or even mutiny).[14] But other military circumstances could influence desertion rates, too. If a regiment was about to move, desertion usually became more of a problem. Local attachments probably account for the reluctance of some soldiers to leave an established posting; we saw earlier that Thomas Sullivan's desertion from the 49th Foot in 1778 owed something to his having married in Philadelphia and an understandable desire not to leave his new wife behind him when the army evacuated the city and marched back to New York.[15] Departure might also raise anxieties in the mind of the soldier about the dangers his new station might bring; when a regiment was about to embark for overseas service, desertion seems to have increased. To avoid an exodus of unsettled and fearful soldiers, the military authorities tried to minimize the notice given to regiments that were about to embark, but even in the short space of time allowed for the 35th Foot to prepare to depart from Cork for North America in the spring of 1775, at least seventeen men deserted.[16] A year later, when it was the turn of the 53rd Foot to go to North America, eighteen men deserted in the month from the regiment's receiving orders to prepare for embarkation and it actually sailing from Cork.[17]

Opportunity needs to be taken into account, as well. As we have seen in the case of Gibraltar, an enclosed outpost, surrounded by an unfamiliar population which spoke a different language, was far from conducive to desertion. On the other hand, a campaign in open country, where the population spoke the same language as the soldiers, offered optimum opportunities. The troops in North America, during the War of Independence, were in just this situation. When they were on detached parties, foraging or on reconnaissance duties, soldiers could slip away relatively easily and be absorbed into local society. Officers usually noted that soldiers who strayed from camp ran the risk of being picked off or captured by the enemy; but sometimes they also recognized that a soldier out of sight of his officers was in a good position to desert.[18] The remote parts of the British Isles, where government struggled to extend its influence, offered good prospects for deserters, too. We have seen that the Catholic population of Ireland helped men who had departed from the army without permission; according to one commentator, the problem was exacerbated by 'the facility of Concealment in the Mountainous Parts of this Country'.[19] In the Highlands of Scotland, local support and elevated topography also favoured desertion. According to one account, penned in 1756, when Lord Home's regiment came into the rugged country near Fort William, 'great numbers of Highlanders enlisted in it, Who upon the Regiments being ordered to England, mostly deserted'. The writer claimed that the deserters still 'infested this Neighbourhood'; the ease with which they could conceal themselves in the surrounding mountains no doubt explains their continued presence.[20]

Other soldiers left the army by more legitimate means. Discharge, a capacious category, accounted for most departures. Members of the rank and file might secure a discharge by negotiating their way out of the service. Well-connected newly-recruited men, rather than desert, could get their family or benefactor to lobby for their discharge. In November 1748, the regimental agent of the 39th Foot requested the discharge of a man recently recruited in Hereford, whose father was a tenant of his and was willing to 'pay any

Listing Charges as far as five pounds'.[21] In September 1781, an even more prestigious patron came to the aid of another enlistee. Sir Henry Dashwood, an Oxfordshire baronet and former MP, wrote to the Secretary at War to secure the release of the son of one of his employees, 'a very sober industrious lad', who, according to Dashwood, had been recruited unfairly. Dashwood urged that the minister order the young man to be discharged at the earliest opportunity.[22] But most members of the rank and file, it scarcely needs to be said, had no such powerful patrons to lobby on their behalf.

Discharge was usually the result of circumstances beyond the control of the soldier himself. Those who had sustained serious injuries and could no longer perform military service usually experienced discharge as soon as they became a burden rather than an asset to the army, even in the midst of hostilities. The same was true of members of the rank and file debilitated by disease or believed to be too old or infirm for further duty. Wartime discharges, then, were far from negligible, despite the army's obvious need for manpower. In the period March to December 1756, when the Royal Fusiliers at Gibraltar experienced a net loss of just six men to desertion, forty were discharged for various reasons.[23] But the largest number of soldiers discharged from the army left at the end of wars, when their regiments were disbanded or slimmed down to a peacetime establishment. In this category, we can surmise, were Thomas Lemman, who left the 67th Foot on 26 November 1763 and Nicholas Silvester, 'Properly Discharged', as he put it, from the 3rd Foot Guards on 23 March of the same year.[24] Such men usually left the army with two weeks' subsistence money and their regimental coat as their only rewards.

Officers

Serious injury might lead a soldier to have to leave the service, but the military authorities showed a great reluctance to part with damaged officers, even when their disabilities made the performance of their duties almost impossible. A captain of the 59th Foot, keen to serve in North America, received permission, 'if you chuse it', to remain at home, 'in consideration of the loss of your Arm in the Service'.[25] The Secretary at War, who conveyed this message to the captain, seems to have been content to allow a one-armed officer to remain in the army, despite the obvious problems that his injury caused. General William Howe showed similar unwillingness to force officers to retire when in December 1776 he allowed Captain Primrose Kennedy of the 44th Foot six months' leave to recuperate from a serious wound he had suffered at the end of August, which 'has render'd you incapable of doing your Duty'.[26] Given that Kennedy had been injured more than four months earlier, he was being given at least ten months to recover from his wounds. Howe was equally tender-hearted when he dealt with Captain William Holmes of the 4th, or King's Own, Foot. In November 1776, John Hopkins of Arundel in Sussex noted in his diary the return to the town of Holmes, who had come back from North America 'being out of his mind'.[27] Howe told the Secretary at War that he did not feel able to 'dismiss' Holmes, so he had 'suspended him from Duty, with my Permission to return to Britain'. Howe effectively passed the buck to the Secretary at War, whom he suggested should 'take such further Steps as may be thought fit'.[28] The Secretary at War instructed that another officer judged to have been 'disordered in his Senses', Edward Wintour of the 49th Foot, should be sent to Bethlehem Hospital 'for Cure if found a proper Object' and 'received back when you think proper to discharge him'.[29]

But if officers tended to be better treated than their men if they were injured or experienced mental collapse, death in service, as we have seen, knew nothing of distinctions of rank. Disease affected officers as well as common soldiers; as General Lord Albemarle remarked of conditions during the siege and occupation of Havana in 1762, 'we have all been Sick, have buried a good many'.[30] Death in action was similarly as likely to befall officers as the men that they commanded. Indeed, during the War of American Independence, some observers believed that officers ran even greater risk, as the rebels pursued a deliberate policy – much to the displeasure of British commentators – of picking off officers.[31] Thomas Anbury, a junior officer in the 24th Foot, recalled seeing the mortally-wounded Brigadier General Simon Fraser on the expedition from Canada in 1777. As Fraser lay dying, according to Anbury, he told his listeners that he had seen the man who shot him: 'he was riflemen and up a tree'. No one doubted that the unfortunate Fraser had been the rifleman's target.[32]

Officers, however, were much less likely than their subordinates to suffer death as a punishment imposed by a court martial. Most of those convicted by general courts martial faced a less final but still career-ending punishment; they were dishonourably discharged and required to leave the army.

Lieutenant William Hamilton faced this ignominy in November 1775, when a general court martial found him guilty of resisting arrest after he had 'offered violence' against his captain and 'Behaving in a Scandalous, infamous manner, unbecoming the Character of an Officer and a Gentleman'.[33] A few months later, Ensign James Foxon of the 10th Foot received the same punishment for stealing from a house in Boston and then trying to bribe another officer to conceal his crime.[34]

Senior officers, it seems clear, spared some of their wayward junior colleagues the humiliation of cashiering and instead encouraged them to resign, saving themselves, their families and their regiments much embarrassment. In the American war, Second Lieutenant Francis Seymour of the Royal Artillery, after being bailed out of the debts he had run up by Earl Percy, assaulted a resident of Boston in 1775.[35] The local artillery commander confronted Seymour with the prospect of a general court martial and the young lieutenant then offered to resign. His lieutenant colonel accepted this offer 'on Account of his family' (he was connected with the Seymours, the dukes of Somerset).[36] Another example, from near the end of the war in America, is Lieutenant Alexander Leslie of the 82nd Foot (almost certainly connected to the Earl of Leven), who seems to have been encouraged to leave his regiment after he 'fell into several scrapes' at Wilmington, North Carolina, in late 1781.[37]

Desertion, an important means of departure from the army for the rank and file, does not appear to have been a route employed by officers or by very few of them, at any rate. That was probably because officers, unlike their men, had the option of resigning their commissions if they wished to leave the service. In the War of American Independence, which divided opinion on both sides of the Atlantic, a few officers resigned on explicitly political grounds. Captain the Earl of Effingham of the 22nd Foot left in full public gaze, ensuring that his letter of resignation appeared in the London press.[38] Major Apollos Morris of the 27th Foot, wrote at length to the commander-in-chief in Ireland, explaining why the war against the Americans was wrong.[39] There may have been more, who objected to the war but decided not to make their unhappiness public. The Earl of Rochford, Secretary of State for the Southern Department, told the Lord Lieutenant of Ireland in September 1775 that 'the King could not but express a Surprise at the great Impropriety of so many Officers requesting to retire when on the Verge of embarking for foreign Service'.[40]

But reluctance to go to North America may not have indicated sympathy for the rebels or opposition to the government's policy of coercion. Some officers displayed a similar reluctance to sail to other overseas postings that were not politically contentious. Regiments ordered for the Caribbean, West Africa and even the Mediterranean garrisons of Gibraltar and Minorca during the War of Independence all had officers that dragged their feet, pleading ill-health and seeking long periods of authorized absence or to leave the army or exchange to a unit remaining in the home territories.[41] Nor was this phenomenon confined to the American war. At least some officers received official support for their attempts to avoid foreign service: in 1746, the Secretary at War indicated that Lieutenant James Paterson of the Royal Regiment of Foot had permission, on the grounds of ill health, to transfer to the same rank in another regiment, which was staying in Ireland.[42] Disapproval was the norm, however. At the end of the Seven Years War, when Samuel Bever published his military guide, he berated officers who were unwilling to serve abroad.[43]

In truth, there were many different reasons for officers to resign. Major Isaac Hamilton of the 18th, or Royal Irish, Regiment, asked permission to retire in July 1775, citing ill health as his motive. But a letter from the Secretary at War to the commander-in-chief in North America suggests that Hamilton was regarded as an inept officer, who might have been encouraged to leave rather than allow him to be in a position of responsibility in a war.[44] We will never know how many officers, who had been tolerated in peacetime, found themselves under pressure to make way for someone more capable once hostilities began. Some officers no doubt genuinely felt that family circumstances made retirement necessary. For Captain Walter Sloane Laurie, who retired from the 43rd Foot in 1775 while in North America, the illness of his elderly parents seems to have been the spur. His hostility to the rebels cannot be doubted; while still in Boston he derided their principles in private letters home.[45] Perhaps one of the most common reasons for quitting the service was debt. Ensign Thomas Gibbons of the 44th Foot asked his lieutenant colonel 'to allow me to sell out on the Terms I purchased at, in order to enable me to discharge my just Debts'.[46] Debt, as we saw earlier, could be a consequence of borrowing to purchase a commission or just to cover the costs of living as a subaltern on poor pay. It often seems to have been made much worse by gambling and heavy spending on drink, the antidotes for many officers to the danger and boredom inherent in a military life.

At least a few resignations proved a costly mistake. Major Henry Basset of the 10th Foot, after 30 years' service, decided to retire because he despaired of promotion after three less experienced majors secured lieutenant colonelcies while he remained unrewarded. Having submitted his resignation in a fit of pique from besieged Boston, he learned a short time later that the king had granted his wish for promotion and made him lieutenant colonel of the 52nd Foot. No doubt rueing his dreadful timing, Basset petitioned for reinstatement. Sadly, as he soon discovered, he was too late. His resignation stood and he was obliged to leave the army, a victim of his own impetuosity and poor transatlantic communications.[47]

Many less impetuous officers ended up no better off than the hapless Basset. Rather than resign, they were obliged to leave because the army no longer needed their services. When new regiments were 'broke', or disbanded, at the end of wars, the officers often had no choice but to leave the army. The additional companies added to old regiments likewise faced disbandment, with their officers obliged to leave active service. But at least some of these officers remained nominally in the army, as they went on the half-pay list, receiving, as the name suggested, half their pay while they waited for a vacancy to occur that would allow them to resume their military careers. They appear in official records with great regularity, as supplicants putting their case for a rapid return to active service and full pay. All too often they had to wait a long time, as promotion in peacetime was much slower than during wars. Many remained stuck on the half-pay list until the next war created new opportunities. Hodson Bernard, a half-pay captain who had served in Ottway's Regiment of Foot until 1748, at the end of the War of the Austrian Succession, when the regiment's additional companies were disbanded, is a good example. In 1754, as hostilities began in the preliminaries to the Seven Years War, Bernard lobbied the lords justices of Ireland for their help in securing him a full-pay post.[48] Countless similar appeals were made by struggling half-pay officers at the beginning of every new wartime augmentation of the army.

After the Army

Once they had left the army, former officers engaged in a variety of activities. Apollos Morris, who resigned in sympathy with the rebels in 1775, took it upon himself to try to broker a settlement between the two sides. He sailed to America, hoping to negotiate with Congress, 'professing myself', as he told General Howe, 'a Friend to G: Brittain as well as the Colonys, & an advocate for a Reconciliation'.[49] Before appealing to the commander-in-chief in North America, Morris had tried to persuade Lord George Germain, the Secretary of State for the Colonies and effective war minister. Victory, he argued, 'can be attended with but transitory advantages, . . . tis certainly our Interest to put a conclusion to the War'.[50] His efforts, needless to say, were in vain, dismissed by both sides as a sign of his eccentricity, though some of his old colleagues, as we will see, suspected that his motives may not have been so lofty. But Morris was a one-off, who pursued a very personal (not to say otherworldly) path. We should turn to more general afterlives.

Those who had no private income to support them no doubt found it difficult. But the more fortunate ones, from well-off families, seem to have moved seamlessly back into civilian life, becoming country gentlemen, living on an income boosted by the sale of their commissions. Those who had never intended service in the army to be anything more than temporary perhaps found it easiest to adapt. Some, such as Thomas Woods Knollis, who served in the army in Portugal at the end of the Seven Years War, became local magistrates. Knollis seems to have remembered his time in the military with some affection; as noted earlier, he took pride in assisting in the recruiting service at the beginning of the American war, when, as a Hampshire JP, he claimed to have endorsed the enlistment of more than 100 men for the 25th Foot.[51]

Still others, frustrated in their desire to pursue a military career, explored other options once the British Army no longer needed them or even while still in British service. Several officers in British regiments in India transferred into the East India Company's military, where promotion was quicker. John Carnac, one of those who made this move, explained his decision thus: 'I was heartily tired of being Seventeen Years a Subaltern in His Majesty's service, without the least prospect of bettering myself.'[52] British regular officers also acquired more senior rank in loyalist provincial regiments during the War of Independence. Of the twenty-six officers in the Volunteers of Ireland, a loyalist corps formed in October 1778, the lieutenant colonel, major, three of the four captains, the captain-lieutenant and three of the eight lieutenants had previously held a lower commissioned rank in a regular regiment. Other loyalist units seem to have contained a similar number of officers who had begun their military careers in the British regulars.[53]

The armies of other states provided opportunities when they seemed to be diminishing in the British. In the closing stages of the Seven Years War, when disbandment of new regiments loomed on the horizon, several British officers chose to transfer into the Portuguese army. The most notable was surely Francis McLean, a lieutenant colonel in a new regiment in the British Army, who was given the same rank in the Portuguese, but soon climbed much higher.[54] He became a general (and a provincial governor), before returning to the British Army in the War of American Independence. Thomas Pelham, who travelled to Portugal in 1775, described McLean as effectively 'Head of the Army'.[55] Apollos Morris, at least one British officer in America suggested, had come across the Atlantic with military advancement rather than peace in mind. Morris was accused of seeking a higher rank in the Continental Army than he could expect in British service; he was reported to have travelled to America 'upon the promise of a Reg^t & being Appointed Adjutant General of the Rebel Army'.[56] Soldiering, as we have seen, was an international profession and in the eighteenth century it was far from uncommon for officers to move from one army to another in pursuit of promotion and better prospects or simply the continuation of a military career that seemed to have been cut short in their own country's army.

The latter was also true of common soldiers, who often chose to offer their services to foreign states when their own no longer needed them. We saw earlier that discharged marines at the end of the War of the Austrian Succession crossed over to northern France, where Scots and Irish regiments in Louis XV's service were posted to entice former British soldiers to join them. The French army's Irish and Scots regiments, the Duke of Newcastle commented bitterly in 1750, were just on the other side of the Channel, 'in order to recruit in Times of Peace and to be ready to invade us, in Time of War'.[57]

Deserters also might gravitate towards other armies once they had left the British. In war zones, it perhaps seemed to make good sense to seek refuge in another army, though those who did so ran the risk of execution if they fell into the hands of their former employers. A Scottish newspaper reported in January 1746 the execution of British deserters who had joined the French and Jacobite forces. The report claimed that 'They are all Irishmen'.[58] Whether the claim was true in this instance is unknowable, but Irish Catholics were perhaps particularly open to encouragement to desert and join the French forces when the enticement came from fellow Irishmen. In 1756, Lord Loudoun, the British commander-in-chief in North America, wrote that an Irish battalion in French service had 'Scattered Letters all round Oswego, this last Spring, promising great Rewards, to any Soldiers that would come over to them'. He continued that the letters succeeded in their intention: they 'drew great numbers of the Irish Recruits, from the two Regiments there, which were mostly Roman Catholicks'.[59] Prisoners of war might be encouraged to change sides, too; Corporal William Todd has left a vivid account of the attempts made to persuade him to join the Irish Brigade when he was captured on a British raid on the French coast in 1758. Todd resisted the blandishments offered to him (including sergeant's rank), noting in his diary that 'I told him [the French officer trying to recruit him] for that I would not serve no Other Nation but my Own'.[60] Others in a similar predicament were almost certainly less resistant.

A variant on joining another army was service in the militia. In wartime, when it was embodied or put on an active footing, the military authorities encouraged the transfer into the militia of experienced regular army non-commissioned officers, who could drill the untrained militiamen. Perhaps more surprisingly, even private soldiers received a discharge from a regular regiment (the 4th Foot) in 1759 in order to become corporals and sergeants in the Devonshire militia.[61] We should also note that non-commissioned officers in British regular regiments often gained commissioned status in American loyalist corps during the War of Independence. The ensigns in the newly-created Volunteers of Ireland in 1778 included a former sergeant major of the 1st Foot, a former quartermaster sergeant of the 35th and a former sergeant in the 7th Foot or Royal Fusiliers.[62]

A lucky few members of the rank and file maintained a connection with the army as pensioners. Chelsea Hospital, established in the seventeenth century, offered a limited number of places to highly recommended soldiers who had been in the army for more than 20 years and sustained wounds that made them unfit for further service. Kilmainham Hospital, in Dublin, did the same for a small number of similarly favoured troops on the Irish establishment. The hospitals had limited room for 'in-pensioners' – Chelsea had fewer than 500 beds – but also offered support to 'out-pensioners', who collected their payments from centres across the country in six-monthly instalments.[63] By 1764, there were some 14,700 Chelsea out-pensioners.[64]

Some men secured a pension only many years after their army service had ended. Roger Lamb, discharged from the Royal Welch Fusiliers on returning from America in 1783, pursued a career as a schoolmaster in his native Ireland before, in January 1809, sending a memorial to the Duke of York, then commander-in-chief, asking for a pension. His request was granted and he was put on the list of Chelsea out-pensioners later that month.[65]

Other discharged soldiers did rather better. The 1779 Recruiting Act, passed at the height of the American war, offered artisans, craftsmen and retailers who joined the army the opportunity, when the conflict ended, to practice their trade in any parish, town or city in the kingdom. The general intentions of the 1779 Act, furthermore, had been anticipated in 1749, in a piece of legislation that allowed soldiers and marines, on leaving the service, to set up in trade without having undergone an apprenticeship.[66] We have some evidence that local authorities disputed the claims to privileges made by former soldiers; but the rights of the ex-servicemen seem to have been upheld.[67] Perhaps the most fortunate were the demobilized soldiers who benefited from land grants. We have seen that a royal proclamation of October 1763, establishing new colonies in Quebec, Florida and the West Indies, offered land grants to former military personnel who had fought in North America in the recently-concluded Seven Years War. Private soldiers received 50 acres, more than many could have ever have dreamed of owning in Britain itself. We know that at least some former members of the rank and file took up the offer of land, especially on the frontier of upper New York; a few of them show up as landowners in later records, notably the papers of the claims commission established after the War of Independence to compensate American loyalists for property lost in America as a result of the claimants' continuing adherence to the Crown.[68] It seems reasonable to conclude that the former soldiers who received land grants felt a particular sense of gratitude to the British state and were unwilling to renounce their allegiance to it. A significant number of them returned to military service in the American war, when they joined loyalist regiments raised to help put down the rebellion.[69]

But many discharged soldiers had a hard time adjusting to post-war conditions. Those who had sustained injuries often had little choice but to rely on hand-outs. Many of the Chelsea out-pensioners fell in this category; too infirm or disabled to work, they had to survive on five pence a day, less than even an unskilled agricultural labourer might expect to earn. Private charity offered support to at least some of those who failed to secure a state pension. Sir John Langham's Charity in London gave money to soldiers and sailors, many of whom had suffered injuries that made employment in civilian life difficult or even impossible. Typical of the applicants were William Kimber, a stone cutter by trade, who had joined the army in 1760 and been injured in the leg at Guadeloupe, 'which has ever since deprived him of Standing at his Business'; and Thomas Roades, who had served in West Africa in the Seven Years War, where he 'Contracted an inveterate Scurvy' and now suffered from 'Gravel and Rheumatism which often Renders him incapable of following his trade as a Journeyman Carpenter'.[70]

Even able-bodied former soldiers often found it a struggle to re-enter the labour market. After large-scale conflicts, when most soldiers experienced demobilization, the number of former military men trying to secure employment was inevitably large. Competition for jobs was therefore fierce. Furthermore, the wartime stimulus to the economy caused by increased government spending on weapons, equipment, uniforms and food, abruptly stopped as public spending was cut in order to reduce the level of taxation. Soldiers, in other words, were competing in a labour market that was both overstocked and shrinking. The consequences can readily be imagined. Many could not find work and were driven to seek parochial poor relief or forced to take to the streets to beg. Jeremy Bentham, the philosopher, noted in 1782 that in London 'I have frequently been importuned by English soldiers for half-pence'; he was almost certainly referring not to serving soldiers but to men who had just been discharged and were still wearing their old regimental coats.[71]

The end of wars caused much nervousness among property owners. They worried that idle hands would turn to crime. Even during wartime, deserters alarmed members of the propertied classes, who imagined – sometimes rightly – that deserters congregated on the fringes of society and turned to crime because they could not reintegrate successfully. In December 1776, Abraham Stanley, a farmer of Newtown, Montgomeryshire, petitioned the Secretary at War requesting him to remove Sir Edward Manley Pryce, an army officer, who had gathered around him 'every lawless Ruffian & Deserter' from far and wide to help him terrorise the neighbourhood.[72] But it was at the end of wars that anxiety about crime became widespread. Fear led to a greater propensity to prosecute and much anxiety that former soldiers, accustomed to the use of arms, lay behind many of the new offences.[73]

Anxiety led to the imposition of more draconian punishments, in an attempt to deter crime; the Murder Act of 1751, which threatened offenders with an aggravated death penalty, can be seen as the culmination of responses to the fear generated in the aftermath of the War of the Austrian Succession. Besides harsher penalties, it was this period that saw new legislation designed to curb the receiving of stolen goods, tighten liquor licensing and the regulation of brothels and gaming houses, all of which were seen as necessary in the context of concerns about the impact of demobilization.[74] There were some more positive moves, too, such as the schemes to encourage discharged soldiers to settle in Nova Scotia and the suggestion by the Prince of Wales that 'disbanded troops' might be given land in the West Indies;[75] but it was not until the end of the next conflict, the Seven Years War, that a more sympathetic approach was much in evidence.

Not only were more extensive land grants given in North America, but the possibility of a similar scheme in the home territories seems to have been discussed in the public realm. In January 1763, the *Gentleman's Magazine* published a letter calling for discharged soldiers, sailors and dockyard workers to be given tracts of land to cultivate and improve on commons, heaths and forests. The author suggested that these land grants 'would make numbers of them comfortable and happy' and would 'lessen the poor rates'.[76] In Scotland, land seems actually to have been allocated to soldiers and sailors on the so-called annexed estates – the property of rebels involved in the 'Forty-Five Jacobite uprising, which had been confiscated by the government.[77] Just as importantly, in the press and prints, soldiers who had served their country faithfully appeared as neglected heroes, often juxtaposed favourably with comfortable civilians who had not been required to make any sacrifices. *The Pluralist and the Old Soldier*, a broadside of 1762, is a good example. It compares the disbanded infantryman, who had lost a leg in the capture of Guadeloupe from the French, reduced to begging on the streets, to the wealthy clergyman who refuses to give the battered old soldier any money. There can be no doubt who 'Tim Bobbin', the author of this broadside, regarded as the more worthy.[78] Around the same time, Oliver Goldsmith, the Irish author and playwright, included a moving passage on a discharged soldier in his *Citizen of the World*.[79]

Public sympathy, perhaps a product of the army's improving reputation following the victories of the Seven Years War, was scant consolation, however, for those former soldiers reduced to eking out a living by begging. It must have been a very bitter conclusion to their involvement with an institution that, whatever its many faults, had given them a sort of pride in their status. It was probably hard enough for many to adjust to the end of the camaraderie of a military career and to overcome the feeling of redundancy and purposelessness that discharge at the close of wars could bring. To have to cope with a lack of money and food and be reduced to begging, was the final indignity for men who had risked their lives in their country's service. In the eighteenth century, for some old soldiers life after the army was grim indeed. Sadly, that remains true even today.

Notes

Introduction

1. Here the key work remains J.R. Western, *The English Militia in the Eighteenth Century* (London, 1965).
2. See, e.g., Glenn A. Steppler, *Britons to Arms: the Story of the Volunteer Soldier* (Stroud, 1992).
3. For these auxiliaries in imperial theatres, see, e.g., Stephen Conway, 'Continental European Soldiers in British Imperial Service, *c.*1756-1792', *English Historical Review*, 129 (2014), 79–106.
4. Sir John Fortescue, *History of the British Army* (13 vols, London, 1899–1930).
5. Charles Clode, *The Military Forces of the Crown: Their Administration and Government* (2 vols, London, 1869).
6. Edward E. Curtis, *The Organization of the British Army in the American Revolution* (New Haven, CN, 1926).
7. H.C.B. Rogers, *The British Army of the Eighteenth Century* (London, 1977).
8. Tony Hayter, *The Army and the Crowd in Mid-Georgian England* (London, 1978).
9. J.A. Houlding, *Fit for Service: The Training of the British Army, 1715-1795* (Oxford, 1981).
10. Glenn A. Steppler, 'The Common Soldier in the Reign of George III, 1760-1792' (Oxford DPhil dissertation, 1984).
11. Alan J. Guy, *Œconomy and Discipline: Officership and Administration in the British Army, 1714-1763* (Manchester, 1989).
12. Peter Way, 'Class and the Common Soldier in the Seven Years War', *Labor History*, 44 (2003), 455–81.
13. Hannah Smith, 'The Army, Provincial Urban Communities and Loyalist Cultures in England, *c.*1714-1730', *Journal of Early Modern History*, 15 (2011), 139–58; and 'The Hanoverian Succession and the Politicisation of the British Army', in *The Hanoverian Succession: Dynastic Politics and Monarchical Culture*, ed. Andreas Gestrich and Michael Schaich (Aldershot, 2015), pp. 207–26.

14. See, e.g., *Soldiering in Britain and Ireland, 1750-1850: Men of Arms*, ed. Catriona Kennedy and Matthew McCormack (Basingstoke, 2013); and *Britain's Soldiers: Rethinking War and Society, 1715-1815*, ed. Kevin Linch and Matthew McCormack (Liverpool, 2014).

15. Tony Hayter was intending to write a book on the army's organization, which, judging by the outline he showed me, would have covered at least some of the ground in the current study.

16. E.P. Thompson, 'The Moral Economy of the English Crowd in the Eighteenth Century', *Past & Present*, no. 50 (1971), 76–136, reprinted in his *Customs in Common* (London, 1991), Ch. 4.

17. Jack P. Greene, *Negotiated Authorities: Essays in Colonial Political and Constitutional History* (Charlottesville, VA, 1994), esp. Ch. 1.

Chapter 1

1. Contemporaries tended to use the term 'inhabitant'. Other alternatives, such as non-combatant, were not in use at the time. In this book, however, 'civilian' will be used, despite its anachronism, as well as inhabitant and non-combatant.

2. The most thorough analysis remains Hiller B. Zobel, *The Boston Massacre* (New York, 1970), but see also the illuminating Neil L. York, *The Boston Massacre: A History with Documents* (New York, 2010).

3. *The Justicing Notebook of William Hunt, 1744-1749*, ed. Elizabeth Crittall (Devizes, 1982), p. 33.

4. Hampshire Record Office, Winchester, Banbury Papers, 1 M44/66, fo. 32.

5. See John Lynn, *Giant of the Grand Siècle: The French Army, 1610-1715* (Cambridge, 1997), Pt. II, esp. Ch. 6.

6. M.S. Anderson, *War and Society in Europe of the Old Regime, 1618-1789* (London, 1988), p. 61.

7. John Childs, *Armies and Warfare in Europe, 1648-1789* (Manchester, 1982), p. 197.

8. 1 Will. & Mar., c. 5.

9. 1 Will. & Mar., session 2, c. 4, sec. 17.

10. Jeremy Black, *Culloden and the '45* (Stroud, 1990), pp. 132, 177–8.

11. See, e.g., Bedfordshire and Luton Archives Service, Bedford, Lucas of Wrest Park Collection, Robinson Papers, L 29/216, 'General Thoughts on America'.

12. Newberry Library, Chicago, Case MS F 8326.2, Orderly Book of Lt. Benjamin Craven, Barrack-master at Staten Island, 19 July 1782.

13. For Scotland, see Victorian Henshaw, *Scotland and the British Army, 1700-1750: Defending the Union* (London, 2014), Ch. 5; for Ireland, see the Army Barracks of Eighteenth-Century Ireland Project (barracks18c.ucd.ie) and Charles Ivar McGrath, '"The Grand Question Debated": Jonathan Swift, Army Barracks, Parliament and Money', *Eighteenth-Century Ireland*, 31 (2016), 117–36 and the same author's *Ireland and Empire, 1692-1770* (London, 2012), Ch. 4.

14. TNA, War Office Papers, WO 1/992, Knollis to Lord Barrington, 12 March 1776.

15. Ibid., WO 1/992, Rev. J. Vashony to Lord Barrington, 26 July 1776. See also WO 1/997, William Man Godschall (a Surrey magistrate) to -------, 10 Sept. 1778.

16. Hannah Smith, 'The Army, Provincial Urban Communities and Loyalist Cultures in England, *c*,1714-50', *Journal of Early Modern History*, 15 (2011), 139–58.

17. For Dashwood's notes, see Centre for Buckinghamshire Studies, Aylesbury, Dashwood Papers, D/D19/5, Notes of Expenses of the War in Germany.

18. See Stephen Conway, 'Checking and Controlling British Military Expenditure, 1739-1783', in *War, State and Development: Fiscal-Military States in the Eighteenth Century*, ed. Rafael Torres Sánchez (Pamplona, 2007), pp. 45–67.

19. *House of Commons Sessional Papers of the Eighteenth Century*, ed. Sheila Lambert (145 vols, Wilmington, DE, 1975), xli. 414.

20. See J.R. Western, *The English Militia in the Eighteenth Century: The Story of a Political Issue, 1660-1802* (London, 1965), esp. Pt II.

21. *Tracts, Concerning the Ancient and Only True Legal Means of National Defence, by a Free Militia* (London, 1781), pp. 47, 74, 77.

22. *The House of Commons, 1715-1754*, ed. Romney Sedgwick (2 vols, London, 1970), i. 142–4; *The House of Commons, 1754-1790*, ed. Sir Lewis Namier and John Brooke (3 vols, London, 1964), i. 138.

23. *The Parliamentary History of England*, ed. William Cobbett and John Wright (36 vols, London, 1806-20), xi. 344 (29 Jan. 1740).

24. Ibid., xi. 918.

25. BL, Liverpool Papers, Add. MS 38,567, fo.30.

26. Childs, *Armies and Warfare in Europe*, p. 175.

27. National Records of Scotland, Edinburgh, Leven and Melville Muniments, GD 26/9/513, William Leslie to the Earl of Leven, 8 June 1773.

28. *Colonel Samuel Bagshawe and the Army of George II, 1731-1762*, ed. Alan Guy (London, 1990), p. 110.

29. National Library of Ireland, Dublin, MS 3750, Order-book, 32nd Foot, 28 Feb., 6 July 1776.

30. *The Harcourt Papers*, ed. E.W. Harcourt (14 vols, Oxford, 1880–1905), x. 182.

31. BL, London, Holland House Papers, Add. MS 51378, fo. 89.

32. Beckles Willson, *The Life and Letters of James Wolfe* (London, 1909), p. 304.

33. *Correspondence of the Reverend Joseph Greene*, ed. Levi Fox (London, 1965), p. 44.

34. *Records of the Borough of Leicester*, vii. *Judicial and Allied Records, 1689-1835*, ed. G.A. Chinnery (Leicester, 1974), pp. 91 and 103.

35. Regimental Museum of the Queen's Lancashire Regiment, Warrington, Plymouth Citadel Order-book, 18 June 1776.

36. See, e.g., TNA, War Office Papers, WO 4/110, p. 177.

37. See, e.g., TNA, Chatham Papers, PRO/30/8/45, John Hubbard to [William Pitt], 28 Dec. 1756.

38. Cited in Christopher Duffy, *The Military Experience in the Age of Reason* (London, 1998 edn.), p. 125.

39. See, e.g., TNA, War Office Papers, WO 1/1007, p. 789.

40. Ibid., WO 1/1007, p. 259.

41. Hampshire Record Office, Winchester, Jervoise Collection, 44 M69 E86, Daniel Paterson to Tristram Huddleston Jervoise, 4 April 1780.

42. Essex Record Office, Chelmsford, Parish Records, D/P 195/1/2.

43. Though, for a case of an apprentice prosecuted for enlisting, see Worcestershire Archive and Archaeology Service, Worcester, Quarter Sessions Order-book, 1773–1790, fol. 87 (7–8 Oct. 1777).

44. *The Diary of Isaac Fletcher of Underwood, Cumberland, 1756-1781*, ed. Angus L.L. Winchester (Kendal, 1994), p. 22.

45. *Documents Illustrating the Wiltshire Textile Trades in the Eighteenth Century*, ed. Julia De L. Mann (Devizes, 1964), p. 40.

46. Dorset History Centre, Dorchester, Ryder of Rempstone Papers, D/RWR/X/4, letter-book of Henry Fox, 25 Oct. 1748.

47. See Thomas Bartlett, '"A Weapon of War Yet Untried": Irish Catholics and the Armed Forces of the Crown, 1760-1830', in *Men, Women and War*, ed. T.G. Fraser and Keith Jeffery (Dublin, 1993), pp. 66–85.

48. See, e.g., Robert Clyde, *From Rebel to Hero: The Image of the Highlander, 1745-1830* (Est Linton, 1998), Ch. 6; Andrew Mackillop, '*More Fruitful than the Soil': Army, Empire and the Scottish Highlands, 1715-1815* (East Linton, 1999).

49. See Stephen Conway, 'Scots, Britons and Europeans: Scottish Military Service, *c.*1739-1783', *Historical Research*, 82 (2009), 114–30.

50. For the cultural impact of the camps established in the French Revolutionary and Napoleonic Wars, see Gillian Russell, *The Theatre of War: Performance, Politics and Society, 1793-1815* (Oxford, 1995), pp. 33–46; for the American war period, see Stephen Conway, *The British Isles and the War of American Independence* (Oxford, 2000), pp. 121–2.

51. John Houlding, *Fit for Service: The Training of the British Army, 1715-1795* (Oxford, 1981), p. 330; Stephen Conway, 'Locality, Metropolis and Nation: The Impact of the Military Camps in England during the American War', *History*, 82 (1997), 549.

52. TNA, Treasury Papers, T 1/543, fo 12.

53. See, e.g., *Calendar of Treasury Books and Papers*, ed. William Arthur Shaw (5 vols, London, 1897–1903), iv. 566, for £1,318 paid to Abraham Cortissos for ammunition bread for the camps in southern England established in 1740; and TNA, Treasury Papers, T 52/41, pp. 83, 139, 238, 243, 297, 378, for payments to George Wright for supplying hay, straw and wood to the camps in 1740–1. For an important recent study, see Gordon Bannerman, *Merchants and the Military in Eighteenth-Century Britain: British Army Contracts and Domestic Supply, 1739-1763* (London, 2015).

54. *Chelmsford Chronicle*, 17 July 1778.

55. Tyne and Wear Archives, Gateshead, Ellison Papers, A19/20, Cuthbert Ellison to his brother, 4 Sept. 1741.

56. *Secret Comment: The Diaries of Gertrude Savile, 1721-1757*, ed. Alan Saville (Kingsbridge, 1997), p. 319.

57. Wiltshire and Swindon Archives, Chippenham, Savernake Estate MSS, 9/34/138. See also, Bodleian Library, Oxford, Charles Rivington Diary, MS Eng. misc. e. 957, p. 1.

58. BL, Hardwicke Papers, Add. MS 35,659, fo. 393.

59. Centre for Kentish Studies, Maidstone, U333 Z1, General Orders, Coxheath Camp, 18 July 1779.

60. Huntington Library, San Marino, CA, Diaries of John Marsh, MS HM 54457/ 6.

61. *Records of the Borough of Nottingham* (9 vols, Nottingham, 1882–1956), vi. 176–7, 181, 186–7, 196, 201–08.

62. See, e.g., West Sussex Record Office, Chichester, Petworth Turnpike Trustees, Minute-book, 1757–1801, Add. MS 2212, p. 268, where there is a reference to George Elliott, a local farmer, 'employed in carrying Soldiers Baggage' in wagons.

63. TNA, War Office Papers, WO 55/2, fos. 25, 120, Charles Frederick to Board of Ordance, 4 Nov. 1755, [Jan. 1758].

64. National Library of Scotland, Edinburgh, Dundas Letter-book, Acc 8425, Dundas to Richard Pierson, 1 May 1761.

65. Centre for Buckinghamshire Studies, Howard Vyse Deposit, D/HV/B/5/4, Weir to George Howard, 24 June 1762.

66. Ibid., D/HV/B/5/13A.

67. Ibid., D/HV/B/5/22.

68. Conway, *British Isles and the War of American Independence*, pp. 80–1.

69. *Woollen Manufacturing in Yorkshire: The Memorandum Books of John Brearley, Cloth Frizzer at Wakefield, 1758-1762*, ed. John Smail (Woodbridge, 2001), p. 54.

70. East Sussex Record Office, Lewes, Sheffield Papers, A 2714/265.

71. Birmingham City Archives, Matthew Boulton Papers, MBP 141, Letter-book of Boulton & Fothergill, 13 May 1778.

72. *The Walker Family: Ironfounders and Lead Manufacturers, 1741-1893*, ed. A.H. John (London, 1951), pp. 11–19.

73. For an example from the Seven Years War, see TNA, Chancery Papers, C 103/202, John Warrington's Account-book, 1760–1.

74. Cheshire Record Office, Chester, Cholmondeley of Cholmondeley Papers, DCH/X/9, 10. See also 17, 21, 42.

75. John Rylands Library, Manchester, Mary Hamilton Papers, HAM/1/20/54.

76. Cornwall Record Office, Truro, DD J 2245, Diary of Thomas Hawkins.

77. *The New Oxford Book of Eighteenth-Century Verse*, ed. Roger Lonsdale (Oxford, 2003), p. 406.

78. *Register of Marriages of the City of Edinburgh, 1751-1800*, ed. Francis J. Grant (Edinburgh, 1922), pp. 440–582 (a sample of those registered under 'M'), suggests a fall in the number of marriages in the Seven Years War, followed by a surge in 1763 and 1764.

79. These conclusions are based on a sampling exercise, extracting information from *Registers of Baptism, Marriages and Burials of the City of Exeter/Exeter Diocese*, ii. *The Parishes of Allhallows, Goldsmith Street, St. Pancras, St. Paul*, ed. H. Tapley-Soper (Exeter, 1933), pp. 23–57.

80. [John Douglas,] *A Letter Addressed to Two Great Men, on the Prospect of Peace* (London, 1760), p. 29.

81. *A Parson in the Vale of White Horse: George Woodford's Letters from East Hendred, 1733-1761*, ed. Donald Gibson (Gloucester, 1982), p. 111.

82. London Metropolitan Archives, Eliot and Howard Family Papers, Acc. 1017/983, Philip Eliot to John Eliot III, 9 Aug. 1759.

83. See Nicholas Rogers, 'Brave Wolfe: The Making of a Hero', in *A New Imperial History: Culture, Identity and Modernity in Britain and the Empire, 1660-1840* (Cambridge, 2004), pp. 239–59.

Chapter 2

1. David French, *The British Way in Warfare, 1688-2000* (London, 1990), p. 38 (Table 2.2).

2. See Thomas Bartlett, 'The Augmentation of the Army in Ireland, 1767-1769', *English Historical Review*, 96 (1981), 540–59; and Alan J. Guy, 'The Irish Military Establishment, 1660-1776', in *A Military History of Ireland*, ed. Thomas Bartlett and Keith Jeffrey (Cambridge, 1996), pp. 211–30.

3. See Stephen Conway, *The British Isles and the War of American Independence* (Oxford, 2000), p. 208; *Journals of the House of Commons . . . of Ireland*, xvii. 97.

4. For recruitment, see below, Chapter 3; for desertions and death by combat and disease, see Chapter 8.

5. Historical Manuscripts Commission, *Rutland Manuscripts* (5 vols, London, 1888–1905), ii. 233.

6. Centre for Kentish Studies, Maidstone, Amherst Papers, U 1350 O38/24, Amherst to Lord Barrington, 18 Oct. 1760.

7. See below, Chapters 5 and 8.

8. *Colonel Samuel Bagshawe and the Army of George II, 1731-1762*, ed. Alan J. Guy (London, 1990), p. 252.

9. J.A. Houlding, *Fit for Service: The Training of the British Army, 1715-1795* (Oxford, 1981), p. 127 (Table 7).

10. Stephen Conway, 'The Mobilization of Manpower for Britain's Mid-Eighteenth-Century Wars', *Historical Research*, 77 (2004), 378–9.

11. Conway, *British Isles and the War of American Independence*, p. 18 (Fig. 1.1).

12. Peter Wilson, 'Warfare in the Old Regime, 1648-1789', in *European Warfare, 1453-1815*, ed. Jeremy Black (Basingstoke, 1999), p. 80 (Table 3.1).

13. Conway, 'Mobilization of Manpower for Britain's Mid-Eighteenth-Century Wars', 378.

14. Houlding, *Fit for Service*, p. 419 (Appendix C).

15. These figures are derived from Wilson, 'Warfare in the Old Regime', p. 80 (Table 3.1).

16. French, *British Way in Warfare*, p. 59 (Table 2.4).

17. Alan J. Guy, *Oeconomy and Discipline: Officership and Administration in the British Army, 1714-1763* (Manchester, 1985), pp. 28–34.

18. See, e.g., TNA, War Office Papers, WO 72/7, Stephen Payne Adye to Charles Gould, 23 March 1776, enclosing minutes of general courts-martial of 18–20 Oct, 7–13 Nov. and 12–28 Dec. 1775; WO 81/13, Gould to Adye, 3 Jan. 1775; and WO 72/8, Gould to Sir William Howe, 20 Jun. 1777.

19. See below, Chapter 4, on 'Military Communities'.

20. National Records of Scotland, Edinburgh, Leven and Melville Muniments, GD 26/9/499.

21. See, e.g., ibid., GD 26/9/504.

22. Guy, *Oeconomy and Discipline*, pp. 140–1.

23. The March 1781 returns, for instance, referred to '6th Boothby's' and '45th Haviland's': BL, Liverpool Papers, Add. MS 38438, fos. 9 and 10.

24. For the connection between local and national loyalties, see Conway, *British Isles and the War of American Independence*, pp. 168–73.

25. See William Faden's 'Plan of New York', in his *North American Atlas: Selected from the Most Authentic Maps, Charts, Plans &c Hitherto Published* (London, 1776).

26. William L. Clements Library, Ann Arbor, MI, 47th Foot Order-book (typescript copy), 7 Aug. 1777.

27. Houlding, *Fit for Service*, p. 410 (Appendix B).

28. Ibid., pp. 411, 413 (Appendix B).

29. Ibid., pp. 18–19.

30. See Shy's pioneering study *Toward Lexington: The Role of the British Army in the Coming of the American Revolution* (Princeton, 1965).

31. Houlding, *Fit for Service*, p. 413 (Appendix B).

32. For this conflict, see M.S. Anderson, *The War of the Austrian Succession, 1740-1748* (Harlow, 1995).

33. Stephen Brumwell, *Redcoats: The British Soldier and war in the Americas, 1755-1763* (Cambridge, 2002), pp. 318–19 (Tables 5 and 6).

34. Ibid., pp. 20, 24.

35. Its world-wide character is captured in Daniel A. Baugh, *The Global Seven Years War, 1754-1763: Britain and France in a Great Power Contest* (London, 2011).

36. For the importance of the ideological element in the preference for amphibious operations, see Richard Harding, 'The Ideology and Organisation of Maritime War: An Expedition to Canada in 1746', in *War, State and Development: Fiscal-Military*

States in the Eighteenth Century, ed. Rafael Torres Sánchez (Pamplona, 2007), pp. 157–77.

37. For British strategy in North America, before and after French intervention, see Stephen Conway, 'British Governments and the Conduct of the American War', in *Britain and the American Revolution*, ed. H.T. Dickinson (Harlow, 1998), pp. 155–79.

38. BL, Liverpool Papers, Add. MS 38437, fos. 22-3.

39. The best strategic overview of the war from a British perspective remains Piers Mackesy, *The War for America, 1775-1783* (London, 1964).

40. BL, Liverpool Papers, Add. MS 38343, fos. 344-5.

41. Ibid., Add. MS 38440, fos. 8-20.

42. Ibid., Hardwicke Papers, Add. MS 35354, fo. 30.

43. Beckles Willson, *The Life and Letters of James Wolfe* (London, 1909), pp. 403–4.

44. TNA, Chatham Papers, PRO 30/8/56, Pt. I, fos. 124-9, Shelburne to Chatham, 26 Sept. 1773.

45. See H.M. Scott, *British Foreign Policy in the Age of the American Revolution* (Oxford, 1990), Ch. 12; Andrew Stockley, *Britain and France at the Birth of America: The European Powers and the Peace Negotiations of 1782-1783* (Exeter, 2001).

46. For more on the European character of the British Army, see below, Chapter 4. For its European-ness at the time of the American Revolution, see Stephen Conway, 'The British Army, "Military Europe" and the American War of Independence', *William & Mary Quarterly*, 3rd series, 67 (2010), 69–100.

Chapter 3

1. Alan J. Guy, *Oeconomy and Discipline: Officership and Administration in the British Army, 1714-1763* (Manchester, 1985), p. 91.

2. Eric Robson, 'Purchase and Promotion in the British Army in the Eighteenth Century', *History*, 36 (1951), 59.

3. Ardchattan Priory, Argyll, Campbell-Preston of Ardchattan Papers, box 34, bundle 514, Campbell to his uncle, 29 January 1778.

4. J.A. Houlding, *Fit for Service: The Training of the British Army, 1715-1795* (Oxford, 1981), pp. 100–1.

5. See, e.g., Peter Marshall, 'Manchester and the American Revolution', *Bulletin of the John Rylands University Library of Manchester*, 62 (1979), 168–86; Andrew Mackillop, *'More Fruitful than the Soil': Army, Empire and the Scottish Highlands,*

1715–1815 (East Linton, 2000); Stephen Conway, 'Entrepreneurs and the Recruitment of the British Army in the War of American Independence', in *War, Entrepreneurs and the State in Europe and the Mediterranean, 1300–1800*, ed. Jeff Fynn-Paul (Leiden, 2014), 111–30.

6.   Historical Manuscripts Commission, *Laing MSS* (2 vols, London, 1914–25), ii. 487.

7.   For more on half-pay, see below Chapter 8.

8.   TNA, State Papers Ireland, SP 63/437A, fo. 88, Blacquiere to John Vaughan, 29 Sept. 1775.

9.   James William Hayes, 'The Social and Professional Background of the Officers of the British Army, 1714-1763', University of London MA dissertation, 1956, p. 100. Hayes considers gentlemen volunteers on pp. 39–40.

10. See, e.g., Huntington Library, San Marino, CA, Loudoun Papers, LO 1607.

11. *Calendar of Home Office Papers of the Reign of George III, 1766–1769*, ed. Joseph Redington (London, 1879), p.54.

12. Hauptstaatsarchiv Hannover, Hann. 47 II Nr. 114, fo. 44.

13. TNA, War Office Papers, WO 4/97, pp. 462–3; WO 4/99, p. 198; British Army Headquarters Papers, PRO 30/55/3, 314.

14. See, e.g., West Sussex Record Office, Chichester, Goodwood MS 58/44 and 48; BL, Leeds Papers, Egerton MS 3443, fos. 110-11.

15. Stephen Conway, 'British Mobilization in the War of American Independence', *Historical Research*, 72 (1999), 69.

16. Stephen Conway, 'The Mobilization of Manpower for Britain's Mid-Eighteenth-Century Wars', *Historical Research*, 77 (2004), 392.

17. TNA, War Office Papers, WO 34/119, fos. 217-19.

18. 19 Geo. III, c.10, s. xli. For the use made of this provision in the act to recruit men for the 104th Foot in Reading, see *Reading Mercury and Oxford Gazette*, 10 June 1782.

19. New York Public Library, Bayard-Campbell-Pearsall Papers, box 13, 'Capt. Campbell's Recruiting Instructions', 15 Dec. 1775.

20. National Records of Scotland, Edinburgh, Abercairney Muniments, GD 24/1/843/57.

21. BL, Haldimand Papers, Add. 21680, fo. 7.

22. National Records of Scotland, Gordon Castle Muniments, GD 44/43/226/35.

23. Ibid., Dalhousie Muniments, GD 45/2/24, 'A Weekly return of recruits raised by Capt. Cosnan for the 45th Regiment of Foot . . . Boston', 2 January 1758, Cosnan to John Forbes, 18 Jan. 1758.

24. John Rylands Library, Manchester, Bagshawe of Ford Muniments, BAG 2/2/71, Campbell to Samuel Bagshawe, 11 March 1758.

25. TNA, War Office Papers, WO 1/992, Haslam to Barrington, 3 Feb. 1776.

26. See, e.g., East Sussex Record Office, Lewes, Sheffield Papers, A 2714/265, 'Song in Honour of the 22d Light Dragoons'.

27. See, e.g., TNA, War Office Papers, WO 26/29, p. 169, for the Secretary at War authorizing short-term enlistments in Dec. 1775.

28. See BL, Barrington Papers, Add. MS 73589, fo. 14, Col. Samuel Zobel to Barrington, 9 March 1776, for the views of an experienced officer.

29. National Records of Scotland, Clerk of Penicuik Muniments, GD 18/4175.

30. Ibid., Cuninghame of Thornton Muniments, GD 21/359, Cuninghame to his brother, 18 March 1751.

31. National Library of Scotland, Edinburgh, Fletcher of Saltoun Papers, MS 16517, fo. 235.

32. BL, Sutton Court Collection, MSS Eur. F 128/23.

33. Stephen Brumwell, *Redcoats: The British Soldier and War in the Americas, 1755-1763* (Cambridge, 2002), p. 319 (Table 6).

34. See *The Correspondence of General Thomas Gage*, ed. Clarence E. Carter (2 vols, Cambridge, MA, 1931–4), I, 122–3, Earl of Hillsborough to Gage, 2 Jan. 1771.

35. Brumwell, *Redcoats*, p. 318 (Table 5).

36. James Hayes, 'Scottish Officers in the British Army, 1714-1763', *Scottish Historical Review*, 37 (1958), 25.

37. TNA, War Office Papers, WO 27/35.

38. Ibid., WO 27/47.

39. See Lister's correspondence and journal in Calderdale Archives, Halifax, Lister of Shibden Hall MSS, SH7 JL.

40. BL, Liverpool Papers, Add. MS 38212, fo. 81.

41. Historical Manuscripts Commission, *Buccleuch and Queensbury MSS* (3 vols, London, 1899–1926), i (1899), 412.

42. BL, Barrington Papers, Add. MS. 73550.

43. *Gunner at Large: the Diary of James Wood, RA, 1746-1765*, ed. Rex Whitworth (London, 1988), pp. 106, 137, 144, for Wood's promotion and that of others in the same unit.

44. *The Journal of Corporal Todd, 1745-1762*, ed. Andrew Cormack and Alan Jones (Stroud, 2001), p. 14.

45. *The Commissariot of Edinburgh: Consistorial Processes and Decreets, 1658-1800*, ed. Francis J. Grant (Edinburgh, 1909), p. 64.

46. TNA, War Office Papers, WO 1/991, Cunninghame to Barrington, 19 May 1776.

47. See Douglas Hay and Nicholas Rogers, *Eighteenth-Century English Society* (Oxford, 1997), p. 9.

48. National Records of Scotland, Agnew of Lochnaw Papers, GD 154/626/2.

49. Royal Archives, Windsor, Cumberland Papers, Box 67/X.35.20.

50. TNA, War Office Papers, WO 1/992, 'List of Recruits Rais'd for the 46th Regiment of Foot', Dublin, 9 Feb. 1776.

51. Ibid., WO 25/537.

52. Library of Congress, Washington, DC, Peter Force MSS, George Chalmers Collection, 8A/25, Military Journal of Walter Homes, 1770–2.

53. BL, Loudoun Papers, Add. MS 44084, fo. 231.

54. Rammerscales House, Dumfries, Bell-Macdonald Papers, Letter-book of Lt. Allan Macdonald, 1781–2, 'Return of Recruits levied for the Macdonald Regt of Highlanders by Lieut Allan Macdonald at Glasgow'.

55. John Rylands Library, Townshend Papers, Eng. MS 940, Charles Tassell to Hunt Walsh, 15 Jan. 1768.

56. Staffordshire Record Office, Stafford, Lyttleton Papers, D 260/M/T/5/52.

57. TNA, War Office Papers, WO 1/1005, George Reynolds to [Matthew Lewis], 24 May 1779; WO 1/1010, James Barker to Lewis, 6 April 1781.

58. Ibid., WO 34/153, fo. 245, Rudd to Lord Amherst, 12 July 1779.

59. Fred Anderson, *Crucible of War: The Seven Years War and the Fate of Empire in British North America, 1754-1766* (New York, 2000), p. 259.

60. Derbyshire Record Office, Matlock, Wilmot-Horton of Osmaston and Catton Papers, D 1355/C 961.

61. William L. Clements Library, Ann Arbor, MI, Gage Papers, Lt-Col. Francis Smith to Gage, 30 June 1775. See also Stirke's own memorial to Gage, 1 July 1775.

62. See below, Chapter 4.

63. National Records of Scotland, Leven and Melville Muniments, GD 26/9/484/29.

64. See below, Chapter 5.

65. For convicts turning down the option of military service, see, e.g., TNA, War Office Papers, WO 4/106, Matthew Lewis to Sir Stanier Porten, 24 April, 1 July 1779. For what looks like self-mutilation intended to make the victims unfit for

military service, see the return of impressed men in the 99th Foot, 8 Nov. 1780, WO 34/225, fo. 267. Several men have written next to their names 'lost his right Thumb'.

66. Edinburgh City Archives, Council Records, SL 7/1/75, pp. 369–70.

67. *City of Liverpool Municipal Archives and Records*, ed. Sir James A. Picton (Liverpool, 1907), pp. 119–20.

68. East Sussex Record Office, Sheffield Papers, A 2714/265.

69. American Philosophical Society, Philadelphia, Journal of Thomas Sullivan, p. 29.

70. John Rylands Library, Bagshawe of Ford Muniments, Letter-books of Lord John Murray, Rev. James McLagan to Murray, 31 May 1777.

71. Barnsley Archives and Local Studies, Spencer Stanhope of Cannon Hall MSS, SpSt 60542/6, Sill to John Spencer, 2 March 1775.

72. Wiltshire and Swindon Archives, Chippenham, Wansey Papers, 314/4/1, Laurence to George Wansey, 5 Aug. 1778.

73. *The Rambling Soldier*, ed. Roy Palmer (Gloucester, 1985), p. 22.

74. See above, Chapter 1 and also Louise Carter, 'Scarlet Fever: Women's Enthusiasm for Men in Uniform, 1780-1815', in *Britain's Soldiers: Rethinking War and Society, 1715-1815*, ed. Kevin Linch and Matthew McCormack (Liverpool, 2014), pp. 155–80.

75. *Rambling Soldier*, ed. Palmer, p. 19.

76. National Records of Scotland, Cuninghame of Thornton Muniments, GD 21/359, Archibald Cuninghame to his brother, 21 Aug. 1749.

77. *English Historical Documents*, ix. *American Colonial Documents to 1776*, ed. Merrill Jensen (London, 1969), p. 641.

78. See Mackillop, *'More Fruitful than the Soil'*.

79. See David A. Kent, '"Gone for a Soldier": Family Breakdown and the Demography of Desertion in a London Parish, 1750-1791', *Local Population Studies*, 45 (1990), esp. Table 1. See also Jennine Hurl-Eamon, 'Did Soldiers really Enlist to Desert Their Wives? Revisiting the Martial Character of Marital Desertion in Eighteenth-Century London', *Journal of British Studies*, 53 (2014), 356–77.

80. Warwickshire Record Office, Warwick, Quarter Session Records, QS 39/8, Minute Book, 1778–81, Easter 1781 session.

81. R.W. Malcolmson, *Life and Labour in England, 1700-1780* (London, 1981), p. 37.

82. Mackillop, *'More Fruitful than the Soil'*, p. 21.

83. Rammerscales House, Bell-Macdonald Papers, Letter-book of Lt. Allan Macdonald, 1781–2, 'Return of Recruits . . .'.

84. Beckles Willson, *The Life and Letters of James Wolfe* (London, 1909), p. 304.
85. BL, Grant Papers, Add. MS 25411, fo. 231, Penuel Grant to Robert Grant, 17 Feb. 1757.
86. *Aris's Birmingham Gazette*, 2 Nov. 1778.
87. *The Correspondence of Sir Roger Newdigate of Arbury, Warwickshire*, ed. A.W.A White (Hertford, 1995), p. 220.
88. Trinity College Dublin, Conolly Papers, MS 3976/525.

Chapter 4

1. See, e.g., two examples from the War of American Independence: *John Peebles' American War: The Diary of a Scottish Grenadier, 1776-1782*, ed. Ira D. Gruber (Mechanicsburg, PA, 1998), p. 254; *Diary of Frederick Mackenzie* (2 vols, Cambridge, MA, 1930), I, pp. 49–50, 80, 91.
2. The concept of an 'imagined community' was coined by Benedict Anderson to conceptualize nations; it applies equally well in the military context: see Anderson's *Imagined Communities: Reflections on the Origin and Spread of Nationalism* (London, 1983).
3. See, e.g., the inspection of the 28th Foot at Limerick in June 1775: TNA, War Office Papers, WO 27/35.
4. Recent scholarship recognizes the essential similarities between European armies in the eighteenth century. See, Christopher Duffy, *The Military Experience in the Age of Reason* (London, 1987) and, especially, Ilya Berkovich, *Motivation in War: The Experience of Common Soldiers in Old-Regime Europe* (Cambridge, 2017), which considers British soldiers alongside those from other European armies.
5. J.A. Houlding, *Fit for Service: The Training of the British Army, 1715-1795* (Oxford, 1981), p. 116 n. 31.
6. The authority on the training of the army is Houlding, *Fit for Service*.
7. See above, Chapter 1.
8. TNA, War Office Papers, WO 1/1006, pp. 521-4, H. Penrud Wyndham to Secretary at War, 11 April 1779.
9. Royal Artillery Institution, Woolwich, MS 58, General Orders, entry of 18 Feb. 1778.
10. See the illuminating discussion in John Keegan, *The Face of Battle: A Study of Agincourt, Waterloo and the Somme* (London, 1991), Ch. 3.
11. TNA, War Office Papers, WO 71/83, pp. 73–85.

12. Ibid., State Papers Ireland, SP 63/458, fo.59, Richard Heron to Sir Stanier Porten, 13 Sept. 1777.

13. Ibid., SP 63/469, fos. 98-116.

14. *Memoirs of the Life of Sir John Clerk of Penicuik*, ed. John M. Gray (Edinburgh, 1892), p. 191; Historical Manuscripts Commission, *Stopford Sackville MSS* (2 vols, London, 1904–10), I, pp. 289, 290.

15. *The Journal of Corporal Todd, 1745-1762*, ed. Andrew Cormack and Alan Jones (Stroud, 2001), p. 187.

16. See Stephen Conway, 'The British Army, "Military Europe" and the American War of Independence', *William & Mary Quarterly*, 3rd series, 67 (2010), 69–100.

17. See, e.g., Joachim Miggelbrink, 'The End of the Scots-Dutch Brigade', in *Fighting for Identity: Scottish Military Experience, c.1550-1900*, ed. Steve Murdoch and Andrew Mackillop (Leiden, 2002), p. 86.

18. BL, Haldimand Papers, Add. MS 21728, fo, 29.

19. Alexander William Crawford Lindsay, Lord Lindsay, *Lives of the Lindsays* (4 vols, Wigan, 1840), 3, p. 319.

20. For British respect for Washington, see, e.g., E. Stuart-Wortley, *A Prime Minister and His Son: from the Correspondence of the 3rd Earl of Bute and of Lt. General the Hon. Sir Charles Stuart, K.B.* (London, 1925), p. 99.

21. Staffordshire Record Office, Stafford, Congreve Papers, D 1057/M/F/32/2, Leighton to William Congreve, 20 April 1777; Historical Manuscripts Commission, *Hastings MSS* (4 vols, London, 1928–47), iii, p. 167.

22. TNA, Cornwallis Papers, PRO 30/11/2, fo. 28, Clinton to Lord Cornwallis, 6 May 1780.

23. For the surrender, see John D. Grainger, *The Battle of Yorktown, 1781: A Reassessment* (Woodbridge, 2005), p. 149.

24. BL, Rainsford Papers, Add. MS 23646, fo. 42.

25. See Hannah Smith, 'The Idea of a Protestant Monarchy in Britain, 1714-1760', *Past & Present*, 185 (2004), 91-118.

26. Stephen Conway, *The British Isles and the War of American Independence* (Oxford, 2000), pp. 14–15.

27. For the exchange of prisoners, rank for rank, see, e.g., Sir Reginald Savory, 'The Convention of Éclusé, 1759-1762', *Journal of the Society for Army Historical Research*, 42 (1964), 68–77.

28. For the situation in the British Army, see Alan J. Guy, *Oeconomy and Discipline: Officership and Administration in the British Army, 1714-1763* (Manchester, 1985), esp. p. 162. For contemporaneous developments elsewhere, see Duffy, *Military Experience in the Age of Reason*, pp. 67–8.

29. BL, Letter-book of John Ramsay, Additional MS 63,819, fols. 4-5.

30. Berkshire Record Office, Reading, Neville Aldworth Papers, D/EN F54, Journal of a Tour of Switzerland and Italy, Oct. 1743.

31. See, e.g., Newberry Library, Chicago, Case MS °E199. M36 1755, Anon. Diary of French and Indian War, 24 Oct. 1758.

32. For uniforms, see Duffy, *Military Experience in the Age of Reason*, pp. 105–7.

33. John Childs, *Armies and Warfare in Europe, 1648-1789* (Manchester, 1982), pp. 107–8.

34. See Duffy, *Military Experience in the Age of Reason*, pp. 230–3.

35. See, e.g., Peter E. Russell, 'Redcoats in the Wilderness: British Officers and Irregular Warfare in Europe and America, 1740 to 1760', *William & Mary Quarterly*, 3rd series, 35 (1978), 629–52. For different views, see Eric Robson, 'British Light Infantry in the Mid-Eighteenth Century: The Effect of American Conditions', *Army Quarterly*, 63 (1952), 209–22; Peter Paret, 'Colonial Experience and European Military Reform at the End of the Eighteenth Century', *Bulletin of the Institute of Historical Research*, 37 (1964), 47–59.

36. See, e.g., David J. Beattie, 'The Adaption of the British Army to Wilderness Warfare, 1755-1763', in *Adapting to Conditions: War and Society in the Eighteenth Century*, ed Maarten Utlee (Tuscaloosa, AL, 1986), pp. 56–83; Matthew H. Spring, *With Zeal and Bayonets Only: The British Army on Campaign in North America, 1775-1783* (Norman, OK, 2008).

37. Huntington Library, San Marino, CA, HM 818, p. 71, Robert Honyman's Journal, 22 March 1775.

38. See Houlding, *Fit for Service*, esp. p. 204.

39. [James Cunninghame,] *Strictures on Military Discipline, in a Series of Letters, with a Military Discourse, in which is Interspersed some Account of the Scotch Brigade in the Dutch Service* (London, 1774), p. 8. For corroboration, see London Metropolitan Archives, London, Jersey Papers, ACC/0510.255, p. 7; BL, Rainsford Papers, Add. MS 23,646, fol. 6.

40. Dundas was the author of *Principles of Military Movements, Chiefly Applied to Infantry: Illustrated by Manoeuvres of the Prussian Troops and by an Outline of the British Campaigns in Germany, during the War of 1757* (London, 1788).

41. See Jeremy Black, 'Sir William Faucett and the Publication of Military Works in the Mid-Eighteenth Century', *Factotum*, 33 (1991), 10–13. Faucitt's name appeared in various forms – Faucitt, Faucett, or even Fawcett: for his letters to his uncle, see Calderdale Archives, Lister of Shibden Hall Papers, SH 7: FAW.

42. Lee Kennett, *The French Armies of the Seven Years War: A Study in Military Organization and Administration* (Durham, NC, 1967), p. 57.

43. Christopher Storrs and H. M. Scott, 'The Military Revolution and the European Nobility, *c.*1600-1800', *War in History*, 3 (1996), 15–17.

44. For some of the difficulties in comparing aristocracies, see John Cannon, 'The British Nobility, 1660-1800', in *The European Nobilities in the Seventeenth and Eighteenth Centuries*, ed. H.M. Scott (2 vols, London, 1995), I, pp. 54–5.

45. Duffy, *Military Experience in the Age of Reason*, pp. 37, 38, 44; Rauf Blaufarb, *The French Army, 1750-1820: Careers, Talent, Merit* (Manchester, 2002), Ch. 1.

46. According to Michael Hochedlinger, *Austria's Wars of Emergence: War, State and Society in the Habsburg Monarchy, 1683-1797* (London, 2003), pp. 305–6, only about half of the officers in the 'German' regiments of the Austrian army came from the Austrian or Bohemian nobility.

47. For the British case, see Houlding, *Fit for Service*, p. 105.

48. See Duffy, *Military Experience in the Age of Reason*, pp. 74–80, for the cult of honour.

49. For more on the British Army's 'gentlemen volunteers', see above, Chapter 2 and Houlding, *Fit for Service*, p. 103.

50. Christopher Duffy, *The Austrian Army in the Seven Years War*, i. *Instrument of War* (Rosemont, IL, 2000), p. 203.

51. See André Covisier, *L'Armée Française de la fin du XVII* siècle au ministère de Choiseul: Le Soldat* (2 vols, Paris, 1964), i, pp. 449–542, for the social background of French soldiers.

52. For different rates of urbanization, see Jan de Vries, *European Urbanization, 1500-1800* (London, 1984), Table 3.6.

53. See, e.g., Glasgow City Archives, Hamilton of Barnes Papers, TD 589/586 and 630; National Library of Scotland, Edinburgh, Albemarle Papers, MS 3730, fol. 14; *Extracts from the Records of the Burgh of Glasgow*, ed. Robert Renwick et al (11 vols, Glasgow, 1881–1916), vii, p. 99; Historical Manuscripts Commission, *Various Collections* (8 vols, London, 1901–13), viii, p. 414; Historical Manuscripts Commission, *Buccleuch and Queensbury MSS* (3 vols, London, 1899–1926), I, p. 412; *Colonel Samuel Bagshawe and the Army of George II, 1731-1762*, ed. Alan

J. Guy (London, 1990), p. 234; William Salt Library, Stafford, S. MS 478B, Milo Bagot to --------, 29 Nov. 1760.

54. Duffy argues that the Austrian army 'had an overwhelmingly rural character' (*Austrian Army in the Seven Years War*, I, p. 203); the same was surely true of the Prussian and Russian armies.

55. Duffy, *Military Experience in the Age of Reason*, p. 92.

56. For the European pattern, see M. S. Anderson, *War and Society in Europe of the Old Regime, 1618-1789* (Leicester, 1988), pp. 122–3; for the British and Irish, see above, Chapter 2.

57. For two examples from the time of the American war, see TNA, State Papers Ireland, SP 63/445, fol. 7 and SP 67/14, fol. 173.

58. See, e.g., Nottingham University Library, Mellish of Hodsock MSS, MeC 24/3/8, for evidence relating to 1731; and Tyne and Wear Archives, Newcastle, Ellison MSS, bundle A30, esp. letter from Henry Thomas Carr to Henry Ellison, 24 Sept. 1749.

59. See, e.g., BL, Pelham Papers, Add. MS 33,126, fol. 299; National Archives of Scotland, Edinburgh, Shairp of Houston Muniments, GD 30/1590/3, 4, 5, Thomas Shairp to his grandfather, 3 Dec. 1767, 25 March and 18 May 1768; Library of Congress, Washington, D.C, Peter Force Collection, Journal of Richard Augustus Wyvill; TNA, SP 63/445, fol. 7, Viscount Harcourt to the Earl of Rochford, 7 Jan. 1775.

60. For Brunswick, see BL, Althorp Papers, Add. MS 75,571, Anna Maria Poyntz to Countess Spencer, 11 Oct. 1766; Cornwall Record Office, Truro, Diary of Thomas Hawkins, DD J 2245; [John Moore,] *A View of Society and Manners in France, Switzerland and Germany: With Anecdotes relating to Some Eminent Characters* (London, 1779), p. 2; for Göttingen, see Gordon M. Stewart, 'British Students at the University of Göttingen in the Eighteenth Century', *German Life and Letters*, 33 (1979), 24–41.

61. George Hanger, *The Life, Adventures and Opinions of Col. George Hanger* (2 vols, London, 1801), I, p. 14.

62. J. E. O. Screen, 'The Royal Military Academy of Lewis Lochée', *Journal of the Society for Army Historical Research*, 70 (1992), 146.

63. E. B. De Fonbanque, *Political and Military Episodes in the Latter Half of the Eighteenth Century: Derived from the Life and Correspondence of the Right Hon. John Burgoyne* (London, 1876), p. 19.

64. TNA, State Papers France, SP 78/232, Pt. I, Joseph Yorke to the Duke of Bedford, 30 Jan./10 Feb. 1749.

65. BL, Hamilton and Greville Papers, Add. MS 42,071, fol. 205.

66. Thomas A. Fischer, *The Scots in Germany: being a Contribution towards the History of the Scots Abroad* (Edinburgh, 1902), pp. 119–20.

67. See, e.g., Stephen Conway, 'The Scots Brigade in the Eighteenth Century', *Northern Scotland*, 1 (2010), 30–41.

68. See BL, Loudoun Papers, Add. MS 44,069, fols. 20, 144.

69. For McLean, see Stephen Conway, 'Scots, Britons and Europeans: Scottish Military Service, *c.*1739-1783', *Historical Research*, 82 (2009), 126–8.

70. BL, Leeds Papers, Egerton MS 3500, fol. 15.

71. Robin Gwynn, 'The Huguenots in Britain, the "Protestant International" and the Defeat of Louis XIV', in *From Strangers to Citizens: The Integration of Immigrant Communities in Britain, Ireland and Colonial America, 1550-1750*, ed. Ralph Vigne and Charles Littleton (Brighton, 2001), p. 413.

72. For the Royal Americans, see Alexander V. Campbell, 'Atlantic Microcosm: The Royal American Regiment, 1755-1772', in *English Atlantics Revisited: Essays Honouring Ian K. Steele*, ed. Nancy L. Rhoden (Montreal, 2007), pp. 284–309.

73. See Sir Reginald Savory, *His Britannic Majesty's Army in Germany during the Seven Years War* (Oxford, 1966).

74. For auxiliaries in America and India, see Stephen Conway, 'Continental European Soldiers in British Imperial Service, *c.*1756-1792', *English Historical Review*, 129 (2014), 79–106.

75. BL, Hardwick Papers, Add. MS 36250.

76. See, e.g., *Journal of Captain Pausch, Chief of the Hanau Artillery during the Burgoyne Campaign*, ed. and trans. William Stone (Albany, NY, 1886), p. 107.

77. *Gunner at Large: The Diary of James Wood, RA, 1746-1765*, ed. Rex Whitworth (London, 1988), p. 42.

78. National Library of Scotland, Edinburgh, Stuart-Stevenson Papers, MS 5375, fo. 38; Hull University Library, Hotham Papers, DD HO 4/19, O'Hara to Sir Charles Thompson, 20 Sept. 1778.

79. See, e.g., National Records of Scotland, Seafield Muniments, GD 248/509/3, Robert Grant to John Grant of Tullogriban, 5 June 1777.

80. BL, Dropmore Papers, Add. MS 69382, fo. 96. See also North Yorkshire Record Office, Darley of Aldby Papers, ZDA/DAR CP/2/10, Robert Soulby to John Brewster, 23 June 1743.

81. Gloucestershire Archives, Gloucester, Papers, D 1833 F2, Rooke to Charles Rooke, 23 Nov. 1776.

82. Emerich de Vattel, *The Law of Nations; or, Principles of the Law of Nature: Applied to the Conduct and Affairs of Nations and Sovereigns* (2 vols, London, 1759–60), ii, pp. 27, 48–52, 89–90.

83. For the laws of war, see Stephen C. Neff, *War and the Law of Nations: A General History* (Cambridge, 2005), Pt. II.

84. See, e.g., Robert Ward, *An Enquiry into the Foundation and History of the Law of Nations in Europe, from the Time of the Greeks and Romans, to the Age of Grotius* (2 vols, Dublin, 1795), esp. I, p. 98.

85. See Stephen Conway, *Britain, Ireland and Continental Europe in the Eighteenth Century: Similarities, Connections, Identities* (Oxford, 2011).

86. *The Correspondence of Edmund Burke*, ed. Thomas W. Copeland et al (10 vols, Cambridge, 1958–78), ix, p. 307 (Burke to French Laurence, 11 April 1797).

Chapter 5

1. Derbyshire Record Office, Matlock, Wilmot-Horton of Osmaston and Catton Papers, D 1355/C 440, Berry to Dorset, 29 July 1732.

2. See, e.g., *Gentleman's Magazine*, 47 (1777), 15–16.

3. Alan J. Guy, *Oeconomy and Discipline: Officership and Administration in the British Army, 1714-1763* (Manchester, 1985), p. 141.

4. TNA, War Office Papers, WO 30/105, 'The Custom and Practice of the Army Concerning Offreckonings', 25 April 1772.

5. National Records of Scotland, Edinburgh, Clerk of Penicuik Muniments, GD 18/4175, Clerk to Sir John Clerk, 24 Feb. 1740.

6. Barnsley Archives, Spencer Stanhope of Cannon Hall MSS, SpSt 60542/9, 13, Shuttleworth to John Spencer, 16 July 1775 and 24 Jan. 1776.

7. National Army Museum, Chelsea, Letters of Lt. Francis Laye, Royal Artillery, to his father, 6807-154, pp. 42, 68.

8. National Records of Scotland, Campbell of Barcaldine Muniments, GD 170/1118/7 and 8/1, Campbell to Duncan Campbell of Glenure, 9 Jan., 22 July 1778.

9. National Library of Wales, Aberystwyth, Picton Castle MSS, 589/1714, copy of Jackson to Walpole, 26 Sept. 1736.

10. National Library of Scotland, Edinburgh, Fettercairn Papers, box 4, Urquhart to Sir William Forbes, 27 Aug. 1778, box 5, Urquhart to Forbes, 3 Jan., 22, 26 Feb., 29 April, 30 July, 30 Dec. 1780, box 6, Urquhart to Forbes, 6 March 1782.

11. Public Record Office of Northern Ireland, Belfast, Hart Letters, D 3077/B/1/5, Hart to John Hart, 23 Oct. 1778.

12. Ballindalloch Castle, Grantown on Spey, Macpherson Grant Papers, bundle 707, Macpherson to William Macpherson, 20 Nov. 1776, to George Macpherson of Invershie, 25 Dec. 1776.

13. Lloyds Bank, Cox & King's Branch, London, 22nd Foot Ledger-book, 1772–1779, fos. 31-2.

14. National Library of Scotland, Fettercairn Papers, box 6, Urquhart to Forbes, 6 March 1782.

15. Alnwick Castle, Northumberland, Percy Family Papers, vol. L, Pt A, fo. 47, Percy to Lord Seymour, 13 Feb. 1775.

16. Trinity College Dublin, Conolly Papers, MS 3976, Dickson to Conolly, 2 July 1783.

17. National Library of Ireland, Dublin, Pomeroy Papers, Henry Watson Powell to John Pomeroy, 3 July 1770.

18. Bedfordshire and Luton Archives Service, Bedford, Lucas of Wrest Park Papers, L 30/12/3.

19. Douglas W. Marshall, 'The British Military Engineers, 1741-1783', University of Michigan PhD dissertation, 1976, pp. 292–5.

20. William L. Clements Library, Ann Arbor, MI, Clinton Papers, Blucke to John André, Nov. 1779, 30 May 1780.

21. Library of Congress, Washington, DC, Miscellaneous MSS, Clerk to [Henry Stachey], 22 Nov. 1778.

22. See William L. Clements Library, Clinton Papers, John Watson to Sir Henry Clinton, 14 July 1781. Watson seems to have been accused of this fraudulent practice.

23. BL, Newcastle Papers, Add. MS 32706, fo. 369, Dewhirst to Newcastle, 31 March 1746.

24. Huntington Library, San Marino, CA, HM 617, fo. 86, Standing Orders of 71st Foot, 30 June 1778.

25. TNA, War Office Papers, WO 1/993, Ridout to Barrington, 10 Aug. 1776.

26. Ibid., State Papers Criminal, SP 44/93, p. 125.

27. Ibid., War Office Papers, WO 12/5797, fos. 16, 42, 44, 57.

28. For the figures see T.S. Ashton, *An Economic History of England in the Eighteenth Century* (London, 1959), p. 232; E.W. Gilboy, *Wages in Eighteenth-Century England* (Cambridge, MA, 1934), pp. 225–86. See also John Rule, *The Experience of Labour in Eighteenth-Century Industry* (London, 1981), Ch. 2.

29. For a contemporary account see [John Williamson,] *A Treatise of Military Finance* (London, 1782). For a modern summary, see Guy, *Oeconomy and Discipline*, p. 172.

30. See below, Chapter 5.

31. *The Lost War: Letters from British Officers during the American Revolution*, ed. Marion Balderstone and David Syrett (New York, 1975), p. 60.

32. Nottingham University Library, Newcastle of Clumber MSS, NeC 1691, Wade to Henry Pelham, 17 Oct. 1745.

33. TNA, British Army Headquarters Papers, PRO 30/55/17, 2151, Augustine Prévost to Sir Henry Clinton, 30 July 1779.

34. BL, Loudoun Papers, Add. MS 44084, fo. 238.

35. *The Papers of Henry Bouquet*, ed. S.K. Stevens et al (6 vols, Harrisburg, PA, 1972–94), i. 91.

36. William L. Clements Library, Wray Papers, William Hall to George Wray, 22 Aug. 1780. A muster of 30 June 1780 reveals the pay for armourers.

37. *Colonel Samuel Bagshawe and the Army of George II, 1731-1762*, ed. Alan J. Guy (London, 1990), p. 110.

38. Lee R. Boyer, 'Lobster Backs, Liberty Boys and Laborers in the Streets: New York's Golden Hill and Nassau Street Riots', *New-York Historical Society Quarterly*, 57 (1973), 282.

39. Tower of London, Royal Fusiliers (City of London) Regiment Museum, MS R-26(a), minutes of a regimental court martial, at Winton, 12 June 1744.

40. Ballindalloch Castle, Macpherson Grant Papers, bundle 393, 'Inventory of Articles found in the Possession of Jos[h] Anderson Private Soldier in the 15th Regim[t] of Foot who was Executed the 6th Decem[r] 1778 – for Plundering'.

41. *The Journal of Corporal Todd, 1745-1762*, ed. Andrew Cormack and Andrew Jones (Stroud, 2001), quoting from pp. 148 and 178. For shortages, see, e.g., pp. 132, 135, 143, 146, 157, 179.

42. National Records of Scotland, Dunglass Muniments, GD 206/2/495/8, Hall to Sir John Hall of Dunglass, 13 Sept. 1758.

43. *André's Journal*, ed. Henry Cabot Lodge (2 vols, Boston, 1903), i. 71.

44. 'A British Orderly Book, 1780-1781', ed. A.R. Newsome, *North Carolina Historical Review*, 9 (1932), 164.

45. BL, Diary of William Digby, Add. MS 32413, fo. 64.

46. William L. Clements Library, 47th Foot Orderly-book, entry of 27 Aug. 1777.

47. Ballindalloch Castle, Macpherson Grant Papers, bundle 772, Letter-book, Grant to [Robert Grant], 5 June 1776.

48. Library of Congress, Washington, DC, Peter Force Collection, Journal of Richard Augustus Wyvill, p. 16.

49. National Army Museum, Laye Letters, 6807-154, p. 42.

50. Sheffield Archives, Bagshawe of Oakes Papers, OD/1542, Samuel Bagshawe's accounts of expense in Ireland, India and England, 1752–5.

51. *Journal of Gen. Sir Martin Hunter*, ed. Ann Hunter and Elizabeth Bell (Edinburgh, 1894), pp. 20–1.

52. National Library of Scotland, Wade Papers, MS 3076, fo. 28, 'Orders for the Encampment at Newbury', 2 July 1740.

53. Huntington Library, HM 617, fo. 95, Order-book of 71st Foot, 15 Aug. 1778.

54. Royal Fusiliers (City of London) Regiment Museum, MS R-26(a).

55. National Army Museum, 6807-260, Order-book of the 3rd Foot Guards, entry of 13 May 1762.

56. National Library of Ireland, Pomeroy Papers, Leslie to John Pomeroy, 3 July 1770.

57. Queen's Lancashire Regiment Museum, Warrington, Plymouth Citadel Orderly-book, entry of 22 Sept. 1775.

58. 'Letters of Robert Biddulph', ed. Violet Biddulph, *American Historical Review*, 29 (1923–4), 90.

59. 'British Orderly Book', ed. Newsome, 298.

60. BL, Mackenzie Papers, Add. MS 39190, fo. 209.

61. John Shy, *Toward Lexington: The Role of the British Army in the Coming of the Revolution* (Princeton, 1965), p. 309.

62. TNA, War Office Papers, WO 71/81, pp. 166–77.

63. Thomas Jones, *History of New York*, ed. Edward E. DeLancey (2 vols, New York, 1879), i. 136–7.

64. Library of Congress, George Washington Papers, 6B vol. IV, captured British Orderly Book, entry of 9 July 1778.

65. Glasgow Archives, Maxwell of Nether Pollok Papers, T – PM 115/180, Maxwell to Dalrymple, 17 July 1761.

66. Centre for Buckinghamshire Studies, Aylesbury, Baker of Penn Papers, D/X 1069/2/116, Brown to [Richard Andrewes?], 30 April 1745.

67. Nottingham University Library, Galway Collection, Monckton Papers, Ga M/28/3. Abercromby to Robert Monckton, July 1758.

68. Barnsley Archives, Spencer Stanhope of Cannon Hall MSS, SpSt 60542/8, Sill to John Spencer, 6 July 1775.

69. Ballindalloch Castle, Macpherson Grant Papers, bundle 707, McPherson to George McPherson of Invershie, 2 Sept. 1776.

70. National Library of Scotland, Halkett Papers, MS 6410, fo. 25.

71. Boston Public Library, Boston, MA, Stanley Letters, MS Am. 228.5.

72. Huntington Library, Loudoun Papers, LO 6556, David Cuninghame to Lord Loudoun, 2 May 1777; National Records of Scotland, Gilchrist of Ospisdale Muminents, GD 153, box 1, bundle 4, William Sutherland to Dugald Gilchrist, 30 May 1777.

73. Nottingham University Library, Galway Collection, Monckton Papers, GaM 98, Albemarle to Monckton, 6 Oct. 1762.

74. Wiltshire and Swindon Archives, Chippenham, Money-Kyrle of Whetham Papers, 1720/1011.

75. TNA, Colonial Office Papers, CO 318/6, fo. 79, Vaughan to Lord George Germain, 13 Sept. 1780.

76. Hampshire Record Office, Winchester, Banbury Papers, 1 M44/40/5.

77. 'The Capture of Quebec: A Manuscript Journal relating to the Operations before Quebec from 8th May, 1759, to 17th May, 1760, Kept by Colonel Malcolm Fraser, then Lieutenant in the 78th Foot (Fraser's Highlanders)', ed. R.O. Alexander, *Journal of the Society for Army Historical Research*, 18 (1939), 162.

78. Tyne and Wear Archives, Gateshead, Ellison Papers, A 19/31.

79. See above, Chapter 1.

80. *The Papers of Henry Bouquet*, ed. Stevens et al, i. 248–9.

81. Derbyshire Record Office, Matlock, Wilmot-Horton of Osmaston and Catton Papers, D 1355/C 1190.

82. TNA, War Office Papers, WO 12/6398, fos. 126-34.

83. National Records of Scotland, Shairp of Houstoun Muniments, GD 30/1590/3.

84. See, e.g., TNA, State Papers Ireland, SP 63/469, fo. 21.

85. Ibid., War Office Papers, WO 4/93, p. 414.

86. Ibid., WO 4/99, p. 185; WO 4/101, p. 96.

87. Ibid., WO 4/101, p. 398; WO 4/102, p. 147.

88. Ibid., WO 4/111, Charles Jenkinson to Lieut.-Gen. Simon Fraser, 6 Sept. 1780.

89. Ibid., WO 1/1010, ----- Daniell to the Secretary at War, 28 Aug. 1781.

90. John Rylands Library, Manchester, Mary Hamilton Letters, HAM/1/20/42.

91. Boston Public Library, Letters of Hugh, Earl Percy, MS G 31.39.4.

92. National Army Museum, Account of the Military Services of James Green, 7201-36, p. 3.

93. *Memoir and Letters of Captain W. Glanville Evelyn*, ed. G.D. Scull (Oxford, 1879), p. 30.

94. George Spater, *William Cobbett: The Poor Man's Friend* (2 vols, Cambridge, 1982), i. 21.

95. W.H. Wilkin, *Some British Soldiers in America* (London, 1914), pp. 240–1.

96. National Records of Scotland, Hamilton Dalrymple Muniments, GD 110/1026/18, John Buchan to Sir Hew Dalrymple, 24 Jan. 1782.

97. Calderdale Archives, Halifax, Lister of Shibden Hall MSS, SH 7 JL/1, p. 27.

98. National Records of Scotland, Cuninghame of Thornton Papers, GD 21/630, Cuninghame to his mother, 9 May 1781, GD 21/629/7, Cuninghame to his sister, 19 June 1781.

99. Ibid., Shairp of Houstoun Muniments, GD 30/1590/11, Shairp to his father, 14 Aug. 1770.

100. Ibid., Montrose Muniments, GD 220/5/301/2, Urquhart to the Duke of Montrose, 3 May 1713.

Chapter 6

1. The originator of the concept was E.P. Thompson: see his 'The Moral Economy of the English Crowd in the Eighteenth Century', *Past & Present*, 50 (1971), 76–136, reprinted in his *Customs in Common* (London, 1991), Ch. 4.

2. See Jack P. Greene, *Negotiated Authorities: Essay in Colonial Political and Constitutional History* (Charlottesville, VA, 1994), esp. Ch. 1.

3. For references to the moral economy, contractual attitudes and negotiated author-ity in the American forces, see, e.g., Charles Patrick Neimeyer, *America Goes to War: A Social History of the Continental Army* (New York, 1996), esp. pp. 117, 132, 163, 164; Wayne Bodle, *The Valley Forge Winter: Civilians and Soldiers in War* (University Park, PA, 2002), pp. 128–9; Gregory T. Knouff, *The Soldiers' Revolution: Pennsylvanians in Arms and the Forging of Early American Identity* (University Park, PA, 2004), p. 101. For more clearly exceptionalist claims, often making a direct comparison with the British Army, see, e.g., Howard H. Peckham, *The War for Independence: A Military History* (Chicago, 1958), p. 204; Alan Rogers, *Empire and Liberty: American Resistance to British Authority, 1755-1763* (Berkeley, CA, 1974), Ch. 6; Douglas Edward Leach, *Roots of Conflict: British Armed Forces and Colonial Americans, 1677-1763* (Chapel Hill, NC, 1986), Ch. 6; Fred Anderson, *Crucible of War: The Seven Years' War and the Fate of Empire in British North America, 1754-1766* (New York, 2000), esp. pp. 145–7, 219–21, 370–2; John Ferling,

Almost a Miracle: The American Victory in the War of Independence (New York, 2007), pp. 17–18; John A. Ruddiman, '"A Record in the Hands of Thousands": Power and Negotiation in the Orderly Books of the Continental Army', *William & Mary Quarterly*, 3rd series, 67 (2010), 747–74.

4. See, esp. Peter Way, 'Rebellion of the Regulars: Working Soldiers and the Mutiny of 1763-1764', *William & Mary Quarterly*, 3rd series, 57 (2000), 761–92, which explores a moment of dramatic defiance; and Stephen Brumwell, *Redcoats: The British Soldier and War in the Americas, 1755-1763* (Cambridge, 2002), pp. 127–36, 313–14, which discusses some of the rank and file's ideas of 'Rights and Resistance' and offers a brief comparison with the Continental army. See also Gareth William Morgan, '"A Clever Little Army": The British Garrison in Boston, 1768-1776', University of Sussex DPhil dissertation, 2004, Chs 4 and 5; and Michael N. McConnell, *Army and Empire: British Soldiers on the American Frontier, 1758-1775* (Lincoln, NB, 2004), esp. pp. 23, 94–5.

5. For soldiers as workers, see esp., Peter Way, 'Class and the Common Soldier in the Seven Years War', *Labor History*, 44 (2003), 455–81.

6. An insightful recent essay by William P. Tatum III touches upon some of the issues covered here, but mainly from the perspective of military law: see his '"The Soldiers Murmured much on Account of this Usage": Military Justice and Negotiated Authority in the Eighteenth-Century British Army', in *Britain's Soldiers: Rethinking War and Society, 1715-1815*, ed. Kevin Linch and Matthew McCormack (Liverpool, 2014), pp. 95–113.

7. West Sussex Record Office, Chichester, Goodwood MSS, 223/3/5, Wolfe to the Duke of Richmond, 25 Oct. 1755.

8. For an apparent example of the last of these reasons, see Peter Brock, 'The Spiritual Pilgrimage of Thomas Watson: From British Soldier to American Friend', *Quaker History*, 53 (1964), 83–4. For more on desertion, see below, Chapter 8.

9. See above, Chapter 5.

10. See, e.g., Bennet Cuthbertson, *Cuthbertson's System, for the Complete Interior Management and Oeconomy of a Battalion of Infantry* (Bristol, 1776), pp. 125, 127; Robert Hinde, *The Discipline of the Light Horse* (London, 1778), p. 99.

11. Roger Lamb, *Memoir of His Own Life* (Dublin, 1811), p. 68.

12. TNA, War Office Papers, Adjutant-General's Letter-book, WO 3/5, p. 49.

13. Ibid., WO 71/89, p. 86, William Naylor to Clinton, 17 April 1779. The fact that Naylor was court-martialled is a reminder that officers did not always accept soldiers' views on discipline.

14. BL, Liverpool Papers, Add. MS 38,214, fo, 323, Anon. to Jenkinson, 3 Nov. 1780.

15. Royal Artillery Institution, Woolwich, Royal Artillery Brigade Orders, 1777–8, MS 57, p. 57.

16. American Philosophical Society, Philadelphia, Thomas Sullivan Journal, pp. 253, 300, 406–7.

17. The British Army was (on paper) some 48,647 strong at the beginning of the War of Independence; in practice probably no more than 36,000 officers and men were actually serving: see Stephen Conway, *The British Isles and the War of American Independence* (Oxford, 2000), p. 13. Between Sept. 1775 and Sept. 1780 alone, more than 73,000 men were added: see BL, Liverpool Papers, Add. MS 38,344, fo. 162.

18. For short-term enlistments during the War of Independence, see notice signed by Lord Barrington, the Secretary at War, 16 Dec. 1775, TNA, War Office Papers, WO 26/29, p. 169.

19. Bodleian Library, Oxford, MS Eng. hist. g.4, p. 137, Order-book of Ensign Hamilton, 3rd Foot Guards, 17 April 1747.

20. National Records of Scotland, Edinburgh, Cuninghame of Thornton Muniments, GD 21/625, Garrison Orders at Louisbourg, 4 and 10 Sept. 1747.

21. National Army Museum, Chelsea, MS 6707-11, Notebook of Lieut. Hamilton, 17 April 1762.

22. We need to be careful not to exaggerate the role of landowners in the enlistment of soldiers for the Highland regiments; Highland landowners used their reputation as men of influence to persuade the government in London to allow them to raise new regiments, but they tried hard to spare their own estates from over-recruiting. See Andrew Mackillop, *'More Fruitful than the Soil': Army, Empire and the Scottish Highlands, 1715-1815* (East Linton, 2000); and Stephen Conway, 'Entrepreneurs and the Recruitment of the British Army in the War of American Independence, 1775-1783', in *War, Entrepreneurs and the State in Europe and the Mediterranean, 1300-1800*, ed. Jeff Fynn-Paul (Leiden, 2014), pp. 111–30.

23. For Highland soldiers and the pull of land in America, see Matthew Dziennik, *The Fatal Land: War, Empire and the Highland Soldier in British America* (Yale, 2015).

24. See, e.g., Centre of South Asian Studies, Cambridge, Cromartie Papers (photocopies), Eyre Coote to Lord Macleod, 31 Aug. 1780, for the unhealthy state of the 73rd Foot and the desire of many of its officers to return to Europe as quickly as possible.

25. Sylvia R. Frey, *The British Soldier in America: A Social History of Military Life in the Revolutionary Period* (Austin, TX, 1981), p. 74. For Highland mutinies as a particular phenomenon, see John Prebble, *Mutiny: Highland Regiments in Revolt, 1743-1804* (Harmondsworth, 1975).

26. National Records of Scotland, Leven and Melville Muniments, GD 26/9/520/14.

27. Paul E. Kopperman, 'The Stoppages Mutiny of 1763', *Western Pennsylvania Historical Magazine*, 69 (1986), 241–54; Way, 'Rebellion of the Regulars'; Brumwell, *Redcoats*, pp. 133–5.

28. BL, Bouquet Papers, Add. MS 21,635, fos. 6-8.

29. See above, Chapter 5.

30. See Robert Ellison to Henry Ellison, 28 June 1747, in 'The Correspondence of Colonel Robert Ellison of Hebern, 1733-48', ed. Edward Hughes, *Archaelogia Aeliana*, 4th series, 31 (1953), 17; National Records of Scotland, Hamilton-Dalrymple of North Berwick Muniments, GD 110/919/12, John Suttie to Sir Hew Dalrymple, 30 June 1747.

31. Brumwell, *Redcoats*, p. 128.

32. *The Correspondence of General Thomas Gage with the Secretaries of State and with the War Office and the Treasury, 1763-1775*, ed. Clarence E. Carter (2 vols, New Haven, CN, 1931), ii. 215.

33. Frey, *British Soldier in America*, pp. 73–4.

34. See above, Chapter 5.

35. Brumwell, *Redcoats*, p. 128.

36. See above, Chapter 5.

37. See above, Chapter 5.

38. TNA, War Office Papers, WO 71/88, pp. 324–34.

39. Frederick Mackenzie to his father, 29 June 1773, in *A British Fusilier in Revolutionary Boston: being the Diary of Lieutenant Frederick Mackenzie, Adjutant of the Royal Welch Fusiliers, January 5-April 30, 1775, with a Letter describing His Voyage to America*, ed. Allen French (Cambridge, MA, 1926), p. 19.

40. See Kathryn Preyer, 'Penal Measures in the American Colonies: An Overview', *American Journal of Legal History*, 26 (1982), 326–53. See also, for the study of a particular colony, Douglas Greenberg, *Crime and Law Enforcement in the Colony of New York, 1691-1776* (Ithica, NY, 1974).

41. Newberry Library, Chicago, Case MS °E 199, M 36 1755, Anon. Diary of the French and Indian War, 24 and 28 Oct. 1755.

42. 'Extracts from Gibson Clough's Journal', ed. B.F. Brown, *Historical Collections of the Essex Institute*, 3 (1861), 104.

43. For punishment in the British service, see Frey, *British Soldier in America*, Ch. 4. For British general courts martial sentences from the American war period, see TNA, War Office Papers, WO 71/80-95.

44. TNA, War Office Papers, WO 71/88, p. 350.

45. See, e.g., *Rules and Articles for the Better Government of His Majesty's . . . Forces* (London, 1778), pp. 39–43.

46. For regimental courts martial, see Glen Steppler, 'British Military Law, Discipline and the Conduct of Regimental Courts Martial in the Later Eighteenth Century', *English Historical Review*, 102 (1987), 859–87.

47. See above, Chapter 5.

48. Royal Artillery Institution, Brigade Order-Book, 1777–8, MS 57, p. 103.

49. TNA, War Office Papers, WO 36/2, fo. 34.

50. See, e.g., the order-book entry of Dec. 5, 1775, in *The Kemble Papers*, I (New York, 1884), p. 269; and Library of Congress, Washington, DC, Washington Papers, Series 6B, vol. I, Captured British Order-book, 21 June 1777.

51. William L. Clements Library, Ann Arbor, MI, General Order-book of the forces under Howe, 23 and 31 Aug., 6 Sept. 1776. It should be said that some of his subordinates criticized Howe for not carrying out his threatened punishments: see, e.g., *A Prime Minister and His Son from the Correspondence of the Third Earl of Bute and Lt. General the Hon. Charles Stuart, K.B.*, ed. E. Stuart Wortley (London, 1925), pp. 99, 116.

52. BL, Mackenzie Papers, Add. MS 39,190, fo. 209.

53. See, e.g., William L. Clements Library, Clinton Papers, Order of 15 Aug. 1780.

54. For an insight into the scope provided by lesser courts martial, see TNA, War Office Papers, WO 72/8, Stephen Payne Adye (deputy judge advocate in America) to Charles Gould (the judge-advocate general), 20 May 1778.

55. Royal Artillery Institution, Royal Artillery Brigade Orders, 1777–8, MS 57, pp. 102, 140, 159–60, 184, 185, 190, 199.

56. *John Pebbles' American War: The Diary of a Scottish Grenadier, 1776-1782*, ed. Ira D. Gruber (Mechanicsburg, PA, 1998), p. 481.

57. William L. Clements Library, Clinton Papers, Ferguson's report, Nov. 1779.

58. TNA, War Office Papers, WO 71/82, p. 231.

59. Douglas Hay, 'Property, Authority and the Criminal Law', in Douglas Hay, Peter Linebaugh, John J. Rule, E.P. Thompson and Cal Winslow, *Albion's Fatal Tree: Crime and Society in Eighteenth-Century England* (Harmondsworth, 1977), pp. 17–63. Hay's argument, it should be said, set off a lively debate: see, e.g., John Langbein, 'Albion's Fatal Flaws', *Past & Present*, 98 (1983), 96–120; Peter King, 'Decision-Makers and Decision-Making in the English Criminal Law, 1750-1800', *Historical Journal*, 27 (1984), 27–54; Peter Linebaugh, '(Marxist) Social History

and (Conservative) Legal History: A Reply to Professor Langbein', *New York University Law Review*, 60 (1985), 212–43. Peter King returns to the issue in his *Crime, Justice and Discretion in England, 1740-1820* (Oxford, 2000).

60. William L. Clements Library, Order-book, Cornwallis's forces, 23 April, 14, 19, 20, 23, 30 May 1781; Library of Congress, British Order-book, Virginia, 4 June 1781; Boston Public Library, Boston, MA, MS qAm 1995, Order-book of Capt. John Hawthorn, Eightieth Foot, 4 July 1781.

61. Historical Society of Pennsylvania, Philadelphia, Sir John Wrottesley's Notebook.

62. Clwyd Archives, Haverfordwest, Gwynne Letters, D/CT/271.

63. BL, Napier Family Papers, Add. MS 49,092, fo. 38.

64. New York State Library, Albany, MS 6744, Order-book, Howe's army, 16 March 1777.

65. Library of Congress, British Order-book, Virginia, 1 and 2 June 1781.

66. William L. Clements Library, 47th Foot Order-book (typescript copy), 7 Aug. 1777.

67. Historical Society of Pennsylvania, 7th Foot Order-book, 21 June 1778.

68. William L. Clements Library, Order-book of the forces under Howe, 29 June 1776.

69. Ibid., 47th Foot Order-book (typescript copy), 18 July 1777.

70. 'A British Orderly Book, 1780-1781', ed. A.R. Newsome, *North Carolina Historical Review*, 9 (1932), 296.

71. William L. Clements Library, Clinton Papers, memo. of conversation, 7 Feb. 1776.

72. National Army Museum, 5904/175, 14th Foot Order-book, 7 June 1776.

73. William L. Clements Library, Order-book of the forces under Howe, 29 June 1776.

74. Isle of Cana, Campbell of Inverneil Papers, 'General Orders on Board the Phoenix Man of War. 22d. December 1778', Campbell's Journal of an Expedition against the Rebels of Georgia, p. 20.

75. 'A British Orderly Book', ed. Newsome, 296.

76. William L. Clements Library, Order-book of Cornwallis's forces, 22 Feb. 1781.

77. Isle of Cana, Campbell of Inverneil Papers, 'General Orders on Board the Phoenix Man of War. 22d. December 1778', Campbell's Journal, p. 20.

78. For a modern and more wide-ranging comparison, see John Childs, 'The Army and the State in Britain and Germany during the Eighteenth Century', in *Rethinking Leviathan: The Eighteenth-Century State in Britain and Germany*, ed. John Brewer and Eckhart Hellmuth (Oxford, 1999), pp. 53–70.

79. Johan Conrad Döhla, *A Hessian Diary of the American Revolution*, ed. and trans. Bruce E. Burgoyne (Norman, OK, 1990), pp. 112, 202.

80. William L. Clements Library, Clinton Papers, Charles Cathcart to Clinton, 5 Nov. 1777.

81. *Revolution in America: Confidential Letters and Journals 1776-1784 of Adjutant General Major Baurmeister of the Hessian Forces*, ed. Bernhard A. Uhlendorf (New Brunswick, NJ, 1957), p. 46.

Chapter 7

1. Piers Mackesy, *The Coward of Minden: The Affair of Lord George Sackville* (Stroud, 1979), p. 44.

2. Historical Manuscripts Commission, *Hastings MSS* (4 vols, London, 1928–47), iii. 179.

3. W.H. Wilkin, *Some British Soldiers in America* (London, 1914), p. 227 (letter of Lt. William Hale, 45th Foot, 30 Aug. 1777).

4. See Adrienne Mayor, *The Amazons: Lives and Legends of Warrior Women Across the Ancient World* (Princeton, 2014).

5. Selekou Olympia, 'Amazon Company', in *Encyclopaedia of the Hellenic World: Black Sea* (Athens, 2008).

6. See Marian Füssel, 'Between Dissimulation and Sensation: Female Soldiers in Eighteenth-Century Warfare', *Journal for Eighteenth-century Studies*, 41 (2018), 527–42.

7. 'A Naval Diary of the Seven Years War', ed. J.C. Dickinson, *Transactions of the Cumberland and Westmorland Antiquarian and Archaeological Society*, new series, 38 (1938), 241.

8. *Scots Magazine*, 21 (1759), 328.

9. The painting is reproduced in *The Oxford Illustrated History of the British Army*, ed. David Chandler and Ian Beckett (Oxford, 1994), facing p. 111.

10. Huntington Library, San Marino, CA, MS 54457, vol. 6, Diary of John Marsh, 6 May 1776.

11. Printed in Linda Colley, *Britons: Forging the Nation, 1707-1837* (New Haven, CT, 1992), p. 243, where it is dated 'c.1770'. Internal evidence, particularly the uniforms, suggests that it was produced between 1778 and 1783.

12. Dror Wahrman, '*Percy*'s Prologue: From Gender Play to Gender Panic in Eighteenth-Century England', *Past & Present*, 159 (1998), 113–60.

13. Jennine Hurl-Eamon, *Marriage and the British Army in the Long Eighteenth Century: 'The Girl I Left Behind Me'* (Oxford, 2014), Ch. 1, examines the army's anti-marriage policies, but notes their uneven and inconsistent application.

14. BL, Grant Papers, Add. MS 25411, fo. 231, Penuel Grant to Robert Grant of Tomore, 17 Feb. 1757.

15. Bedfordshire and Luton Archives Service, Bedford, Russell Papers, box 769, Seaford to [Bedford?], 12 Oct. 1745.

16. William Salt Library, Stafford, Congreve Papers, S MS 522, Gower to [William Congreve], 19 Nov. 1745; S MS 47/18/9, [Congreve] to [Gower], 31 Jan. 1746.

17. The most detailed and authoritative account is provided in Hurl-Eamon, *Marriage and the British Army*, esp. Ch. 5.

18. *Dublin Journal*, 6–8 July 1746.

19. London Metropolitan Archives, Westminster Sessions Papers, WJ/SP/1742/04/02, Poor Law examination, 1 May 1742.

20. *Poor Law Records of Mid Sussex, 1601–1835*, ed. Norma Pilbeam and Ian Nelson (Lewes, 2001), p. 154.

21. Hurl-Eamon, *Marriage and the British Army*, Ch. 5 considers separation.

22. BL, Sutton Court Collection, MSS Eur. F 128/23, Andrienne Carnac to John Carnac, 14 Feb. 1760.

23. Ibid., Dropmore Papers, Add. MS 69382, fo. 93.

24. John Rylands Library, Manchester, Bagshawe of Ford Muniments, BAG 2/2/187, Martha Forde to Samuel Bagshawe, 6 July 1757.

25. BL, Blenheim Papers, Add. MS 61667, fo. 1.

26. Ibid., fo. 51, 23 Sept. 1758.

27. Huntington Library, Agnew Letters, HM 2929, Agnew to Elizabeth Agnew, 7 May [1775].

28. *Correspondence of Emily, Duchess of Leinster*, ed. Brian Fitzgerald (3 vols, Dublin, 1949–57), iii. 226.

29. Staffordshire Record Office, Stafford, Congreve Papers, D 1057/M/F/26, Congreve to Congreve, 6 May 1776.

30. BL, Dropmore Papers, Add MS 69382, fo. 135, Mary Russell to Charles Russell, 21 July 1743.

31. See Stephen Brumwell, *Redcoats: The British Soldier and War in the Americas, 1755–1763* (Cambridge, 2002), pp. 120–2.

32. Mackesy, *Coward of Minden*, pp. 254–8.

33. In his contemporaneous ballad 'Battle of the Kegs'.

34. National Library of Scotland, Edinburgh, Robertson-MacDonald Papers, MS 3945, esp. fos. 28, 46, 52 and, for the quotation, from a letter of 10 June 1780, fo. 61.

35. Northumberland Archives, Newcastle upon Tyne, Ridley of Blagden Papers, ZRI 30/4a.

36. National Records of Scotland, Edinburgh, Cuninghame of Thornton Muniments, GD 21/629/7, letter of 19 June 1781.

37. *Baroness von Riedesel and the American Revolution: Journal and Correspondence of a Tour of Duty, 1776-1783*, ed. Marvin L. Brown Jr. (Chapel Hill, NC, 1985), p. 52.

38. Bedfordshire and Luton Archives Service, Lucas of Wrest Park Papers, L 30/12/17/14, Carr Clerke to Lord Polwarth, 10 Sept. 1777.

39. *Gunner at Large: The Diary of James Wood, RA, 1746-1765*, ed. Rex Whitworth (London, 1988), p. 32.

40. National Records of Scotland, Rose of Kilravock Muniments, GD 125/22/17/11, 'Return of the Honable Colonel Commandant Simon Frasers Reg^{t}', 17 Oct. 1757.

41. Serena Zabin, *The Boston Massacre: A Family History* (New York, 2020), p. 97.

42. J.W. Jackson, *With the British Army in Philadelphia* (San Rafael, CA, 1979), p. 83.

43. Historical Society of Pennsylvania, Philadelphia, Dreer Collection, Daniel Weir letter-book, pp. 8–10, 81.

44. TNA, War Office Papers, WO 60/26, Pt. II, 'Women, 44 Regim^{t} on board the Baltic Merch^{t}', return made at New York, but covering 29 May–24 Aug. 1778.

45. Ibid., British Army Headquarters Papers, PRO 30/55/32, 3713, 'Return of the Number of Men, Women and Children, of the British and Foreign Regiments, New Levies and Civil Departments, Victualed at New York and the Out Posts', 20 Aug. 1781.

46. Ibid., War Office Papers, WO 4/96, p. 364.

47. Historical Society of Pennsylvania, Dreer Collection, Daniel Weir Letter-book, p. 20.

48. TNA, Admiralty Papers, ADM 110/3, fo. 89, victualling board to Thomas Corbett, 17 Dec. 1742.

49. New-York Historical Society, New York City, Joseph Reed Papers, Journal of John Miller, 17 Nov. 1777.

50. William L. Clements Library, Ann Arbor, MI, Clinton Papers, Ferguson's 'Proposed Plan', filed under Nov. 1779.

51. 'A British Orderly Book, 1780-1781', ed. A.R. Newsome, *North Carolina Historical Review*, 9 (1932), 378.

52. TNA, War Office Papers, WO 71/80, p. 358.

53. Ibid., WO 71/81, pp. 393–400.

54. Ibid., WO 71/82, pp. 203–10.

55. Bedfordshire and Luton Archives Service, Lucas of Wrest Park Papers, L 30/12/17/3, Clerke to Polwarth, 13 July 1776.

56. Roger Lamb, *An Original and Authentic Journal of Occurrences during the Late American War* (Dublin, 1809), p. 143.

57. Northumberland Archives, Ridley of Blagden Papers, ZRI 30/4a.

58. See Sylvia R. Frey, *The British Soldier in America: A Social History of Military Life in the Revolutionary Period* (Austin, TX, 1981), p. 20.

59. Peter Way, 'Venus and Mars: Women and the British-American Army in the Seven Years War', in *Britain and America Go to War: The Impact of War and Warfare in Anglo-America, 1754-1815*, ed. Julie Flavell and Stephen Conway (Gainesville, FL, 2004), p. 52.

60. National Library of Scotland, Letters to Margaret Mercer, Acc 5396/2, 18 Jan. [1757].

61. Hampshire Record Office, Winchester, Banbury Papers, IM 44/14/2 and 4, Barrington to Lady Wallingford, 10 Jan. 1760, Bedford to Lady Wallingford, 7 Dec. 1760.

62. National Records of Scotland, Miscellaneous Gifts and Deposits, GD 1/481/13, C. Power to Patrick Boyle, 27 Aug. 1779.

63. *The History of Parliament: The Commons, 1754-1790*, ed. Sir Lewis Namier and John Brooke (3 vols, London, 1964), ii. 168–9.

Chapter 8

1. York City Archives, Acc. 163, Dr William White's Diary, entry of 12 May 1782.

2. National Records of Scotland, Edinburgh, Broughton and Cally Muniments, GD 10/1421/7/338, letter from an unnamed army officer at St Lucia, 15 July 1780.

3. *The Deserted Village: The Diary of an Oxfordshire Rector, James Newton of Nuneham Courtenay, 1736-1786*, ed. Gavin Hannah (Stroud, 1992), p. 120.

4. Newberry Library, Chicago, Case MS°E199, Anon. Diary of the French and Indian War, 1755–8.

5. Berkshire Record Office, Reading, Downshire Papers, D/ED 037, 'Casualtys in the Royal Fuz[rs] from 31st March 1756'.

6. See, e.g., BL, Buckinghamshire Papers, Add. MS 40178, fo. 29, Nugent Temple to Thomas Townshend, 8 Nov. 1782.

7. M.S. Anderson, *War and Society in Europe of the Old Regime, 1618-1789* (London, 1988), p. 165.

8. 'The Letters of Captain Nicholas Delacherois, 9ᵗʰ Regiment', ed. S.P.G. Ward, *Journal of the Society for Army Historical Research*, 51 (1973), 12.

9. See above, Chapter 3.

10. West Sussex Record Office, Chichester, Goodwood MS 223/16, Wolfe to the Duke of Richmond, 10 July 1757.

11. *The Official Diary of Lieutenant-General Adam Williamson Deputy-Lieutenant of the Tower of London, 1722-1747*, ed. John Charles Fox (London, 1912), p. 117.

12. TNA, War Office Papers, WO 71/86, pp. 84–91.

13. Ibid., WO 71/90, pp. 26–34.

14. See above, Chapter 6.

15. See above, Chapter 6.

16. TNA, State Papers Ireland, SP 63/ 447, fo. 25.

17. Ibid., SP 63/453, fo. 172.

18. See, e.g., the comments of Francis Downman, an artillery officer, on 31 Aug. 1777: *The Services of Lieut.-Colonel Francis Downman, RA, in France, North America and the West Indies, Between the Years 1758 and 1784*, ed. F.A. Whinyates (Woolwich, 1898), p. 31.

19. BL, Buckinghamshire Papers, Add. MS 40178, fo. 29, Nugent Temple to Thomas Townshend, 8 Nov. 1782.

20. National Library of Scotland, Edinburgh, Erskine Murray Papers, MS 5075, fo. 60, Mungo Campbell to the lord justice clerk, 25 May 1756.

21. *Colonel Samuel Bagshawe and the Army of George II, 1731-1762*, ed. Alan J. Guy (London, 1990), p. 80.

22. BL, Liverpool Papers, Add. MS 38217, fo. 50, Dashwood to Charles Jenkinson, 25 Sept. 1781.

23. Berkshire Record Office, Downshire Papers, D/ED 037, 'Casualtys in the Royal Fuzʳˢ from 31ˢᵗ March 1756'.

24. Corporation of London Record Office, Miscellaneous MSS, box 206, items 65 and 95, Sir John Langham's Charity applications.

25. TNA, War Office Papers, WO 4/93, p. 35.

26. Ibid., WO 1/10, fo. 36, Howe to Kennedy, 3 Dec. 1776.

27. West Sussex Record Office, Chichester, Add. MS 12091, Diary of John Tompkins, 16 Nov. 1776.

28. TNA, War Office Papers, WO 1/10, fo. 2, Howe to Lord Barrington, 13 Aug. 1776.

29. Ibid., WO 4/105, p. 80, Charles Jenkinson to the President, treasurers and governors of Bethlehem Hospital, 29 Jan. 1779.

30. Nottingham University Library, Galway Collection, Monckton Papers, GaM 98, Albemarle to Robert Monckton, 6 Oct. 1762.

31. See, e.g., Essex Record Office, Chelmsford, Round MSS, D/DRg 4/30, Thomas Falconer to Charles Gray, 9 Aug. 1775.

32. *With Burgoyne from Quebec: An Account of Life in Quebec and of the Famous Battle at Saratoga*, ed. Sydney Jackman (Toronto, 1963), p. 184.

33. TNA, War Office Papers, WO 71/82, pp. 158–88

34. Ibid., pp. 292–302.

35. For Percy's paying his debt, see above, Chapter 5.

36. TNA, War Office Papers, WO 55/1537, fos. 63 and 139, Samuel Cleaveland to Viscount Townshend, 10 May 1776, Seymour to Cleaveland, 15 Dec. 1775.

37. Ballindalloch Castle, Grantown-on-Spey, Macpherson Grant Papers, bundle 203, John McPherson to John McPherson, 27 Dec. 1781.

38. John Almon, *The Remembrancer; or Impartial Repository of Public Events*, i (1775), 262–4.

39. TNA, State Papers Ireland, SP 63/438, fo. 115, Gen. John Irwine to Earl Harcourt, 1 Sept. 1775.

40. Ibid., SP 67/15, fo. 52, Rochford to Harcourt, 6 Feb. 1775.

41. See, e.g., TNA, War Office Papers, WO 4/94, p. 374, Barrington to Ensign James Benson Tulhill, 1 Oct. 1775. Tulhill was in O'Hara's Corps, a unit that was then serving in Senegal.

42. Derbyshire Record Office, Matlock, Wilmot-Horton of Osmaston and Catton Papers, D 1355/C 717, William Yonge to the lord lieutenant, 16 April 1746.

43. [Samuel Bever,] *The Cadet: A Military Treatise* (2nd edn., London, 1762), pp. 241–3.

44. See William L. Clements Library, Ann Arbor, MI, Gage Papers, Hamilton's memorial of 22 June 1775; BL, Barrington Papers, Add. MS 73550, Barrington to Gage, 22 June 1775.

45. William L. Clements Library, Gage Papers, Laurie to George Clerk, 6 June 1775; Glasgow University Library, Bannerman MSS, Laurie to [John Roebuck,] 23 June 1775.

46. William L. Clements Library, Gage Papers, Gibbons to Lt.-Col. James Agnew, 24 July 1775.

47. TNA, Colonial Office Papers, CO 5/115, fo. 153.

48. Derbyshire Record Office, Wilmot-Horton of Osmaston and Catton Papers, D 1355/C 1642, Bernard's memorial, n.d., but Sept. 1754.

49. Trinity College Dublin, Conolly Papers, MS 3974-84/452, Morris to Howe, 17 Feb. 1777.

50. William L. Clements Library, Germain Papers, Morris to Germain, 29 Dec. [1775.]

51. Hampshire Record Office, Winchester, Banbury Papers, Letter-book of Thomas Woods Knollis, 1 M44/66, fo. 32, Knollis to his brother Samuel, 29 June 1776.

52. John Rylands Library, Manchester, Bagshawe of Ford Muniments, BAG 2/2/83, Carnac to Samuel Bagshawe, 4 March 1758.

53. TNA, War Office Papers, WO 34/111, fos. 16 (Royal Highland Immigrants) and 27 (Volunteers of Ireland).

54. BL, Loudoun Papers, Add. MS 44069, fo. 20, 'List of Officers with their Ranks at home and the Ranks proposed for them in the Service of the King of Portugal'.

55. Ibid., Pelham Papers, Add. MS 33126, fo. 178, Pelham to his father, Oct./Nov. 1775.

56. Library of Congress, Washington, DC, Journal of Christopher French, 19 Dec. 1776.

57. Nottingham University Library, Newcastle of Clumber MSS, NeC 938.

58. *Caledonian Mercury*, 24 Jan. 1746.

59. *Military Affairs in North America, 1748-1765: Selected Documents from the Cumberland Papers in Windsor Castle*, ed. Stanley Pargellis (Hamden, CN, 1969), p. 232.

60. *The Diary of Corporal Todd, 1745-1762*, ed. Andrew Cormack and Alan Jones (Stroud, 2001), p. 229.

61. Devon Record Office, Exeter, Bedford Papers, L 1258/M/55/M, bundle 1, Lt-Col John Mompesson to the Duke of Bedford, 23 May 1759.

62. TNA, War Office Papers, WO 34/111, fo. 27.

63. See Andrew Cormack, *'These Meritorious Objects of the Royal Bounty': The Chelsea Out-Pensioners in the Early Eighteenth Century* (London, 2017).

64. See Stephen Brumwell, *Redcoats: The British Soldier and War in the Americas, 1755-1763* (Cambridge, 2002), pp. 298–9.

65. Roger Lamb, *Memoirs of His Own Life* (Dublin, 1811), p. 289.

66. Richard Connors, 'Parliament and Poverty in Mid-Eighteenth-Century England', *Parliamentary History*, 21 (2002), 210–11.

67. See, e.g., *Oxford Council Acts, 1752-1801*, ed. M.G. Hobson (Oxford, 1962), pp. 144–5.

68. See, e.g., TNA, Audit Office Papers, Loyalist Claims Commission, AO 12/27, fos. 93-4, claim of Anthony Wallister.

69. Ibid., AO 12/32, fo. 29, claim of John Smith.

70. Corporation of London Record Office, Sir John Langham Charity Papers, Miscellaneous MSS, box 206, items 57 and 91.

71. University College London, Bentham MSS, box lxxxvii, fo. 71, essay on 'Indirect Legislation'.

72. TNA, War Office Papers, WO 1/995, Stanley to Barrington, 21 Dec. 1776.

73. See, e.g., J.M. Beattie, 'The Pattern of Crime in England, 1660-1800', *Past & Present*, 62 (1974), 47–95; and the same author's *Crime and the Courts in England, 1660-1800* (Oxford, 1986), pp. 213–35.

74. See Nicholas Rogers, 'Confronting the Crime Wave: The Debate over Social Reform and Regulation, 1749-1753', in *Stilling the Grumbling Hive: The Response to Social and Economic Problems in England, 1689-1750*, ed. Lee Davison et al. (Stroud, 1992), pp. 77–98.

75. 'Leicester House Politics, 1750-60, from the Papers of John, Second Earl of Egmont', ed. Aubrey Newman, Royal Historical Society, *Camden Miscellany*, 23 (1969), 192.

76. *Gentleman's Magazine*, 33 (1763), 16–17.

77. Annette M. Smith, *Jacobite Estates of the Forty-Five* (Edinburgh, 1982), pp. 145–56.

78. Reproduced in Brumwell, *Redcoats*, p. 291.

79. Oliver Goldsmith, *The Citizen of the World; or, Letters from a Chinese Philosopher, Residing in London, to His Friend in the East* (London, 1762), letter cxix.

Further Reading

This book, as a mere glance at the notes will show, has drawn extensively on primary materials – letters, journals, diaries, reports, order-books, memorials and petitions and court-martial proceedings – which were produced at the time. Many are still in unpublished form; they exist as little-read manuscripts in archives and libraries. As the manuscript sources are not always easy to access, I have excluded them from this essay, though anyone keen to explore them should be able to use my notes as a starting point – the first reference in each chapter to a repository (such as the National Records of Scotland or the Berkshire Record Office) notes where these are located (in the first instance, Edinburgh; in the last, Reading).

Other primary sources used in the book are in print, either because they were published during the period we are studying (such as pamphlets and treatises) or they were published subsequently, from manuscript materials which were arranged and annotated by an editor (as with some correspondence, journals, diaries, order-books and so on). I refer to some published primary sources at the end of this essay, on the basis that they should be easier to access for the general reader than is archival material and in the hope that they will prove of interest to anyone wanting to begin their own research on the eighteenth-century army. Most of this brief account, however, focuses on secondary sources – books, articles and essays written by historians about our subject or aspects of it. The approach that these historians take is in all cases different from mine – often very different – which is why I recommend reading them. They cover ground I omit or touch upon only briefly.

To put the army in context, readers might want to find out more about soldiers that this book chose not to include. J.R. Western's *The English Militia in the Eighteenth Century: The Story of a Political Issue, 1660-1802* (London, 1965), is an impressive – and still unsurpassed – account of the militia in England and Wales. Volunteers – amateur soldiers who defended their own communities during wartime emergencies – are covered in Glenn

Steppler, *Britons to Arms: The Story of the Volunteer Soldier* (Stroud, 1992). The most important contingent of the German auxiliary troops who fought alongside the British Army in the American War of Independence receives thorough analysis in Rodney Atwood's exemplary *The Hessians: Mercenaries from Hessen-Kassel in the American Revolution* (Cambridge, 1980). The East India Company's army is the main concern of T.A. Heathcote, *The Military in British India: The Development of British Land Forces in South Asia, 1600-1947* (Manchester, 1995). Comparisons between British and German armies and their relationship to their respective states is the subject of an illuminating essay by John Childs in *Rethinking Leviathan: The Eighteenth-Century State in Britain and Germany*, ed. John Brewer and Eckhart Hellmuth (Oxford, 1999), pp. 53–70. Christopher Duffy's book on *The Military Experience in the Age of Reason* (London, 1987), puts the British Army in a proper European context, while Ilya Berkovich, *Motivation in War: The Experience of Common Soldiers in Old-Regime Europe* (Cambridge, 2017) shows conclusively how much British soldiers shared with soldiers in other European armies.

A small army of scholars has written on the British Army itself. I mention here merely a sample of a substantial literature. Inescapable is Sir John Fortescue, *History of the British Army* (13 vols, London, 1899–1930). It now seems very old-fashioned and largely concentrates on campaigns and battles, but Fortescue's study remains valuable in many ways. The same is true of Charles Clode, *The Military Forces of the Crown: Their Administration and Government* (2 vols, London, 1869); not an easy read, but fundamental to anyone wishing to come to grips with the eighteenth-century British Army. More recent is H.C.B. Rogers, *The British Army of the Eighteenth Century* (London, 1977). Mention should also be made of some of the collections of essays published in the last few years, which together provide a fresh picture of the army – *Soldiering in Britain and Ireland, 1750-1850*, ed. Catriona Kennedy and Matthew McCormack (Basingstoke, 2013) and *Britain's Soldiers: Rethinking War and Society, 1715-1815* (Liverpool, 2014) are particularly rich. A brief but shrewd analysis of the army appears in Alan J. Guy's essay on 'The Army of the Georges, 1714-1783', in *The Oxford Illustrated History of the British Army*, ed. David Chandler and Ian Beckett (Oxford, 1994).

For the different aspects of the army in our period, I found the following works especially helpful. On the army's training, J.A. Houlding, *Fit *for Service: The Training of the British Army, 1715-1795* (Oxford, 1981) is magnificent – and much more informative about the army in general than its title suggests. For the administration of the army and the role of its officers, Alan J. Guy, *Oeconomy and Discipline: Officership and Administration in the British Army, 1714-1763* (Manchester, 1985) is invaluable and a brilliant guide to tortuous matters such as army finance. Glen Steppler, 'British Military Law, Discipline and the Conduct of Regimental Courts Martial in the Later Eighteenth Century', *English Historical Review*, 102 (1987), 859–87, makes excellent use of a little-used source, regimental courts-martial records. On the specific subject of promotion, see the article by Eric Robson, 'Purchase and Promotion in the British Army in the Eighteenth Century', *History*, 36 (1951). Tony Hayter, *The Army and the Crowd in Mid-Georgian England* (London, 1978), rigorously analyses the army's support for the civil power in putting down riots and disturbances. The army as a consumer of goods and services is the focus of Gordon Bannerman's meticulous study, *Merchants and the Military in Eighteenth-Century Britain: British Army Contracts and Domestic Supply, 1739-1763* (London, 2015). Hannah Smith has ploughed new ground with her study of 'The Army, Provincial Urban Communities and Loyalist Cultures in England, *c.*1714-50', *Journal of Early Modern History*, 15 (2011), 139–58, which explores the part the army played in bolstering and encouraging support for the government; see also her essay on 'The Hanoverian Succession and the Politicisation of the British Army', in *The Hanoverian Succession: Dynastic Politics and Monarchical Culture*, ed. Andreas Gestrich and Michael Schaich (Aldershot, 2015), pp. 207–26. Peter Way has published a series of insightful articles and essays on the common soldier as a working man: see particularly his 'Class and the Common Soldier in the Seven Years War', *Labor History*, 44 (2003), 455–81 and 'Rebellion of the Regulars: Working Soldiers and the Mutiny of 1763-1764', *William & Mary Quarterly*, 3rd series, 57 (2000), 761–92. Women's role in the army is covered authoritatively in Jennine Hurl Eamon, *Marriage and the British Army in the Long Eighteenth Century: 'The Girl I left Behind Me'* (Oxford, 2014). Erica Charters, 'The Caring Fiscal-Military State during the Seven Years War, 1756-1763', *Historical Journal*, 52 (2009), 921–41, demonstrates the efforts made to preserve the lives of soldiers in one particular conflict.

The army in different settings is the subject of many fine works. The army in Ireland receives illuminating coverage in Charles Ivar McGrath, *Ireland*

and Empire, 1692-1770 (London, 2012), Chapters 4–6 and Alan J. Guy's chapter on 'The Irish Military Establishment, 1660-1776', in *A Military History of Ireland*, ed. Thomas Bartlett and Keith Jeffery (Cambridge, 1996). Victoria Henshaw, *Scotland and the British Army: Defending the Union* (London, 2014) looks at the army in Scotland; Andrew Mackillop, *'More Fruitful than the Soil': Army, Empire and the Scottish Highlands, 1715-1815* (East Linton, 2000) and Matthew Dzennik, *The Fatal Land: War, Empire and the Highland Soldier in British America* (Yale, 2015) consider Scottish soldiers in the British Empire. The disastrous West Indian campaigns of the British Army in the war against Spain that began in 1739 and merged into the War of the Austrian Succession is the subject of Richard Harding's insightful *Amphibious Warfare in the Eighteenth Century: The British Expedition to the West Indies, 1740-1742* (Woodbridge, 1991). In the absence of a monograph on the army's European campaigns in the War of the Austrian Succession, we are reliant on Rex Whitworth's not entirely dependable biography of *William Augustus, Duke of Cumberland* (London, 1992). M.S. Anderson, *The War of the Austrian Succession, 1740-1748* (London, 1995), has some interesting material on the armies involved, including the British, in Chapter 2.

Stephen Brumwell, *Redcoats: The British Soldier and War in the Americas, 1755-1763* (Cambridge, 2002) provides an insightful analysis of the army in North America and the West Indies during the Seven Years War. For the European campaigns of the same conflict, Sir Reginald Savory, *His Britannic Majesty's Army in Germany during the Seven Years War* (Oxford, 1966) remains useful, though see also Piers Mackesy, *The Coward of Minden: The Affair of Lord George Sackville* (London, 1979), which focuses in a very measured way on one notorious episode. The British Army in North America after the Seven Years War is covered in a brilliant book by a pioneer of the new military history, John Shy, *Toward Lexington: The Role of the British Army in the Coming of the Revolution* (Princeton, 1965). See also, for different and interesting interpretations, Michael N. McConnell, *Army and Empire: British Soldiers on the American Frontier, 1758-1775* (Lincoln, NB, 2004) and Sylvia R. Frey, *The British Soldier in America: A Social History of Military Life in the Revolutionary Period* (Austin, TX, 1981). Matthew Spring, *With Zeal and Bayonets Only: The British Army on Campaign in North America, 1775-1783* (Norman, OK, 2008), puts the spotlight on the War of Independence.

There is no shortage of revealing printed primary sources, which give readers the chance to form their own judgements based on first-hand evidence. Treatises and pamphlets give us insights into contemporary systems and attitudes. For systems, see, for example, Humphrey Bland, *A Treatise of Military Discipline* (London and Dublin, 1727); Samuel Bever's *The Cadet: A Military Treatise* (2nd edn., London, 1762); Bennet Cuthbertson's *Cuthbertson's System, for the Complete Interior Management and Oeconomy of a Battalion of Infantry* (Bristol, 1776); and John Williamson's *A Treatise of Military Finance* (London, 1782). For attitudes, see *Observations on the Present State of England* (London, 1773), an impassioned plea, almost certainly written by a junior officer, for an improvement in the pay of subalterns.

Among the many published collections of correspondence, the following give a good flavour of the army and its soldiers – *Colonel Samuel Bagshawe and the Army of George II, 1731-1762*, ed. Alan J. Guy (London, 1990); *The Albemarle Papers*, ed. Charles Sanford Terry (2 vols, Aberdeen, 1902); *Military Affairs in North America, 1748-1765: Selected Documents from the Cumberland Papers in Windsor Castle*, ed. Stanley Pargellis (Hamden, CN, 1969); *The Life and Letters of James Wolfe* (London, 1909) and *The Correspondence of General Thomas Gage*, ed. Clarence E. Carter (2 vols, Cambridge, MA, 1931–4). *The Papers of Henry Bouquet*, ed. S.K. Stevens et al (6 vols, Harrisburg, PA, 1972–94) covers the Seven Years War and its aftermath in North America, a period when the army adapted to local conditions with much success.

'The Letters of Captain Nicholas Delacherois, 9th Regiment', ed. S.P.G. Ward, *Journal of the Society for Army Historical Research*, 51 (1973), reveal much about different aspects of a junior officer's life; see also *'To Mr Davenport': being Letters of Major Richard Davenport (1719-1760) to his Brother*, ed. C.W. Frearson (London, 1968). Order-books, which listed regimental, brigade and general orders, are also available in print: see, for instance, the order-book of British forces in Germany, 1758, in 'Manuscripts of M.L.S. Clements', Historical Manuscripts Commission, *Manuscripts in Various Collections* (8 vols, London, 1901–14), viii; and 'A British Orderly Book, 1780-1781', *North Carolina Historical Review*, ix (1932), 57–78, 163–86, 273–98, 366–92. For some particularly fine military diaries, written by lower-ranking officers, see *The American Journals of Lieutenant John Enys*, ed. Elizabeth Cometti (Syracuse, NY, 1976); *Diary of Frederick Mackenzie*

(2 vols, Cambridge, MA, 1930) and *John Peebles' American War: The Diary of a Scottish Grenadier, 1776-1782*, ed. Ira D. Gruber (Mechanicsburg, PA, 1998).

The rank and file, inevitably, is less well covered; compared with their officers, very few common soldiers left any record of their activities and thoughts. One way of filling the gap is to engage with soldiers' songs and ballads; a selection is reproduced in a very useful compilation, *The Rambling Soldier*, ed. Roy Palmer (Gloucester, 1985). We do have some first-hand testimony written by the lower ranks, however. *Gunner at Large: The Diary of James Wood, RA, 1746-1765*, ed. Rex Whitworth (London, 1988) tells us about the experiences of an artilleryman who was promoted to officer status. Roger Lamb's *Original and Authentic Journal of Occurrences during the Late America War* (Dublin, 1809) and *Memoirs of His Own Life* (Dublin, 1811) are undoubtedly helpful, but as with all biographical accounts published during the author's lifetime, not necessarily reliable in every detail. For the recorded thoughts of a member of the rank and file, which remained unpublished until recently and seems authentic in all regards, even in its linguistic oddities, we are fortunate to have the very detailed *Journal of Corporal Todd, 1745-1762*, ed. Andrew Cormack and Alan Jones (Stroud, 2001).

Index

This index refers only to material in Chapters 1 to 8. It excludes the preliminaries (Preface, Introduction, etc.), the Notes and the Further Reading. For the most part, it focuses on categories and concepts, not on individuals. I have not included the army itself as a category, as many of the references are to aspects of its history; nor have I created an entry for Britain or British, terms used throughout the text.